BOBBY
ROBSON

MY AUTOBIOGRAPHY

BOBBY ROBSON

Farewell but not Goodbye

MY AUTOBIOGRAPHY

BOBBY ROBSON

with Paul Hayward

HODDER

Copyright © 2005 by Bobby Robson

First published in Great Britain in 2005 by Hodder and Stoughton
A division of Hodder Headline

A Hodder paperback

1

A CIP catalogue record for this title is available from the British Library

ISBN 13 978 0 340 82347 7
ISBN 10 0 340 82347 X

Typeset in Linotype Sabon by
Rowland Phototypesetting Ltd,
Bury St Edmunds, Suffolk

Printed and bound by
Clays Ltd, St Ives plc

Hodder Headline's policy is to use papers that are natural,
renewable and recyclable products and made from wood grown
in sustainable forests. The logging and manufacturing processes are expected
to conform to the environmental regulations of the country of origin.

Hodder and Stoughton Ltd
A division of Hodder Headline
338 Euston Road
London NW1 3BH

CONTENTS

ACKNOWLEDGEMENTS

Although I have written about phases of my career in previous books, this is the definitive story of my life, from the mines of Langley Park in County Durham to my five years in charge of Newcastle United.

Many people have helped me thread together the narrative of my seventy-two years and I would like to thank, in particular, Roddy Bloomfield at Hodder and Stoughton, the *eminence grise* of sports publishing, who commissioned this book and kept us chugging along with his support and encouragement.

Gabrielle Allen performed wonders with the picture research. The photographs she has selected should provide an insight into the changing face of football, and British life, since my birth, in 1933. Marion Paull, Hodder's expert copy editor, was also a key player, as was my wonderful secretary, Judith Horey, who plans my days and helped me double-check the manuscript.

I spent many enjoyable hours with Paul Hayward, whose job it was to turn into prose the stories and memories that poured from me as we recounted first my childhood years and then more than fifty seasons in the game. My very special thanks to him.

My thanks also go to my valued Agents Tim Sice and Robert Kirby.

This story would not exist, of course, without the love and support of my family – my dear departed parents, my four brothers, three sons, many grandchildren and the head of the clan, Elsie, my wife for fifty years.

To my dear wife Elsie
and our three sons

Photographic Acknowledgements

The author and publisher would like to thank the following for permission to reproduce photographs:

Action Images, AFP/Getty Images, Agencia Feriaque/Empics, AP/Empics, Matthew Ashton/Empics, Barratts/Empics, Beamish The North of England Open Air Museum, Shaun Botterill/Getty Images, Colorsport, Ken Coton, Andrew Cowie/Colorsport, John Dawes/Daily Star, L'Equipe/Offside, Mark Leech/Offside, Manuel Lopes, Tony Marshall/Empics, Steve Morton/Empics, Newcastle City Council, Phil O'Brien/Empics, PA/Empics, Popperfoto.com, Peter Robinson/Empics, Neal Simpson/Empics, Sport & General/Empics, Aubrey Washington/Empics, Witters/Empics.

All other photographs are from private collections.

GOING UNDERGROUND

L AMP, hobnail boots, tin hat, haversack packed with pliers, screwdrivers and spanners – these were my first tools. Before the white lights of the world's biggest football stadiums shone on my endeavours, my working life began in darkness. When I was fifteen and a half years old and a football addict leaving school to earn a living underground, Wembley, the Maracana and the Nou Camp glowed in a distant galaxy. The single ray of brightness that lit my path came from the lamp clamped to my metal hat. I was a raw boy, following my father into the subterranean corridors of the Langley Park colliery, the heart of our small mining village, some four miles from the cathedral city of Durham.

I was a Geordie lad and another clean recruit for the National Coal Board, who employed some 650 men to excavate the Busty and Brockwell seams in a community that came into being, in the mid-1870s, solely to hack coal from the walls of this vast underground fuel store. In those post-war years pit ponies had yet to be fully liberated from the mines. As I dig for memories now, I peer back fifty-six years and see myself as a trainee electrician, walking to the mouth of the shaft with an older man detailed to be my 'mate', who would teach and protect me as I served my apprenticeship deep below the fields and football pitches of my beloved North East. I hear the clank of the switch and feel the metal floor plunge, sucking us into the blackened cavern from where we began our long walk to the coalface, trouble-shooting along the way.

We electricians would arrive at our depot at 7 a.m. to find out what was on the agenda, what repairs were needed. We'd be told where the target area was and head there before the men who extracted the coal formed their long queue to descend. Sometimes our destination would be a three-mile walk from the pit shaft, and we would trudge there, not with our backs straight but leaning forward to avoid banging our heads on the low dark ceiling. On those long treks I learned how to walk with a stoop – bent double, sometimes, supporting my pack as I went. There was no hitchhiking underground. We were fined if we snatched a ride on one of the coal trucks that crept up behind us on rails. The only way to know they were coming was from the rumble in the dark. Every 300 yards or so a recess allowed you to evade the hurtling wagons, and in these alcoves you were able to stand erect and stretch the muscles in your back.

The lamp was attached to the tin hat, with a heavy alkaline battery at the back of the helmet. It was claustrophobic and pitch black if your light went out – and I mean pitch black. The area around the pit shaft was always lit but the farther you went towards the coalface the darker it became. One of our duties was to lay cables for lighting and cutting equipment; another was the constant cycle of repairs to lights and machinery that kept the men on the front line, gouging out fuel for the country to burn. We would be down the pit for a minimum of six or seven hours a day, and come back up at around three. Then we had an hour of tidying up before clocking off at 4 p.m. I would walk home over the bridge, and be through the front door by twenty-past, totally black, ready to turn my thoughts to the sporting passion that was to raise me to the surface once and for all.

My electrician's apprenticeship was served mostly below the surface. We learned our skills on the job. My work mattered to me and I was determined to be good at it because there was no guarantee I was going to make the grade as a footballer. Two or three evenings a week I would go off to night school in Durham, where I studied electrical engineering, maths and technical drawing. My brother Tom did the same. I had graduated to S1 level, as it used to be called, when I signed for Fulham and left that blackened world behind.

In total, I spent eighteen months underground – a year and a half of going down there every working day – a teenager, an adolescent, following the path of virtually all the young men in our village. Fate kept me safe. Apart from a few collisions between my head and a girder or a low ceiling, the odd slip on uneven ground and some cut fingers, I didn't have any accidents, but the occasional close shave compounded the constant sense of lurking danger. I knew plenty about electrical currents, so I was always careful around the cables and wires.

Mercifully, there were no serious pit accidents in my time below the soil of Langley Park, although my father lost an eye after a mishap underground. He ended his mining career with a glass replacement, which at first glance was almost indistinguishable from a real eye. It must have left him feeling terribly scarred, yet we never discussed either the accident itself or how he felt about having such an obvious physical disability – not once.

For a fifteen-year-old, exhaustion was the heaviest burden. At the end of a shift I would be utterly worn out making the long journey back to the lift shaft. Again, it never entered my head to jump on a passing wagon, because my instinct was always to follow the rules. Some miners would leap in the empty carts rattling towards the coalface but they had to keep their heads down because the trucks were made to measure, and so any raising of the forehead could result in decapitation. Coming back, of course, the trucks were full of coal, which left no room for stowaways. My mate, who oversaw my education, taught me well. He was a real professional, disciplined and conscientious. He didn't play about. There were some great characters to be found along those narrow shafts – tough guys, hardy guys, who loved sport. Their strength was conveyed not through words but actions. They played cricket and bowls and dominoes and knew their football inside out. I can see them now, taking each other on at one game or another, or supping a pint and sucking a cigarette.

Like all working-class lads, I had to take my turn as the butt of colliery humour. I particularly remember a little trick my older colleagues played on me, the sort of thing that happened to all boys in their first week. A woodwork shop, an electrical shop and an engineering store were to be found around the pit head. One day one of the electricians told me to call in at the fitting shop for something called a long-stand.

'See the boss and tell him you need a long-stand,' he said. 'You'll get one there.' It was my first week. I was a mere kid and in no position to challenge an order. So off I went to discharge this important mission.

'I need a long-stand,' I told the chap behind the counter.

'No problem,' he said. 'Stand there, in the corner.'

I shuffled over to the spot he had pointed to and waited for thirty minutes before it dawned on me, and then only because the guy in charge called over.

'How long have you been there?' he asked.

'Half an hour,' I replied.

'Well, that's your long-stand,' he said. 'Now get back to your shop.'

In my day, there was no such thing as a colliery bath, or bathrooms in colliery houses, so I would wash at home in the family's tin tub. It made a shocking mess. I don't know how my mother coped, what with my dad and me having to wash ourselves from black to white every night. A miner never felt that the grit and dust were quite gone from his skin or his hair but in my eagerness to put the day's work behind me, I was pretty fastidious in washing the muck from every pore and hair. I would ask my mother to leave the room as soon as I was ready to lower myself into that tin bath and would then kneel to wash my hair.

By the time the Coal Board started putting bathrooms in colliery houses, I was already a professional footballer, so I never did experience the luxury of a proper enamel bath in my parents' home, in privacy. Those bathrooms, which were created by taking a slice out one of the bedrooms, signalled the end for the outside toilet – a little torture chamber in the coldest winter months.

This world has provided a reference point for me throughout my time in football. Once, I even used it to impress on my employers how lucky they were. At Ipswich Town, where I was manager for thirteen years, I took the whole board of directors down a shaft, at Swadlincote, near Burton-upon-Trent. My brother Tom arranged it for me. By then, Tom had gone very much up in the mining world. He had become chief engineer for the Coal Board in his district. Johnny Cobbold, the eccentric and somewhat aristocratic Ipswich chairman, was a sight to behold as he dropped below ground in overalls and tin hat. It was as if he and the other directors had entered a parallel universe.

It is a fairly well-known fact that my father, Philip Robson, worked for fifty-one years in the mining industry and missed only one shift – just one. Hewing coal and sweeping it on to a conveyor behind him – that was my dad's life until he was promoted to deputy and then overman. So there are no prizes for spotting the origins of my own appetite for hard graft. Throughout my time in football I have thrived on the routine of turning up for work early and throwing all my energy into a job. I have had very few breaks from work in my fifty-six years of toil – like father, like son.

Dad never drank, which might help to explain his incredible

5

stamina, his extraordinary strength. He would go to the working men's club each Thursday night for the whist drive but confine himself to a soft drink or a cup of tea. He was a union man, a Labour man, but not active in politics. From time to time people ask whether I still identify with my working-class background and the answer is that I couldn't fail to do so because I was brought up to be loyal to socialist principles – unity, self-reliance, helping others. Conservatives were people who had far more money than us and couldn't possibly understand our lives underground. Through thrift, Dad taught me the value of a sixpence. It's not in my nature even now to throw money around.

I worked hard but my heart was elsewhere. I wanted to be a footballer. Those six words are found in the memoirs of all football men. They establish the basic truth but fail to convey the depth of the craving that takes men into the sport. A teacher once asked us to write a composition on what we wanted to be when we grew up. 'A footballer,' I wrote, aged twelve, without hesitation. All of us who make it into the professional game are led there by our hearts. It's a compulsion we have to obey.

Mine was formed in the streets, the backyards, the school playing fields of Langley Park, County Durham, where we moved soon after I was born, Robert William Robson, in nearby Sacriston on 18 February 1933 – the year Hitler came to power in Germany. My mother Lillian bore five boys in all, and with my brothers Tom, Philip, Ronald and Keith I always had playmates.

My memory starts with the war years, which began when I was six and ended when I reached twelve. I remember vividly the flares lighting the sky over Newcastle, as the German bombers tried to pick out the heavy industrial targets of the Tyne, and I can recall the searchlights scanning the blackness for a German fuselage to strike. It was a panorama of strange light that wasn't meant to be there. I can remember feeling afraid, scared of being bombed, as we were gathered up before taking cover. The village was near Durham, of course, a relatively safe distance from the real German targets around the Tees, Wear and Tyne. In August 1940, the Luftwaffe launched bombing raids against the North East from their bases in Norway and Denmark. The skies above our biggest cities featured prominently in the Battle of Britain. In 1941, the Newcastle Goods Station was destroyed by enemy bombs. The Germans carried out detailed aerial reconnaissance before attacking train stations, engineering plants and iron and chemical works.

In Langley Park we were never bombed, but we could hear the rumbles above the industrial heartland of Tyneside. We had air-raid shelters in the yard, and the smell and feel of a gas mask will never leave me. Dad was in the Home Guard and the Ambulance Service. He had a passion for First Aid. I remember his tin hat, his haversack and the rifle he was given to ward off German soldiers, who, thank heavens, never made it up our shores. His patch was our village and his brief was to help defend Langley Park.

None of the Robson men were summoned for full military duties. The eldest of my siblings, Tom, was only thirteen, so plainly none of us were going to attract the attention of the recruiting sergeant. At Fulham, when I started my playing career, I failed my medical for National Service on account of a perforated eardrum. In fact, as boys we didn't even play at war, as many lads of that time did. Football and cricket dominated our playtimes. On the back walls of the outside lavatories, we would chalk the posts and crossbars of our goals, and there wasn't a car in the street to hinder our activities. Today's children have lost a very great deal by not being able to play in the road.

We'd play football in the schoolyard before the bell went, football at break times and football after lunch. It was a reflex, an instinct. Later, I went to a school in a neighbouring village and would use the time before the bus left at 4.30 p.m. to arrange games with a tennis ball. Between the ages of eleven and fifteen, I played for Langley Park on Saturday mornings. At fifteen, I was sufficiently well advanced to start turning out for the Under-18s.

Cricket was played in the backyard against a metal dustbin. I was always a keen cricketer. I don't think I'd have made county standard, but by the time I went away, at seventeen, I was a pretty decent batsman. The village had practice nights in the summer and I'd always be sure to attend. At Fulham, I played a couple of games each pre-season with my fellow professionals.

School was strict. At Waterhouses Modern Intermediate, discipline was imposed by a whack of a cane across the hand. There was no escape from the rod. If the hand withdrew slightly as the cane came down, the stick would be used to tap the knuckles back up so it could register a clean strike next time round. If you were really naughty, you were 'tanked' across the backside.

I was afraid of the headmaster, Mr Cowell. He was a good teacher but ruled by fear. The ultimate classroom threat was, 'Go to the headmaster's study, immediately.' That was the last thing you wanted to hear. Oh no, it was best to keep away from there.

I was especially fond of two of my teachers. Miss Hendry, who was a real lady, took us for English, history and geography, but my mentor was David Gilliland, a Sunderland supporter. He taught us cricket and football and took the trouble to arrange matches for us, even though the school had no official team. David came to see me play once or twice and wrote me the occasional letter. When I went back to Newcastle as manager, I invited him to watch some games, which he did, putting aside his allegiance to Sunderland – no easy job, in these parts. He died recently and I was sad to miss his funeral. We had an away game that day. I'm sure he would have understood.

A good teacher will always stay in the memory. Even the name has a certain resonance that lasts all through life. I still have a photograph of our team in 1946–47, with quartered, collarless shirts and heavy woollen socks. Mr Gilliland is at the back, with his side-parting, round spectacles and tweed suit.

I liked school and never played truant but I wasn't an academic type. My dad allowed us to play in the backyard until seven o'clock every night, and I would use that time to practise heading and other skills. Then he would call us in to do our homework and get washed. I'd be in bed by nine. I broke the curfew and failed to be back on time just once, when the funfair came to our village, and I'll never forget the tanking he gave me that day after he had marched out of the house to find me. Among the rides and amusements, I saw him scanning the crowds with a stern look on his face, and skidaddled before his eye caught mine. I sneaked home, thinking I was being clever, but that didn't diminish his wrath when he came back through our front door. He took off his belt and whacked me. It was the only time he did that. He was kind, but firm – a disciplinarian.

We didn't have many books in the house, which is something I regret because I love reading now. Instead, we would listen to music on the radiogram. The songs of Frank Sinatra, Vic Damone, Nat King Cole, Bing Crosby, Lena Horne and Judy Garland filled my head. They were a window on the world. On trips to the swimming baths in Durham I would always buy a record, 78rpm in those days. Later, when I came home from Fulham for the summer, I asked Mum, 'Where have you put all those records I bought? I'd like to take a few back with me to London.'

'I've given them all away,' she replied, surprised. 'They were gathering dust in the cupboard so I gave them to the rag and bone man.'

'What! Gathering dust? Mum, they were worth a fortune.'

My mother was solely a housewife – a cook and a housewife. There was never any thought of her having her own career. She

9

never went to work. She devoted her life to my father and her boys. I can't remember a single argument between her and my father, so I think it's safe to describe it as a happy marriage. She was lovely, always immaculately turned out. Until the last meal of the day was cooked, eaten and washed up, she would wear a pinafore. Then she would change into a dress for the evening. I never saw her in trousers. She kept the house spotless, dusting and polishing every day, and re-laying the fires. On one side of the coal fire was the boiler and on the other was the oven. She made her own bread and cooked suet dumplings and steak and kidney pies wrapped in cloth. Sometimes I would help her knead the dough for the loaves.

My parents started out as Methodists and I was expected to attend Sunday school. Later, my father became a regular Church of England man. He switched sides and did a lot of charitable work for the local parish. Towards the end, religion was a major component of his life. He and the vicar became great friends and allies. When Dad died, they allowed our family to place his ashes on the right side of the path leading into the church, in a very prominent spot. It was a sign of how highly they valued him. Later, they allowed my mother's ashes to be put alongside those of her departed husband – Philip and Lillian Robson, together in a spot that was normally reserved for vicars.

I am not a religious man by nature but I married a devout Roman Catholic. Elsie goes to church at least twice a week. In the villages of the North East, in those days, friction still existed between Catholics and Protestants. For a while, my parents were upset that I'd chosen to marry a woman from the other side of the divide. They felt uncomfortable about me straying into that unknown world. It may shock the modern reader but that was a very common response at the time. Yet, in all our married life, Elsie and I haven't once fallen out over religion. Our kids were educated in Catholic schools. I love her very much and I was always happy to endorse her judgement whenever religious issues affected our lives.

My brother Tom, who became chief engineer for the National Coal Board, is now in his late seventies and lives in the Midlands at Swadlincote, where the famous boxer Jack Bodell came from. Like me, he left school before his sixteenth birthday. By eighteen he was married. He and his wife Marion were great ballroom dancers. They used to go to the Oxford Galleries dancehall in Newcastle and really dazzle. Tom's as solid as a rock, a great brother and a football man who has followed me and been proud of my achievements.

Tom and Marion had three children. Philip, the youngest one, contracted muscular dystrophy and died in his late twenties. At Wembley, Tom would push Philip to the turnstiles in his wheelchair, leave it outside the gate and carry his son, on his back, to his seat. Wherever Ipswich were playing, I would phone our opponents to find out what they could do for my brother and his disabled son. Tom did everything he could for Philip.

My brother Philip became a bricklayer. He was conscripted into the army and sent to Korea where he was blown up out on patrol in the jungle. The first of the six squaddies tripped the wire on a booby-trap and was killed, along with the second in line. Philip came third in line and survived. He was in Korea one minute and woke up in Tokyo the next. I remember being at home when my mother received a telegram from the War Office telling us that Philip had been wounded in Korea and was recovering in a Tokyo hospital. She was distressed out of her mind – tearful but thankful that he was still alive.

Philip went on to become a master builder and constructed some beautiful homes. At Ipswich, I bought a piece of land in Capel St Mary and Phil built a lovely house for me, which I called Durham House, masterminding it via his own business in Slough. Later in life, he got fed up working outside in winter and he and his wife Maureen, who had a kidney problem and needed dialysis, moved to Stowmarket where they bought a newsagent's and tobacconist's. When Maureen died Philip never married again. We lost him to a stroke during Euro 2004.

Ron was the brainy one. He went to grammar school in Durham and matriculated, as they used to say in those days. He became secretary to the local colliery manager. He was cut out for administration. Ron played football with me for Langley Park and was good. He played defensive left-half, whereas I was more attack minded. He was quite ambitious and eventually took a position down in London, leaving the North East with his wife Brenda. Misfortune struck when eye trouble forced him to give up administrative duties, so he went back to the North East and bought a grocery shop in Langley Park. He and Brenda worked their socks off and expanded the business, making it into the biggest shop in the village before passing it on to their son.

Ron loved it when I came back to the area to manage Newcastle. He came to many of the games, but he was deeply hurt – even more so than I was – when the club called time on me four games into the 2004–05 season. He vowed never to go to St James' Park again.

Keith was born five years after me. As a young boy, he developed rheumatic fever, which is a minor ailment now but was quite serious in those days, and didn't go to school for months while he was recovering. He was a bright boy, a scholar, who got a good education, despite his problems, and ended up as a draughtsman, working on oil rigs off Aberdeen. Sadly, he died young. At breakfast one day, on holiday, he suddenly hit the table, rolled over and was dead in seconds. A ruptured aorta struck him from nowhere and carried him off. He was the youngest yet died first. It was a terrible shock to us, a disaster. His children saw their father pass away at the table. Andrea, Keith's wife, was inconsolable at the funeral. I've never seen a widow so distraught. Every day for a year she would take a stool, plant it by Keith's grave and talk to him for an hour. She was very devoted, but she came to terms with it, eventually, after three or four years, and married again. Life goes on.

My mum and dad stayed in Langley Park after he retired. They didn't move up the social scale at all. In fact, they downsized. Dad made a profit on the house we lived in and they moved into rented accommodation for ex-miners. It had one bedroom, a little lounge, a small kitchen and a bathroom. That seemed to suit them. Dad used to come to all my games for the village youth team. When I went to Fulham as a young professional, he would come to see me play whenever we had a game in the north – Sheffield, Newcastle, Middlesbrough. Mum would often come, too, and they would trek as far as Yorkshire. The Midlands were a bit beyond them because they didn't have a car. They went by train, which wasn't always convenient.

Later, though, Dad never missed an England game in my time as manager. It was a strange feature of his visits to Wembley that he would never stay overnight, no matter how much I encouraged him with offers of luxurious hotels. He wanted to get home. To fulfil that urge he would take the Flying Scotsman, which left at midnight. I used to get him a couple of refreshment tickets, so he could have the meal that the FA provided in those days. After the game and the press conference, he would come to see me and we would sit and talk for a while, but then he would join the throng making their way into the night. I tried to book taxis for him but he wasn't having any of that. He would walk to the tube station up Wembley Way and make his way to King's Cross, where he would board a train that got him to Durham at something like 5.30 on the Thursday morning. From there he would get a taxi home to Mum.

The simplest explanation for his refusal to stay overnight was that he couldn't stand being away from my mother. He must have been exhausted by the time he went through that front door but my father was a very strong man, spirited and physically robust. As I said, he missed one shift in fifty-one years, and none at all in the last forty-two years of his working life. That's an incredible record. He was a colossus around the house. He did all the painting and decorating with impressive skill. I'd come home to find him putting a false grain in the doors or mending our shoes, soles and heels, on his last. I remember him putting the prong, which has a steel hook in for the stitching, right through his finger, which was inside the shoe. The only way to remove it was to rip it out, flesh and all. For weeks he had a huge hole in his finger. Half of it was gone. I can see it now. It didn't stop him going to work, of course. Strange how these images stay with you through life.

We were close, my dad and me, and the arrival of a telephone at home enabled us to confide in each other more. Until then we had communicated by letter. It's incredible that a piece of equipment that's taken for granted now had such a profound effect on the lives of working folk. Generally, I would ring home a couple of times a month. Dad didn't really give me advice about my career. He wanted me to stand on my own two feet.

He was a great dad. I was always aware of him following me and supporting me. His pride shone through. During my England playing days I gave him one of my caps, and he and my mother put it in a little glass case, which they placed in the hallway of the house. Anyone paying a visit would have seen it straight away. He showed it to everybody. 'Dad, don't do that,' I would say, squirming. 'Don't be daft,' he would reply, and wait for the next knock at the door.

Of course, it was Dad who exposed me to the football addiction that was so rampant in the North East, and I became one of the pilgrims who flocked to St James' Park every other Saturday without fail. We started our regular visits just after the war, in

1946–47. Dad would lead my brother Ronnie and me on to the 10 o'clock bus to Marlborough Street station. It was twenty or so miles and took an hour, through Chester-le-Street and Low Fell. We would have a cup of tea and a ham roll – that's all we could afford – and be at the gate by 12.15. We were first in line, and I mean first. I can see us standing there as clearly as the hand in front of my face.

I can remember the players equally well. I saw Len Shackleton's first match. Albert Stubbins was my favourite, closely followed by Jackie Milburn, Bobby Cowell, Joe Harvey, Frank Brennan, Bobby Mitchell, Tommy Pearson, Charlie Wayman and Alf McMichael.

Those trips provided the inspiration for me in my ambition to be a footballer. This was the game I loved, on an immense stage, watched by huge legions of Geordies, all willing Newcastle on. This was the passion that was to animate my life but I never dreamed I would ever play on that turf. Me, on that sacred grass? You must be kidding. As it turned out, I played there many times with either Fulham or West Bromwich Albion, and they were really big days for me – special. All the lads were allowed tickets and I would scrounge them off team-mates to accommodate the ten or twelve family members who wanted to be at the game.

For us, in childhood, holidays were spent at Whitley Bay or Blackpool, a much bigger treat. A bus would pull up in the village to take the colliery families to the seaside, where we would stay in a guesthouse. In those days, half the village would decamp to Blackpool. Later, Mum and Dad would take their breaks with Elsie and me. We would invite them down to stay in Ipswich, or wherever we were, at least once a year. Often I would go up to Langley Park and then drive them south.

They are lost to me, now, of course. Only death could separate them. Dad went first, when I was managing PSV Eindhoven. Ron rang me in Holland and said, 'I've got some bad news.' I knew what it was but made a wrong guess about which parent.

'What, our mother?' I asked.

'No. Dad,' he said.

'My dad's died? I can't believe it.'

'Neither can I,' said Ron.

I thought he was indestructible. I thought he would live to be a hundred. He used to get up at six every morning to polish and dust. He did all the housework after he retired. He loved it. After he had given my mum a cup of tea and a slice of toast he would go to Ron's grocery shop to bag potatoes. He'd weigh them and slide them into 2lb and 3lb bags. Dad had them all arranged when people came in for their potatoes. Ron used to give him £10 worth of goods in return and that suited Dad.

His death was terribly sudden. Mum had asked for a glass of water and Dad had placed it on her bedside table, turned and hit the floor without warning. The doctor told us he would have been dead in two seconds. He suffered a massive rupture of his aorta, as did my brother Keith. Dad was as strong as an animal but he hit the deck in seconds, in his pyjamas. He was eighty-seven.

Mum lived on for a while but passed away just before the 1994 World Cup, aged eighty-four, while I was in Porto. She had bad feet towards the end and wasn't comfortable walking. Ron called in every day – he was the only one of us who lived nearby and was fantastic in that respect – but the social services advised her to have an alarm by the side of her bed with a string she could pull in an emergency. When they came to put the cord in and rang the door bell, Mum got up to answer the door, caught her feet in her skirt and fell over, breaking her femur. In hospital she went downhill and never came out. Exactly the same thing happened to Elsie's mum. She broke her femur, went into decline and never made it out of hospital.

I had been due to come home to see Mum in a week's time. In

fact, I was flying back to England the very next day but that awful message from Ron beat me to it – 'bad news, Mum's died.' Twenty-four more hours and I would have been by her side. She died before I could get there. In my grief, I didn't go to the World Cup, for only the second time since 1958. Mum's death just broke me in two.

The Langley Park mine closed thirty years ago and the village has mellowed into a quiet, pretty place. It featured in the hit movie 'Billy Elliot' as well as 'The Fast Show' and 'Ripping Yarns'. I can drive there from our new home near Chester-le-Street in less than half an hour. The colliery band still get together and play tunes that keep the past alive.

2

TALES FROM
THE RIVERBANK

Most clubs sent a scout, but Fulham dispatched the man himself. Bill Dodgin snr came to our family home, seated himself in the front room and explained why I, a seventeen-year-old lad from the mines, should travel hundreds of miles south to start a new life in London. He was quite a salesman. I was about to exchange a terraced house for Craven Cottage.

In those weeks of sifting through my options I could have chosen to join Sunderland, Middlesbrough, Newcastle, Lincoln, Blackpool, Huddersfield or Southampton, where, coincidentally, Bill Dodgin had been in 1948–49 when the Saints expressed a firm interest in taking me on. By 1950 Bill had become the manager of Fulham and he remembered my name and the scouting reports that had made it down to the south coast. So up he came to Durham on the train and knocked on our door, saying that I shouldn't sign for anyone but Fulham. The club had a reputation for nurturing bright youngsters and I liked his enthusiasm and sincerity. He impressed me, so I took a gigantic leap into the unknown.

My schoolboy forms had been held by Middlesbrough but the offer they made me after my seventeenth birthday could not compete with the riches Bill Dodgin laid on our table. Boro proposed to pay me £4 in winter and £3 in summer, while Bill enticed me with the maximum straight away – £7 during the season and £6 in the summer, which was twice the amount I was earning at the colliery.

I suppose it might seem perverse, even now, that I turned down my beloved Newcastle to start a new life in the capital, and decided to play for Fulham, with whom I had no emotional connection. The fact is that Newcastle made no appreciable effort to secure my signature, unlike Bill, who encouraged me to think I would be highly regarded from the moment I stepped off the train.

Most managers understand the importance of wearing out shoe leather in pursuit of young talent. It worked for me at Ipswich and it certainly paid off for Alex Ferguson, who spent many precious hours studying good youngsters and then investing time with their parents to persuade them that Manchester United was the right academy for their boys.

I had never been out of the Langley Park area and had never spent time away from my mum and dad. Suddenly I was in digs, in one of the world's biggest and most vibrant cities. I still don't know how I was able to pull my roots from the ground at such a tender age. I must have been tougher than I knew.

When the deal was confirmed, I caught the rattler south from Durham and set up home at 56 Inglethorpe Street, where I was introduced to my great mucker, Tom Wilson, who later became a successful businessman and a Fulham director. Between them, Tom and Jimmy Hill were credited with saving the club from eviction when its future at Craven Cottage was in doubt.

Tom and I shared a room for five years and were inseparable. We were best man at each other's wedding. I had a single bed and very few clothes – four shirts, a sports jacket, socks, handkerchiefs and a couple of pairs of shoes. I'll never forget that first address in Inglethorpe Street. I suppose I associate those modest digs with making the transition from a boy to a man because from there I set out in life as an adult. Lloyds Bank on Putney High Street was one of my first ports of call. When it came to opening a current account, Bill Dodgin took me over the bridge and showed me how to deposit the princely sum of £1. The bank is still there.

In those early days I felt the nag of homesickness but it soon subsided. The hardest part of my new existence was getting up early on my own before Tom had even stirred. For me, there wasn't the luxury of becoming a professional sportsman over-night. I was a 'spark' by trade and, although there were no mines in London, I still had to join the armies of working men who scuttled to work at first light. When the agreement was struck with Fulham, my dad insisted that I carry on my trade as an electrician, so when I arrived in London I took a job with a firm based in Victoria. Their big project was the Festival of Great Britain site, on the Embankment. The view was nicer than the one at Langley Park colliery but the work was far more onerous. While I helped to put power into those buildings, my own body was being drained of energy.

The routine was that I would get up at 6 a.m., walk through the park to the tube station, get off at Victoria and then take a mini-bus to the site. For a kid of seventeen it was gruelling. The reward was around £3 a week. I was drawing two salaries, which gave me a financial advantage over my young team-mates, but I found it arduous. The fatigue was diminishing me as a player. After work I would go straight to training three nights a week. I needed to work full-time on my fitness and my skills. Even in Fulham reserves, I was playing against full-time professionals who seemed to be sharper and stronger than me.

Eventually, I sent up a distress flare and my mum and dad came down to discuss my predicament with the club, who put them up in digs – not in a hotel but in some rooms close to Craven Cottage. When we were all assembled I made my bid for freedom. Bill Dodgin, my father and I sat down to talk about my career, where it was going and where it wasn't, and why I was finding it so hard. My father could see how keen I was to give football my full attention. I was totally focused on that ambition and it must have impressed him. I made my pitch.

'Dad,' I said, 'I'm playing against good players who seem to be ahead of me – fitter than me, stronger than me. I'd rather try full-time and fail than do it part-time and fail anyway.'

After a moment's thought, Dad conceded the point.

'OK, son, it's your life. I wish you wouldn't do it, but I can see your problem. Maybe this will give you the best possible opportunity to succeed in the game.' Inside I rejoiced.

I'll always be in debt to my father for tackling that tricky issue in such a constructive and compassionate way. It scared him to think of me abandoning my trade for such a risky profession. It contradicted all his instincts as a working man. His own life had been devoted to a single task, which he performed with great consistency and stoicism. That day, though, he set me up for life. He saw that it would be wrong to strangle my dream. He set me free.

Mum and Dad stayed in London for a few days and I made sure I showed them round. They hadn't seen my digs or the club or any other aspect of my life in the south. Those first few years were mainly about exploration. For recreation, Tom and I would walk over the bridge into Putney or go for a Knickerbocker Glory. There was an Italian coffee shop and bakery called Zita's next to Putney Bridge station and every Friday, after we found out which team we were in, we would walk through the park and indulge ourselves with a mountain of fruit and ice cream.

Occasionally, we would jump on a bus to Piccadilly – 'the Dilly' as Londoners of that time called it – and amble around, gaze at Eros and press our noses against the windows of the posh shops on Regent Street, such as Burberry and Aquascutum. The Café Royal gave us a scent of the good life as we floated past. We watched a lot of football, too. I went to see Tottenham in the European Cup and called in on Chelsea, Brentford and

Queen's Park Rangers. I also saw Sinatra twice, Nat King Cole at the Palladium and Danny Kaye. We had a strong urge to see the stars of the day and didn't eat out very much because we couldn't afford to – we saved our money to go to the shows.

I didn't have a girlfriend at Fulham. In that sense my heart never left the North East. My great romantic attachment was not to a London girl but a beautiful nurse I happened to bump into on one of my visits home. It was the Christmas and New Year holiday when I met Elsie at the local village hop. That night, after a few dances, I took her home, kissed her, on the step, and waved her goodnight. In those days, passion was outweighed by decorum.

The next day I took Elsie to the pictures, in the snow, and from then onwards I carried on my love affair with her through letters, because I couldn't afford to go home much, not during the season at any rate. In summer, I would head back north to see Elsie and pass the remaining hours playing cricket, my other sporting love. In the early years, our romance was conducted over the phone and in print. I wrote almost every day, hardly ever missed.

Elsie was training to be a State Registered Nurse at Sunderland infirmary. Getting time off was very hard for young members of her profession. During my five years at Fulham we saw each other very little but in spirit we were firmly entwined. She was equally regular with her correspondence. We must have been great customers for Basildon Bond. I would tell her about my day, what happened at training, what I had for lunch, the usual things. I would tell her I missed her and that I wished she was there with me. She was my real girlfriend. I didn't have another at Fulham.

As we got older, she came down a couple of times and stayed in the digs where Tom and I once lived. By then I had moved out. Naturally, Elsie's mother had given her approval. That was the etiquette in those days. Prior consent was required. Once the permission of the girl's parents had been granted there was a duty to make proper and transparent arrangements with a reputable landlady. I courted Elsie from eighteen years of age to the day I married her, in 1955.

That first summer, in 1950, Fulham had been promoted and had forked out for some decent players – Ian Black the goalkeeper, Charlie Mitten, Eddie and Reg Lowe. These were big names, bought from big clubs. Jim Taylor, Harry Freeman, Dougie Platt and Bedford Jezzard are other names seared into my memory. I was a raw kid who hadn't played anywhere near this exalted level but because I was a prodigy, the club paid me a fair bit of attention. In the office, I encountered a young fellow called Johnny Haynes, who, at sixteen, had signed for Fulham that summer, and was paying his way by licking stamps. Johnny spent his entire first-class playing career, from 1952–70, at that atmospheric stadium beside the Thames. The other starlets in my first season were Bob Taylor, Tony Barton and Roy Dwight, who happened to be related to Elton John. In my second period at Fulham, Tony Macedo, George Cohen, Alan Mullery and Bobby Keetch were the top players.

In 1950 it wasn't easy to break into that Fulham first eleven but once I stopped getting up at 6 a.m. and trying to be an electrician as well as a footballer, a remarkable improvement was evident in my game. I became more robust, more muscular, more energetic. Whatever level you play at, having a certain physical prowess is important. In football there is no escaping the need to run, make contact, challenge, put your foot in, get knocked over and get back up. In all these areas I developed, simply because I was training in the morning and resting in the afternoons. I was a full-time professional footballer with the appropriate reserves of energy.

To illustrate how long ago it was, and how much football has changed since then, the 1950 World Cup was won by Uruguay in front of 199,854 spectators at the Maracana Stadium in Rio de Janeiro. In my first season at Fulham, 100,000 watched Pegasus beat Bishop Auckland at Wembley in the Amateur Cup final. Pegasus were a collection of Oxbridge graduates who did not play in a league and had no ground of their own, yet they were able to attract 100,000 fans to Wembley. When I first laced up heavy leather boots as a professional, the Corinthian ideal was still going strong. In that same year, Jackie Milburn, Wilf Mannion, Stanley Matthews, Stan Mortensen and Tom Finney were the stars of the England team. Spurs won the championship playing push and run. Newcastle beat Blackpool 2–0 to win the FA Cup and Arsenal's Leslie Compton made his England debut aged thirty-eight years and two months. Football was another universe from the one I joined when I finally took up a post in the Premier League as manager of Newcastle.

I made my debut towards the end of that first season, against Sheffield Wednesday, and my dad came down to see me take my bow. I wish I could have done more to repay his faith. I hardly touched the ball that day. I found it so, so hard. I was the star apprentice but I was incapable of imposing myself on the game. I had maybe seven touches all afternoon. I was playing real men's football against solid professionals who really knew the game. I was coming up to my eighteenth birthday and was all at sea. Any serious player reading this passage will recognise that feeling. Supporters who immediately condemn young players for not being good enough should remember that a large measure of disorientation comes with promotion to the first eleven. It takes time for the shock to wear off and for a boy's confidence to grow.

Rejoining the squad the following season, I was a bit more developed, more comfortable with London life and with my team-mates. Deep down I was less lonely. I had a great friend in

Tom. We were very close and went through all the rites of passage together. Fulham was a nice club, a social club. Their most famous chairman was a comedian. I'm not being rude. Comedy was Tommy Trinder's trade. When we were relegated in 1968, with me as manager, Tommy observed, 'The reason why Fulham have never won the league championship is that we could never work up enough speed. That's why we've dropped back into the Second Division – to get a longer run at it.'

I was a wing-half – a midfield player who combined defence with attack. My better half was the attacking. I had an eye for a goal, I could shoot and I had a bit of pace, a dribble and a feint. My heading was so-so. Under the system many teams operated then, you had two wingers and a centre-forward with two inside-forwards. Then you had two wing-halves, two full-backs and a centre-half. When Hungary came to Wembley in 1953 and demolished us with their 4–2–4 formation, that's when English football was compelled to change.

I was a goalscorer. I got goals throughout my youth. My instinct was to surge forward out of midfield. Sure, I doubled back, chased the opponent in possession and got my toe in, but all that was secondary to the work I most enjoyed. Johnny Haynes was more of a passer whereas I liked to ghost up along-side Bedford Jezzard and cause defenders trouble. I'd played an awful lot of football in the North East before I arrived in London. I'd performed for the school team and the local club team and I'd played in the street and on rough ground. I'd played with a ball and I'd played with a piece of coal and a lump of flint. It wasn't an academy education, with special diets and isotonic drinks, but it was a good education all the same. By the time I reached London, I had grasped the basic technical repertoire of the game.

Bill Dodgin would regale us with couple of simple slogans. 'The ball is round, make sure you pass it around' was one, and

'Happy when you win, smile when you lose' was another. That went out of the window later in life. If you smile when you lose nowadays, you're accused of not caring. In defeat, some supporters prefer you to look suicidal.

Of the great Fulham characters, Jimmy Hill was one who stood out. Jimmy was an extrovert. I liked Jimmy. I thought he was lively and honest and had a point of view. He was educated and enthusiastic. In fact, he could talk better than he played, but he wasn't a bad player either. He was a hard working, player's player, with a tremendous engine. Jimmy was tireless. He could run all day. I hope he'll forgive me for saying that he didn't have the greatest of first touches and he wasn't the best passer of a ball, nor was he great in the air. It was his energy and his love for the game that made him such a dynamic presence on the pitch.

Jim was good to be with. It was within his powers to dominate a party or a train journey. He loved a game of cards and he would finish the crossword before anyone else. He loved to train. He was unselfish and, boy, did he love to score goals. If he got one, he would run three miles to celebrate. He would have run all the way to the West End if he could have got through the gates. You had no chance of catching Jimmy to share the thrill of a Fulham goal. He would set off in any and every direction. It was quite a coup if you managed to catch him to shake him by the hand. I was always very fond of him. He was straight as they come and would do anything for you. If he could offer any advice, he would, without expecting anything in return.

Ron Greenwood, another big name of that time, was a bit more dour. Ron was solid, intelligent, and he knew football, as did Jimmy. They were both students of the game. I wasn't at all surprised that Ron became an England manager because he studied the sport as an academic would. If Ron was your friend, he would be there for ever. Jim was flighty and cocky and always had something to say. Ron was down to earth and said less, but whatever he said stayed with you.

Charlie Mitten was a Fulham 'card'. He loved his greyhound racing, did Charlie. After a game at Plymouth, while we waited for the sleeper back to London, Charlie dragged us to the local dog track and forced us all to divvy up two quid to back his selections, which included an animal called Red Biddy that Charlie considered a certainty. We didn't get a penny back. Charlie even used to bring his dogs into the Fulham physio's room for treatment.

'Off those tables, you two,' Charlie barked at Johnny Haynes and me one day as we were trying to overcome injuries in time for Saturday's game. 'I've got to get this dog fit for Wimbledon.' Moments later, the greyhound was up on the treatment table with electronic pads on its muscles and a muzzle round its face to stop it biting the physio. I think we were playing Arsenal on the Saturday.

In his first week at Fulham, Charlie came in with a tailor's tape measure and started taking all our details.

'What's this for?' we asked.

'Raincoats,' he said. 'I'm going to get you all a nice new macintosh. I've got fantastic contacts in Manchester and I'm going to bring all the coats down for you. One each.' Great, a free mac – they still haven't arrived.

Naturally, Tommy Trinder's presence as chairman set the tone for all this hilarity and exuberance. My best recollection of Tommy comes from the days when our forward line was Robson, Haynes, Jezzard, Charlie Mitten and Arthur Stevens. One afternoon, Tommy came into the dressing room in a beautiful cashmere camel coat to do his usual 'You lucky people' speech, and Arthur responded, 'If any of us had a coat like that we'd be lucky.'

'Tell you what, if you get three goals today, you can 'ave it,' said Tommy and the deal was done.

After twenty minutes, Arthur banged one in and ran over to the directors' box with a single finger raised at Tommy Trinder. When he got a second, he made the same run to where Tommy was sitting, this time with two digits raised. In the second half we were all laying the ball on for Arthur to get the third. When he finally completed the hat-trick, he sprinted diagonally across the pitch, waving his two index fingers and exclaiming, 'One-two-three!' After the match, Tommy removed the camel coat and gave it to Arthur.

We never became a serious, championship-challenging club – Fulham was a house of fun, where the emphasis was on companionship and entertainment, and perhaps we lacked the drive that champions possess. The financial clout was also missing. We were always behind Arsenal, Chelsea and Tottenham. Yet the club did employ some outstanding players from 1950 to the mid-1970s. Johnny Haynes, George Cohen, Alan Mullery, Rodney Marsh and Allan Clarke is quite a roll call. In the seventies, Mullery, Bobby Moore, George Best and Marsh laid on some champagne days. It was a happy, convivial club, to which Tommy Trinder attracted his entertainment pals. We played to gates of 27,000, which made us bigger than Queen's Park Rangers and Brentford, but less formidable than the really big London clubs. We were the middle-class in the London hierarchy.

Eventually, I worked out that I would have to get away from Fulham if I was to adorn my career with medals. I knew we were good enough to make inroads into the Cups, but I also felt that once the heavy knock-out stages started it would be cheerio to Fulham. At one point, Newcastle offered £60,000 for Johnny Haynes, Bedford Jezzard and me, which was the biggest single transfer offer the game had seen. Naturally, I fancied going back to my roots, but with typical bravado the board turned it down.

Fulham and I were finally separated in 1956, when West Bromwich Albion came in with an offer of £25,000. That was big money, only £9,000 below the transfer record. West Bromwich were a strong, steady club. Two years previously, they had won the FA Cup and finished second in the League. They bought me to replace Reg Ryan, a roly-poly midfielder who chugged and chugged away, because they needed someone with fresher legs.

Before I moved into that second major phase of my playing career, I dug the most solid foundation of my life, one that supports and sustains me to this day. In 1955, the Robsons assembled at Esh village church, 120 yards from where I came to live four decades later as manager of Newcastle United. The wedding wasn't a grand affair, although I suppose it had some glamour, given that I was the local boy made good, marrying a beautiful girl from the village.

By this time I was an established Under-21 international and had been on two ambassadorial Football Association tours, one to the West Indies in 1955 and another to South Africa in 1956. The modern Premiership manager would recoil at the thought of those tours. I played in fifteen of the eighteen games and was on the go for ten weeks of the summer 'break'. The reward was one week off before pre-season training started with our clubs.

Elsie and I have been married for fifty years but our union might have ended within days – before the end of the honeymoon, in fact – because our boating trip to celebrate the wedding came within touching distance of calamity. With the ceremony behind us, we spent a few nights at the Waverley Hotel in Edinburgh before we came south again and hired a cruiser to go up the Thames to Oxford with two friends, Don and Helen Sinclair, who argued quite a lot. 'What a couple to come on honeymoon with,' I complained to Elsie one night.

One day we berthed at Henley on Thames and were having a picnic on a small patch of grass when Elsie announced that she needed something from the boat – a jug of milk and a cup, as I recall. The rest of us were chatting away when I heard a faint but unmistakable plop. The boat had moved away from the bank just as Elsie was climbing aboard and she had dropped straight down the gap between the hull and the wall. What made it more of a problem was that Elsie couldn't swim. Oddly, there was no accompanying scream, but I was sure I had heard the plop of an object striking water, and looked up to see a hand poking out of the river – just a hand, nothing else. In one movement I was off my feet and throwing myself down on the bank to yank her out. If I hadn't looked, she might have been submerged forever. She was OK but in deep shock. Ours might have been the shortest marriage on record.

—— 3 ——

LA-DI-DAH

VIC BUCKINGHAM, my new manager at West Bromwich Albion, was an extrovert and a dandy who sported a handkerchief that dropped six inches out of his top pocket. He was a very cultured man, well spoken, and used words I had never heard. A typical Vic Buckingham instruction would be: 'Stay off this pitch. This pitch is inviolate!' I would think: 'What colour did he say the pitch was? It looks green to me.'

In his team talks Vic used to say to us, 'Look, I don't want us to go la-di-dah-di-dah-di-dah with the ball. I want to go la-di-dah-di-dah-BONK!' He always got the bonk in there at the end, the strike at the climax of the passing move. Coaches these days would call it 'end product'. The build-up play had to have a purpose, a sting in the tail.

Vic was a fine coach. His training methods were sound, as befitted a man who learned the art of push and run under the master, Arthur Rowe, and was good enough to work at Barcelona and Ajax. There's some irony in the fact that I followed his steps. He went to Ajax, I went to PSV Eindhoven. He went to Barcelona, I went to Barcelona. Vic was a man of the world. He was one of the FA's senior coaches and thinkers. I liked his team talks. They were short and concise and conveyed all his gravitas.

Push and run was pioneered by the Tottenham Hotspur teams of the early 1950s. Under Arthur Rowe, Spurs won the title in 1951, twelve months after being promoted from the Second

Division. The ball was swept around the pitch by Ron Burgess, Eddie Baily, Alf Ramsey and Bill Nicholson. Push and run meant playing first touch football as far and often as you could. You'd move the ball and then run into space, knowing the lay-off was probably going to come your way. You'd hit the target, get the rebound and then play it again. It involved movement and retaining possession.

You couldn't play that way for ninety minutes, of course. Every now and then you might need to take an extra touch or two, or perform a little turn or wriggle to get yourself out of a tight position, but it was very attractive football. It was up to us to take up good positions and form triangles with our passing – full-back to right-half to outside-right and back to the right-half. Then you would change the play. It required accuracy and vision and a good first touch.

Push and run was new to English football. Its roots were on the Continent. Around this time we were starting to become more receptive to foreign influences. In my first spell at Fulham I attended all the international matches at Wembley. The manager would come in to the dressing room and say, 'Hands up if you want to go to Wembley on Wednesday night. Right, seventeen, that's enough for a bus,' and off we went, to learn and be entertained. When I moved to West Bromwich, Wembley wasn't quite so accessible, although I did go to London a few times under my own steam.

What I noticed, studying these international games, was that continental teams played a different style from us, with short, controlled passing. We tended to hit it long and exploit the second ball. The continentals had better technique and a better mastery of the ball. They didn't always win but they were playing a more sophisticated version of the game. I felt they were teaching us a lesson, which Hungary certainly did when they broke our record of being unbeaten at home against European opponents, smashing England 6–3 at Wembley in 1953. More than 100,000 spectators witnessed that turning point for English football, and afterwards Billy Wright, the England captain, said graciously, 'The Hungarians produced some of the finest, most brilliantly applied football it has ever been my privilege to see. The ball did precisely what they wanted. They were relentless. They were superb.'

Six months later, Ferenc Puskas and his pals repeated the dose, demolishing England 7–1 in the People's Stadium in Budapest. Only Merrick, Wright, Dickinson and Sewell had kept their places from the Wembley game. Our problem was that we needed to change attitudes, not individual players.

Back at club level, I liked West Bromwich and the Black Country people. I joined some fine players, including Joe Kennedy, Ray Barlow, Ronnie Allen, Derek Kevan, Jimmy Dudley, George Lee, Frank Griffin and Maurice Setters. With their help, I graduated to the full England team after serving my apprenticeship, in 1956, with the Under-23 and B-sides. Derek Kevan and Ronnie Allen were already valued members of Walter Winterbottom's team. West Bromwich was also where I formed one of my life's great friendships, with Don Howe, who went on to become one of the country's most distinguished coaches. Don and I hit it off straight away. He was married, ambitious, cultured and didn't go to the pub. He had a strong, stable character. We were kindred spirits.

Don and I played for England together and embarked on coaching careers side by side, after Walter Winterbottom had picked us out from the mass of players who passed through his hands. 'Look, what are you two going to do when you stop playing?' he asked us, initially in 1959. At first the question sounded odd, unnecessary. Like most footballers, we thought we would play forever. Age would pass us by. We lived for today. 'Yes, but the thing is that it won't last forever,' Walter said. 'I want you both to come to Lilleshall, get on the courses and get yourselves qualified. I want you both to stay in the game. The game needs to be taken on by players with good international experience. You don't have to be a great player to be a good coach, but it's an advantage if you are and you have that advantage. You're international players. Come to Lilleshall and be teachers, coaches, managers. Take the game on.'

Plainly, Arsene Wenger wasn't a great player but Bobby Charlton was, so there is no hard and fast rule about what makes a good manager. Arsene is Arsenal's most successful coach, yet the tracksuit never felt quite right on Bobby Charlton. In general, having had a decent playing career helps with your understanding of a match and what you might need to do to change its course. It also helps with man management, communication, your tactical approach and your judgement of players in the transfer market and at youth level. A truism of football management is that your 'buys' and 'sells' will determine whether you keep your job.

Tactically, there are only three or four systems of play, so a new coach is not working his way through a menu of ten or fifteen styles. Handling the media is another important skill. Toughness in team selection is vital. Alex Ferguson has always had that. He was never afraid to leave out David Beckham, even when it created a media furore. I once talked to Alex about this. He said, 'I've got a lot of good players, Bobby, and I have to give them a chance in the team. You can't function with just eleven good players.' In the Premiership nowadays, the bottom six will have around fourteen good men, and the rest are bit-part players. Manchester United will have nineteen or twenty top players. I like to think I left Newcastle United with a huge pool of talent. On top of all that, Alex has been able to lay down rules of conduct and really apply them. Let's not forget energy and enthusiasm, either. Alex was always first into the training ground in the morning.

As the FA's Director of Coaching, Walter Winterbottom ran some excellent coaching courses. Twenty years later I was to assume the same dual role, as England team manager and director of coaching for the game as a whole. Lilleshall, where Alan Wade appointed me as a staff coach, had become a greenhouse for future English managers. Don Howe, Dave Sexton, Howard Wilkinson and Terry Venables all passed through the FA's academy in Shropshire.

Coaching fascinated me. I worked not only for the FA but also the Surrey Coaches' Association, which I helped to form, and Pearl Assurance, who had me coaching their works team one night a week. The problem with Pearl was that fifty insurance men would turn up for the sessions, so I used to ask Bobby Drake to come with me to take twenty-five players off my beat. I would write out the training schedule and instruct Bobby to supervise his half.

For two years after leaving West Bromwich to return to Fulham, I travelled up to Oxford University to coach the Dark Blues for the sum of four guineas per afternoon. We trained at Iffley Road, where, of course, Roger Bannister ran the first sub-four minute mile. My routine on Tuesday and Thursday after-noons was to drive the fifty or so miles from Fulham to Oxford to knock a lot of highly educated boys into shape. The lads understood the vernacular of football but had never taken instruction from a proper coach.

I was extremely conscientious in my work and wouldn't have missed those visits to the old university town for the world. The lads were eager to learn. Their whole season revolved around the Varsity match, which was staged at Wembley in front of a small crowd of 8,000, in contrast to the rugby, which sold out Twickenham. I gave them shape and a style of play, and explained the responsibilities that came with each position. A vital component of football teaching is coaching the back four –

when to hold the line, when to move up, what the full-backs should do to help out if an opponent bursts through the middle, when to play square, when to go slightly diagonal, and so on.

All sorts of ingredients go in to successful football coaching, many of them tiny. Take throw-ins. Retaining possession at throw-ins is one of my obsessions. Few things bother me more than my team giving the ball away from our own throw-in.

Oxford University was really my birthplace as a football coach. Those mostly well-bred high-fliers helped me as much as I helped them. As an international footballer, I was guaranteed instant respect. These were my first steps on the road and I put my heart and soul into the process of improving this university eleven. I was a professional player in the morning and a coach in the afternoon. Through the inadequacies of the boys, I had my own private coaching laboratory, and it helped me understand the process of coaching set-pieces, shooting and technique. Oxford won two Varsity matches while I was there.

Academia was not entirely alien to me. In 1953, after Hungary had annihilated England at Wembley, Jimmy Hill, Ron Greenwood and I signed up for an FA course in London's Paddington Street. The 'Magical Magyars', as they were known, jolted a few of us into wanting to know more, and I suppose I ought to thank them for that, even though a later encounter with Hungary's greatest player, Ferenc Puskas, in Canada in 1967, soured my memory of him.

Before Don and I could reach for the tracksuits after that approach from Walter Winterbottom, we had work to do at West Bromwich and I learned a great deal from the esteemed Vic Buckingham. Our team was packed with real footballing men and one such was Ronnie Allen, another 'thinker'. He was a great player with two excellent feet. At 5ft 6in, he couldn't give you the prodigious leap of an Alan Shearer or Ruud van Nistelrooy, but anything within his range would be glanced or accurately poked into the net. He was a natural sportsman, a small man who could hit a golf ball 300 yards. He was an Ian Woosnam. Each time we passed a golf course on the train or the team bus, Ronnie would look out the window, point and say, 'Out in thirty-two, back in thirty-three.' 'Oh, right, well done, Ron,' somebody would mumble. Ronnie was a boaster, you see, but a nice one, which helped him get away with it. In football in those days, the real bigheads were told to shut up. Ronnie was our scratch golfer, who used to play the resident professional at Sandwell golf club and beat him.

Like me, Ronnie did a bit of extra work selling nuts and bolts and steel strips for the Repton Engineering Company. This was the Black Country after all, packed with factories and foundries. For two or three years, after training I hit the pavements to earn a few bob.

Elsie and I went into digs at first but then moved into a club house at 75 Copthorne Road before eventually gambling on buying a house in Handsworth that cost £2,500. I'd saved £500 in cash for the deposit. Eager to accumulate a fighting fund, I would hand my weekly wage to Elsie and she would give me a couple of quid back as spending money. That's what men did in those days. Elsie would spend the money I gave her on food, milk, carpets, curtains, whatever we needed. I didn't need much for myself. I never went out on my own and I certainly didn't go to pubs. Never. That marked me out from many of my team-mates, who liked a pint, but I was being true to my upbringing, in which alcohol didn't feature. Going out to us meant seeing a film, shopping or going into Birmingham to have a look around. Elsie paid all the bills.

We didn't have a car. I walked the fifteen minutes to work. To me, the £2,500 we spent on that house was a fortune. It worried the life out of me. All I could think of was breaking my leg and having a huge mortgage hanging round my neck. How on earth was I going to pay that back? To boost our income, Elsie took a job as an industrial nurse with the Deritend Stamping Company, where she worked until three o'clock. The conveyancing solicitor who put us on the property ladder was a certain Bert Millichip, who went on to become chairman of the FA and my main point of contact in the England job.

For me, these were momentous years, on the pitch and in my family life. In the same season that I made my full international debut, an even bigger privilege came my way with the birth of our first son, Paul, who emerged into the world, after a complicated pregnancy and early birth, at Dudley Road hospital in June 1957. Our second son, Andrew, was born at the same hospital in March 1959 – not that I witnessed the magic moments, the way players do these days. The day Elsie went into hospital to have Andrew, I played against Blackpool in the afternoon. In today's world, a player in that situation would make a strong case to be in the maternity ward so he could hold his wife's hand and see his son or daughter emerge into the light. If you'd suggested such a thing in the 1950s they would have looked at you as if you were insane.

At five o'clock, after we had tussled with Blackpool, I strode back into the changing room to be told by the club secretary, 'Bobby, at three fifteen your wife gave birth to a boy and they're both in good condition.' Quite apart from the club's reluctance to release you on a match day, hospitals in those days were not keen to have anxious fathers clogging up the delivery room. I've never seen a baby being born, not even on television.

With parenthood comes a heightened sense of financial responsibilities. Suddenly a footballer is representing a family at the negotiating table and not just his own sporting ambitions. Money, or the comparative shortage of it, was to drive a wedge between me and West Bromwich Albion after Jimmy Hill and the PFA (Professional Footballers' Association) won their campaign for the abolition of the maximum wage. This victory over the artificial restriction on market forces pushed Johnny Haynes up to £100 a week – a landmark in the English game – but the revolution left many of us still fighting to have our deals renegotiated and our wages increased.

The PFA asked for a rise in the minimum wage across the board from £20 to £25. The football management committee said no. As captain of the club and an England international, I pointed out to the West Bromwich Albion board that Sheffield Wednesday, for example, were offering £30 a week and a bonus scheme relating to attendances. If the gate went up to such and such a level, the players would get an extra pound or two. Deals were being struck. New ground was being broken. West Bromwich offered me £25 a week plus £5 if I played. I wouldn't get the £5 if I was injured. I couldn't help comparing that unfavourably with what Johnny Haynes was being paid at my old club.

Johnny's was the most famous wage ever paid to a footballer. To work out why, you don't need to look beyond Tommy Trinder, who understood showbusiness and the pulling power of a big name. Fulham might not be able to match Arsenal in the market but Tommy was trying to show that his club had style and audacity. The message was, 'We've got the best player in the country, nobody's going to touch him, and we'll pay him whatever we have to.' They rendered Johnny unbuyable because nobody else was paying that sort of money. Tommy made a famous statement to the press: 'Johnny Haynes is a top entertainer and will be paid as one from now on. I will pay him £100 a week to play for Fulham.'

Meanwhile, I confronted the West Bromwich chairman, Jim Gaunt. 'I deserve more. I want more. I'd like you to consider it,' I said. 'If this is what you're paying me, the captain, what are you going to pay the people behind me? They're not going to get much of a rise if I'm top of the tree and you're offering me £25.'

I was fighting for the whole team. I felt I had a right to do that, but Jim wouldn't budge.

That summer of 1962 I asked for a transfer and was stripped of the captaincy by the manager, Archie Macaulay, who had succeeded Vic Buckingham. Archie gave the armband to Don Howe. I had a wife and two kids and maybe five years left in the game, and I was being underpaid. Elsie supported me, even though we had no clue where we were going until Fulham came in and offered me £45 plus £5 – a massive increase that doubled my existing salary. They also paid a £20,000 transfer fee.

West Bromwich blocked my testimonial, which was supposed to be for loyal and meritorious service, and tried to tell me I had been disloyal after six years of hard work. 'I'm not being disloyal,' I protested. 'It's you who's being disloyal.' I didn't receive the full amount. We settled on a proportion of the sum I would have been due.

When Fulham brought me back to London, Bedford Jezzard was in the hot seat as manager. They were still a social club, not for introverts. Take Tony Macedo, our goalkeeper. One morning, Tony came into training full of new ideas, having seen American basketball player Meadowlark Lemon perform his tricks for the Harlem Globetrotters on 'Sportsnight' the previous evening. Meadowlark Lemon could perform an especially elaborate sleight of hand, pretending to throw the ball and then dragging it back into his palm. His marker would be baffled and sent the wrong way. Tony took a fancy to this stunt.

That Saturday, we played Spurs at White Hart Lane in front of 47,000 spectators. We were winning 1–0 when Bobby Keetch turned to collect a ball hit over the top of our defence, and played it back to Tony in goal. In those days, of course, the keeper could pick up the ball. Now, he has to kick it.

As Tony gathered the ball, Jimmy Greaves started to encroach on his space, so our goalkeeper tried the Meadowlark Lemon trick on Jimmy – except that the ball slipped out of his hands and went straight to Greaves, one of the most lethal finishers in the history of English football. Bang, Jimmy buried it in the back of the net. Bobby Keetch fell over in disgust and Johnny Haynes came back to give him a right rollocking. We drew the game 1–1.

Tony had a wonderful knack of delaying his dives until the last moment. He would catch the ball right at the last second. 'My God, what a save that was!' people would exclaim but the truth was that he could have caught it much earlier with ease. With good judgement and a sense of theatre he made himself look the most spectacular goalkeeper in England. Often the public couldn't spot it but the other players knew Tony's game.

Bobby Keetch, meanwhile, gravitated towards high society. He was a handsome boy and a lady's man. He was one of the first players to have a car. It wasn't his, though. It belonged to a titled lady he was escorting, and she would dress him up in pinstriped suits to go with it. The car had a turntable on which you could play records. 'Here lads, come and listen to this,' Bobby would say as he rolled into training, and he'd play us a Frank Sinatra record.

During an overnight stay in Worthing, I remember him talking to his aristocratic girlfriend on the telephone in the most suggestive language imaginable.

'Bobby, you can't talk to a lady like that,' I told him.

'No, it's all right, she likes it,' he reassured me. Then he phoned down to the bellboy to tell him a letter would be coming for him the next morning. In the envelope was a £50 note from the Duchess.

When Bobby was suspended for two weeks one season, we had a whip round to keep him in funds. In those days, players weren't paid if they were banned from playing. Bobby came in one morning, beaming.

'I had a fantastic night last night, lads,' he grinned.

'Oh yeah, where did you go, Bobby?' we chorused.

Then he explained how the bill at the restaurant or nightclub where he had spent the evening had cost him eighty quid. We were aghast.

'That was our money,' we protested. 'We're paying your wages and you've splashed it out like that.'

Bobby told wonderful stories. The lads would come in early just to listen to him. I recall him setting off on the tale of a romantic encounter.

'Hey lads, listen to this,' he began. 'You know when you go to a party and you see a wonderful girl, and she catches your eye – you smile at her and she smiles at you – and then you go over to introduce yourself? Well, that happened to me last night. You know what I said to her?' We all waited. '"I couldn't half **** you."'

'What!' we cried, but Bobby rolled on.

'Do you know what she said? She said "Where?"'

Many years later, during Euro '96, I walked into the Hilton Hotel and spotted Terry Venables sitting alone at the bar, crying.

'You won't believe what's happened,' Terry said. 'Bobby Keetch died last night.'

Rodney Marsh was a young swinger in those days. He hero-worshipped Denis Law. On TV one night, Rodney saw Law take an in-swinging corner that hit the near post, bounced out and was then smashed into the goal on a perfect arc by Denis, who was following up his own ball in the box.

'Lucky bastard,' said Johnny Haynes in training the next day.

'What do you mean, lucky bastard?' Rodney piped up. 'He did that on purpose. Furthermore, I can do it as well.'

'Ah, shut up,' the lads all groaned but Rodney's mind was made up. Off we went to the pitch at Craven Cottage. Rodney carefully placed the ball on the corner spot, and proceeded to do exactly what Denis Law had done for the TV cameras, first time. He smashed it into the net on a rebound that came out at the perfect angle for the shot.

Rodney's boundless self-confidence was not unchallengeable, though. For a bet, he reckoned he could give me yards for years on a sprint round the perimeter of the pitch. I was a lot older than Rodney but I had good heart and lung condition. All the lads came to watch Robson versus Marsh.

Well, Rodney gave me a ten-yard start and by the second corner I was forty yards clear. He gave up, stopped running. 'Just respect your elders, Marshy,' I said. At Fulham and later Ipswich I liked to say, 'Put your caps on the table. When you've got more caps than I have, I'll let you talk.' Rodney remembered the race when he came to speak at Shay Given's cancer charity dinner in Newcastle in 2004.

Not long after I arrived, tension arose between the manager and the board. The sale of Alan Mullery to Spurs for £72,500 was hardly likely to improve strained relations, and in that phase of Fulham's colourful history, Rodney Marsh was also sold to London rival Queen's Park Rangers. So Bedford Jezzard was soon on his way and who should replace him but Vic Buckingham.

The truth is that my playing career fizzled out in my final five years at Fulham, and I ended my time on the pitch without a significant honour to my name, which disappoints me even now. In all my time as a footballer, I didn't win a thing. Playing against Manchester United in an FA Cup semi-final was the closest I came to taking part in a showpiece event. In the League, fourth place with West Bromwich was as good as it got. The teams I played for never quite got the better of the Busby Babes or the great Wolves sides put together by Stan Cullis, or Spurs, Burnley or Aston Villa. These were the pre-eminent clubs of my era. I'm sure my lack of success on the pitch gave me an extra competitive edge when I swapped a playing kit for a tracksuit. I had a void to fill, a gap on my mantelpiece to decorate. I was hungry to wrap my fingers round some prizes.

I had been determined, on principle, to leave West Bromwich, although it hurt me to walk away from so many good team-mates. Don Howe supported me on my decision and I was sure I was making the right move. I knew and liked Fulham. We were back in Surrey when our third son, Mark, was born – in Epsom in April 1963. In 1967 I read in the papers that Arsenal might come in to prolong my career but nothing materialised and foot-ball was to take me much further afield, to Canada and the Vancouver Royals.

4

1966 AND ALL THAT

ON a trip to Wolverhampton racecourse in November 1957 I landed the biggest winner of my early professional life. No horses or bookmakers were involved. As I was leaving the track after a good day out with some West Brom team-mates, I peeled away to buy the evening paper and scanned the stop-press column, where players looked in those days to find out who had been summoned for international duty. There I spotted an announcement: 'The England team to play France is as follows . . .' and there was my name – R. Robson.

Seriously, in the 1950s that was how you found out whether you had been picked to play for your country. This was a world without mobile phones, emails, text messages and faxes – nor did we have a telephone at home, so I had to wait until I got back to the house to tell Elsie I was going to play for England against France at Wembley. I knew the team was being announced that day, and had gone to the races with Don Howe, Brian Whitehouse and Ronnie Allen – who fancied himself as a tipster – knowing that it might be worth my while to stop for a copy of the local paper as I left the nags and the bookies behind.

All over England, presumably, top footballers were rushing up to newspaper vendors and pressing coins into their hands. After that undignified scramble, the next step was for the club to receive a letter from the FA confirming the invitation. When you next came into work, the secretary would tell you when and how to report for duty. No correspondence from the FA ever came directly to your house. The club secretary was the conduit. If England were at home, the order was usually to assemble at Hendon Hall hotel, in Hendon, north London, two days before the match.

So I entered the international firmament of the full England team and encountered, on my first day in the camp, Duncan Edwards, Tom Finney, Billy Wright, Tommy Taylor and the other legends of that age. I confess that I wondered whether I was good enough to be among these gods of the English game but my anxiety soon subsided. After a couple of games I began to feel I belonged in that company. Players who can't cope with international football feel more and more disorientated and merely wait for the moment when they're discarded. The ones who were born for it soon feel part of the furniture.

The forward line for my debut was Bryan Douglas, Bobby Robson, Johnny Haynes, Tommy Taylor and Tom Finney – not bad, I thought. I'm not sure what the others thought of me but from my vantage point I was deeply honoured to be part of such a distinguished quartet. My other team-mates that day were Eddie Hopkinson, Don Howe, Roger Byrne, Ron Clayton, Billy Wright and Duncan Edwards.

For the pre-match meal I sat next to Tom Finney, who was a lovely fellow, and thought it might be wise to seek his advice on the subject of first-night nerves.

'What's it going to be like for me, Tom?' I asked.

'It's going to be difficult,' he said. 'Bobby, you're playing against the best players in France, one of the best teams in Europe. Every player is international standard. Remember, though, you're playing with the best players in England, which equals things out.' Then he smiled. 'If you get yourself in a pickle, just give me the ball and I'll keep it for ten minutes until you get your confidence back.'

If he was trying to make me laugh, it worked. Tom was hilarious. 'Frigging' was his preferred curse. 'That frigging referee' or 'that frigging ball'. He never swore once in all the time I spent with him. Later, I played with Tom in an old-timers' charity match in Yugoslavia, where we were joined by John Charles and Stanley Matthews. Oh yes, I've played with some legends. Stanley was charming and down to earth and very hospitable, a silver-haired icon.

Nat Lofthouse, with whom I never played, was another great person – honest, dead straight. He once asked me to speak, as England manager, at a corporate do at Bolton Wanderers. That night I told a story about waiting for the FA Cup third-round draw in my Fulham playing days. Of all the teams you didn't want to meet, Bolton were top of the list by a mile. Their back line was ferocious. Anything that moved, they kicked – no exceptions. So if you heard your name read out in the draw – 'Number eight, Fulham, will play . . .' – you'd cry, 'Oh please don't say Bolton Wanderers . . .'

Burnden Park was the worst place in the world to go. The pitch was built up on to a kind of plateau, and Tommy Banks, their enforcer in chief, would hit you over the slope and into the ditch below. Those guys were rascals. Nat owned up to it in an interview around the time I went to Bolton to speak. 'In the fifties there were plenty of fellas who would kick your bollocks off,' Nat recalled. 'The difference between then and now is that they would shake you by the hand at the end and help you look for them.'

Nat might have been referring to old Tommy Banks. I played with Tommy for England, and I remember Walter Winterbottom saying to him one day, 'Tommy, I want such and such a player put out of the game. Do you understand?'

Tommy thought for a moment and then said, 'Do you mean today, or for life?'

'No, no, no, Tommy,' Walter replied, his face contorting with horror. Tommy wasn't discouraged.

'Are you fookin' sure, Walter?' he asked.

Jimmy Greaves was another colleague I loved. Walter would describe some elaborate moves to us, passing moves, involving several players, and then say, 'At the end of all that, Jimmy will score a goal.' Jimmy would sit there listening, saying nothing, before finally piping up, 'Do you want me to score with my left foot, Walter, or my right?' What a player. He would play onside-offside on the shoulder of the last defender, and he had a spin that would launch him over the ground at incredible speed. Jimmy ran without touching the ground and was an exemplary finisher. He was left-footed, essentially, but could knock it in just as well with his right. Gary Lineker was a good touch player and so were Kenny Dalglish and Denis Law. Ronaldo is a good touch player, too. Jimmy was up there with those guys and the tragedy of his career was that he didn't play in the World Cup final of 1966. Roger Hunt took his place on the big day.

I didn't mind Jimmy not chasing back in games, because when you had the ball he always demanded it. He was forever offering you a target. He was mustard with anything knocked over the top. 'Just stick it in there and I'll get on the end of it,' he would say. He had the searing pace to carry him into shooting positions. Johnny Haynes was perfect for him because he saw the pass so early. Johnny could put it on the spot for Jimmy to bury.

Back in my debut game in 1957, Bryan Douglas was a clever little bugger, a jinking player, and as my nerves began to settle Bryan pulled one back for me to hit first time and there it was in the back of the net. Tommy Taylor scored twice and I got the other two in a 4–0 win. What a start to my England career. I wasn't to know that two goals on my debut offered no guarantee of a starting place in the next game. Who would have guessed that? Against Scotland, I was moved aside and saw my place awarded to a young guy who was making waves up in Manchester. Bobby Charlton, I think he was called.

This was the least of the tragedies associated with my first game for England. The real calamity was that it turned out to be the last for Duncan Edwards, Roger Byrne and Tommy Taylor, who all perished four months later in the Munich Air Disaster of 1958. The thought chills me to this day. In a sense, I passed the Busby Babes on life's escalator, and soon they would be lost to us, leaving me with haunting memories of the day I played for England with some of the finest players of our generation.

I had played against them at club level a few times, of course, and I have no hesitation in endorsing the claim that Duncan Edwards was a colossus. 'Boom Boom', as the supporters called him, was a big hulk of a lad with two great feet. They were so good, in fact, that he wouldn't have been able to say which one was superior. Duncan purred over the ground, bringing the ball upfield with immense power, and was a master of the long pass, the long-range shot. He was also good in the air. This young kid from Dudley was going to be a phenomenon. He was in the England team by the age of nineteen. Later, I drew an entirely valid comparison between Duncan and Kevin Beattie, whom I managed at Ipswich Town.

The Munich catastrophe took me a long time to get over. I distinctly remember the announcement on television. For some reason, I recall Eric Houghton, the Aston Villa manager, giving his reaction on a television set I had hired from Radio Rentals. It affected me very deeply – the wreck of the Elizabethan airliner on the runway, the shroud of snow over the mangled metal, the roll call of death, all those boys snatched away from us, those young lives. In the violence of that crash on 6 February 1958, Roger Byrne, Geoff Bent, Eddie Colman, Mark Jones, David Pegg, Tommy Taylor and Liam 'Billy' Whelan were among the first casualties. Duncan Edwards hung on for a fortnight but lost the fight for life. Matt Busby, with a crushed chest, was in a critical condition for a time but survived. Bobby Charlton was thrown from the plane still strapped to his seat.

Duncan was something of a local hero in our parish, even though Wolves and West Bromwich Albion had failed to prevent him joining Manchester United. The country went into mourning for several days. Given the proximity to the war years, it may be that people of that time were better equipped to cope with bereavement than we are today, and were able to rationalise death, but still a terrible void opened and the grief was savage. In footballing terms alone, the Busby Babes were the finest team in the country and a beacon to all ambitious clubs. They embodied the principle that a team could be constructed from the bottom up, through good talent spotting and coaching.

I marvel still at Bobby Charlton's ability to recover from his ordeal. One image of him struggling against his trauma, his memories, remains razor sharp. On England's flight to Sweden for the 1958 World Cup, I remember Bobby starting to rock and sweat in his seat as our plane entered a thick bank of cloud and began to be buffeted by turbulence. The two of us got on well. We were two Geordie lads. Bobby took my place in the England side but later we played together as well. I was sitting next to him on that flight, and Bobby, who was in the window seat, was starting to perspire and clench his hands.

'You're all right, Bobby,' I told him, as gently as I could.

'Yeah, I'm all right,' he repeated. 'Just get this bloody plane down.' God only knows what visions were coming back to torment him.

He was strong. He got on with it. There was immense sympathy for him in the England camp but we didn't press him to discuss that awful night in Munich. We tried to help him look forward. I remember playing against him in the FA Cup, not long after Jimmy Murphy had attempted to put the remaining parts of the United team back together, while also bringing in reinforcements, in what must have been one of the most daunting missions in football management. United were engulfed by public sympathy. Twenty thousand were locked out that night. In a kind of mass hysteria, the overwhelming sadness generated and the support they received helped United overcome their grief. A boy called Albert Quixall came in, along with Eddie Clamp, and the team recovered some of its old strength. The post-Munich United even made it to Wembley that year, losing the FA Cup final to Bolton Wanderers 2–0. Four of the original Busby Babes played that day – Charlton, Viollet, Gregg and Foulkes. Two goals by Nat Lofthouse spoiled the fairytale.

Until Alf Ramsey took over and imposed his own authority on the FA, the England team was picked by an international selection committee. Its members came from individual clubs and their trick was to make sure a player or two from their own teams appeared in the starting eleven. For political reasons, then, you ended up with a couple of players from Leeds, two from Bolton and so on. Major Wilson Keys, who was the West Bromwich Albion chairman, was an influential member of the FA and doubtless had his say on whether I should be given a chance. These men weren't idiots. They could only suggest the names of authentically good players. Still, Walter was left to do the best he could with players who had been chosen for him by men in suits.

For the 1958 World Cup, the FA unexpectedly cut the squad from twenty-two to twenty, and Stanley Matthews and Nat Lofthouse were the two who missed out. Yes, you read that correctly. Don't ask me why two of our finest players were left at home. The tournament was a let down for us, and a huge disappointment for me personally. One of the great regrets of my playing career is that I never shared a pitch with Pele. Here's the irony – I played in our group game against Brazil but neither Pele nor his fellow magician, Garrincha, were selected for the match. We drew 0–0. That was my one big chance, although of course I couldn't have known that Pele would go on to become the world's most illustrious footballer. He was seventeen at the time. I took no notice of him sitting on the touchline in that wedge of yellow and green, the colours that would become the most evocative in the game.

That summer, Brazil became football's spiritual home. By the time I encountered them again, as England manager, Pele's homeland was instantly recognisable as the most creative in world football. The aura, the romance, established itself swiftly after 1958, and achieved its zenith twelve years later with the 1970 World Cup. The hypnotic power of Brazilian football can undermine even the best prepared teams. In 2002, in Shizuoka, Sven-Goran Eriksson's England team seemed daunted at times by the artistic tradition coming at them in waves, even when Brazil were reduced to ten by the dismissal of Ronaldinho, who has developed into a sublime player. I look at him and gasp at the tricks, the pace, the power, the dinks, the little sprints – marvellous.

Pele burst to prominence in that 1958 World Cup with no prior reputation. He meant nothing to me but Garrincha did. So did Didi, who was my direct counterpart in our group game. My word, I found him hard going. He was the toughest opponent I had faced up to that point in my career. Later, I got better – harder, wiser, more experienced – and nobody frightened me by the end of my career. I was so pleased to be in the England team to face Brazil that I didn't think much about what Didi would be like. I was twenty-five and had some confidence and stature, playing in the top six of the old First Division, competing against Manchester United and the rest, but I couldn't get near that blasted Didi. I couldn't get the ball off him. He was quick, elusive, and I couldn't work out where he was.

I had two goals disallowed in that tournament. One was against Russia when Derek Kevan was adjudged to have fouled Yashin, the goalkeeper, and my swivelled finish was cancelled out by the Hungarian referee. The press did point out that Hungary was under the heel of Soviet Russia in 1958, and described the disallowing of my goal, as I recall it, as 'a political decision'. We drew 2–2 with the USSR, 0–0 with Brazil and 2–2 with Austria, a match where we again had a goal disallowed. In a subsequent play-off against the USSR we went down 1–0 and headed for the airport.

However sharp the pain, I fell in love with the World Cup that summer. I was intoxicated by this great gathering of nations, this rolling festival of games. Part of the joy of being a participant was being the centre of attention. I can almost feel, on my skin, the official blazer, shirt and tie that marked you out as a player in the drama. Free kit, free boots, tracksuits to keep – it was unheard of. To have two pairs of boots and a bag to carry them all in was the stuff of fantasies. You felt special. The match fee was £50, at a time when we were on £20 or so a week.

Nobody had an agent and commercial tie-ups didn't exist, but players were just starting to understand their commercial value to clubs and to the FA. One day I directed what I thought was a little joke at our manager. 'Walter,' I said, 'as England matches are being televised now, do the players get any extra money for being on TV?' Walter laughed but later we were given a £5 fee, which pushed us up to £55 per appearance – an extra fiver, pure heaven.

Nowadays the logic is reversed. The reward for playing for England is a fraction of what's handed over the counter each week in the Premier League. Our eyes were just being opened to commercial possibilities. Cigarette cards attracted my interest and set off a train of thought. Open a packet of fags or sweets and a picture of an England footballer or cricketer might fall out.

I said to the manager, 'Walter, Wills' cigarette cards are being used to encourage people to keep buying their products. How can they use me like that to make money? Why don't you look into it?' Walter wrote to them and we ended up getting a three-guinea fee for our image rights. They weren't called that, then, of course, but the same principle applied. We thought the three guineas were marvellous. I suppose I was a bit of a trailblazer.

After the 1958 World Cup, I became a regular member of the England first eleven. Between October 1960 and May 1961 I was part of an excellent run of six consecutive victories, during which we scored forty goals. The highlight was the demolition of Scotland, the 'auld enemy', 9–3 at Wembley in the early summer of 1961. The star of the show was Jimmy Greaves, who was on something of a rampage. His hat-trick was at the expense, chiefly, of poor Frank Haffey, the Celtic goalkeeper. Johnny Haynes was another to torment the Scots, ripping their defence apart from the inside-left position. Johnny got two, as did Bobby Smith, and Bryan Douglas and I topped it up to nine. It was Scotland's record defeat.

My goal was England's first. I came out of midfield and hit one first time, on a pull back. I was playing in newish boots and by the end of the match I had a whopping blister on the big toe of my right foot. Squeezing my shoe on after the game was eye-wateringly painful and I still had the journey back to the Midlands ahead of me – not in an FA limo, mark you, but by train and bus. Later, fleets of plush cars would wait for the players beneath the Twin Towers, and fan out across the country to deliver their precious cargo back to their families. For us, in 1961, it was off to the train station. You had to produce your ticket and any other documentary evidence to get your expenses from the FA. Walter would dish out the money and record every item of expenditure on an expense sheet. Taxis were discouraged as far too extravagant.

So off I headed, with a raw, twanging toe, to Euston, to catch the train to Snowshill station in Birmingham, and then on by bus to our house in Handsworth. My toe was beeping like a hazard light. Nevertheless, I walked from the bus stop at Handsworth Road all the way home, which took ten minutes. I had to take my shoe off in the end. I remember thinking, 'I played for England against Scotland yesterday. I played right-half and scored the first goal, and now I'm walking home in my socks.'

The modern reader will assume that a train journey home after a 9–3 win at Wembley was one long round of autograph signings and acclamation. Think again. This was before the mass media age. There was no Sky TV or daily blizzard of newspaper coverage to make our faces instantly recognisable. There was no superstar syndrome, no obsession with celebrity. We could blend into a crowd, pretty much, and board a bus unmolested. These days, a club would go crackers if one of their players came home with a bad blister, via public transport.

Painful journeys aside, those were my best years as a player, from 1959 running up to 1962, when luck just turned against me and deprived me of my place in the England team. The beneficiary was young Bobby Moore – not a bad guy to lose your place to. The Chile World Cup of 1962 was a calamity for me, although I went there as a recognised team member. Bobby Moore was nineteen and he was taken along, as far as we could tell, to be blooded, to be given a chance to stroll across football's biggest stage. Bobby's talent was obvious but that's not what put me on the sidelines for the whole of the tournament.

We stayed in a place called Coya, an old mining community in the hills, a long way from the hub of Chilean life. Walter had been on a scouting mission to find us a base and had settled on this extremely remote location. Today's England players would have rebelled. They would have taken one look and run back down the hill. We lived in two sets of houses, or huts, separated by a ravine, which one of the groups had to cross, via a bridge, to take meals. To get down from the hills you had to descend on a small mining train. There was very little to do, except read books, play head tennis and tell each other tales. One day Walter informed us that the villagers were putting on a concert for us. It was a rare chance to escape our boredom, so arms shot up in the air, volunteering to attend.

In those days, on trips to South America you had to be careful about what you consumed. The affliction we feared most was 'Chile-itis' otherwise known as the runs, or Montezuma's revenge. We were swallowing huge sulphur tablets once a day to counteract any possible ill effects, which were like eating slabs of chalk. Religiously, Harold Sheperdson, the trainer, would come round at breakfast and force the sulphur pills down our throats. 'Come on, eat it, eat it,' Harold would chant.

Peter Swan was a member of our squad. He was a good lad, so how he ever got involved in the match-fixing scandal of 1964–65 I will never know. In January 1965, Peter was among ten professional footballers who were found guilty at Nottingham Assizes of fixing the results of games. Peter and Tony Kay were the two England players to go down. In Chile in 1962, Peter developed a reluctance to take those sulphur tablets, which he hid from the England staff, and, you guessed it, he went down with Chile-itis. He became so dehydrated that he had to be taken to hospital to have fluid pumped into him, but not before he had let his hair down at the village concert, a rare and brief indulgence that was to rebound on him spectacularly.

Obviously, we couldn't understand a word of the concert in the village hall, but we could recognise the beauty of the local girl who got up on stage to sing a folk song while swinging an exotic scarf round her head. When she stepped off the stage to invite one of us up on to the boards to enhance the routine, most of us recoiled, through shyness, but Peter, who was the closest thing we had to a Paul Gascoigne, volunteered, and was soon bouncing on to the stage with a grin. Within no time he was swinging the scarf round his head and throwing himself into the routine.

Click, click, click. Unknown to us, a photographer had wedged himself at the back of the village hall, and had taken what he assumed to be some perfectly innocent pictures of an England player joining the locals in a bit of harmless fun. Back in Sheffield, meanwhile, Mrs Swan was about to give birth to Peter's child. A few days after the concert, she was leafing through the pages of the Sheffield local paper when she came across a picture of her husband cavorting on stage with a Chilean temptress. Mrs Swan had no hope of getting through to the England camp by phone, so she wrote to him, along these lines: 'Here I am at home, having your baby, and you're out there enjoying yourself with a beautiful Chilean lady . . .' Peter showed us the letter. What she didn't know was that by then he was confined to his bathroom and his bed and was completely unable to leave his room, except to be taken to hospital.

Before it became that serious, Don Howe and I said to one another, 'Let's cross the ravine and see how Swanny is.' We banged on the door but got no reply, so in we went. The bed clothes were rumpled but there was no sign of Peter. We found him sitting on the loo, doubled up.

'How are you?' we asked.

'How am I?' he replied, weakly. 'I'm at death's door, and I'll tell you something else. My wife's just written to me, and she thinks I'm having a whale of a time!' My God, he was ill. He was disappearing.

He wasn't the only one who left Chile with bad memories. My own international career began to unravel the day Walter received an invitation from the local parks team to take part in a friendly match on the practice ground, which was actually very good. Walter asked us what we thought, and again we signalled our approval. Why not? Sure, we'd give them a game. We were bored. We knew the World Cup was edging closer, but surely this was only training in a different form. Walter asked for volunteers. My hand went up – big mistake.

My role in this Anglo-Chilean diplomatic exercise ended painfully and prematurely when one of the local players nicked me in a tackle and caused me to go over awkwardly. My foot blew up like a football. I had chipped a bone in my ankle. That's how Bobby Moore was promoted to the England team.

Before Chile, we had stopped off in Peru, where Walter had played Bobby ahead of me, which was fine, because the manager doubtless needed to see how Bobby would perform at that level. We won 4–0, with a hat-trick from Jimmy Greaves. Before that, I had played in a 3–1 win over Switzerland – our last game before heading to South America – and had been pleased with my performance. Johnny Haynes and I were playing 4–4–2, and we knew each other well. None of this was any use to me when the x-ray in a hospital in Coya revealed the damage to my ankle bone.

'Two to three weeks,' said the doctor.

'Oh, no, don't tell me that,' I said.

My ankle was sound again for our last match in Chile, the 3–1 defeat by Brazil in the quarter-finals, but I wasn't quite fit enough to force my way back into the team. So my international playing career ended with the match against Switzerland, and there was to be no second chance to test myself against Pele. I never played for England again, and Bobby Moore never looked back.

Bobby was a handsome boy and a smashing person. I loved him. He was very respectful, very polite and trained well. He was the guy you wanted your daughter or sister to marry.

In 1962, I never thought he would be the golden boy of English football. Later, I marvelled at the breadth and speed of his development. He was a studious player, not a vigorous one. He never hunted opponents to bury them with a tackle. He waited for people to come on to him and then dealt with the threat. He didn't like the idea of people getting in behind him and reasoned that, if he chased strikers around the field, he would leave space for others to run into. Bobby worked out that the hole in front of you is less dangerous than the hole behind you. He read the game exceptionally well. He knew when to press, when to drop off, and had a good, early pass, which he didn't spoil with over-elaboration. If the pass wasn't on, he could 'cuddle' the ball and run five yards with it before playing it to someone else.

He was always going to be a left-half because he didn't quite have the ability to play midfield. His qualities were anticipation, reading the game, judgement and a firm, clean tackle. He could breast the ball down rather than head it into nowhere – which you see a lot of centre-halves do. He was a thoughtful player, even at nineteen, and polished all those little skills while learning to concentrate hard on the specific disciplines of defending – hence his exceptionally low error ratio. The one he made against Poland in 1973 in World Cup qualifying stands out precisely because he made so few. Bobby Moore made fewer mistakes than any defender I've seen in my life.

As we returned to our clubs and began looking ahead to the World Cup of 1966, I was still hopeful of working my way into Alf Ramsey's England team, this time as a defender because I had moved back at Fulham to settle in the back four. Like Bobby, I could read the play and allowed strikers to come on to me with the ball. I knew when to drop off and when to intervene with a tackle. Also, I had a bit of skill from my days as a striker and midfielder, so I felt comfortable and confident in possession. Vic Buckingham converted me and I did well in that position, but the call never came.

On that magical, sun-buttered day in 1966, I took my eldest son, Paul, to Wembley, and felt the competing emotions of joy and envy. I loved every second of the game itself. When Geoff Hurst smashed our fourth, unanswerable goal into the roof of West Germany's net, I was on my feet, like everyone else, but throughout the match an internal voice had been saying, 'That could have been me out there.'

I played for England for five years, won twenty caps and scored four goals. The golden period for me was 1960–61, when we beat Northern Ireland 5–2, Luxembourg 9–0, Spain 4–2, Wales 5–1, Scotland 9–3, Mexico 8–0 and Italy 3–2. Quite a run – and I played in all those games. Play for five years now and you'll get seventy caps. Forty years ago, a cap was for real, awarded only if you started the game and finished it as well.

There is no escaping the sense I have that my international career was unfulfilled. I missed the 1962 World Cup through injury, even though I was there, and the glorious English tournament of 1966 by a narrow margin of selection. My happiest memory, probably, was scoring the first goal in the 9–3 win over Scotland, which Elsie managed to miss. 'Did you see my goal?' I gushed after the game. 'No,' she said. 'Sorry. I got delayed on the way to the ground.'

On English football's greatest day, I confess, I gritted my teeth and shook my head. I was in the top division with Fulham. I felt I could handle anyone. I could have played that day in 1966.

5
ROUGH SEAS

T HE first, painful phase of my coaching life started with a
luxury cruise to Canada and ended in a London labour
exchange with me signing on the dole. But for a chance call from
my old friend Dave Sexton, in January 1969, I might have slipped
off the edge of football. Dad might have been entitled to wag his
finger and tell me he had been right all along about keeping my
hand in as an electrician.

Just about all the pitfalls of football management were laid
out before me in my first two spells in the dug-out – deceit,
litigation, bankruptcy and the terrible cruelty that chairmen
inflict on managers when they throw them aside before they have
had time to grow into the job. This brutal crash course in the
politics of football management equipped me well for England,
Barcelona and Newcastle.

The first club to offer me work was Southend United, who
wanted me to join them as player-manager on less than I was
earning at Fulham. The interview took place at Brentwood,
where Trevor Bailey, the England cricketer who doubled up as
club chairman, was in action for Essex. I love cricket and a
county ground was an unusually tranquil venue for a job interview. At tea, Trevor told me he wanted me to coach and play
simultaneously, but I didn't go for that and instead fell into the
arms of the Vancouver Royals, who were part of the embryonic
North American Soccer League.

I've had a nomadic life in football management. Looking back, I suppose my willingness to uproot the family to try my luck in Canada provided early evidence of my restlessness, or reckless-ness, call it what you will. It would have been easy for a man from the Durham coalfields not to take risks, but an intrepid streak meant I was always ready to jump on a boat or a plane. When I left the England job in 1990, I travelled round Europe for the best part of ten years, absorbing the cultures of Holland, Portugal and Spain. Fortunately, those adventures were a good deal more successful than my little Canadian expedition, which taught me hard lessons about the vulnerability of the wandering coach.

Vancouver sent a representative over to see me and he seduced me into believing that this was a chance too good to miss. The city itself felt very English and was certainly appealing with its harbours, bays and golf courses. British immigrants peppered the community and around 12,000 kids played school football. 'Soccer' was making inroads against ice hockey, baseball and American football. Vancouver were a franchise in the expansion of the planet's most popular game in its most powerful nation.

We went by boat, the SS *Oriana*, which was later converted into a troop ship during the Falklands War. The club bought us first-class tickets and we crossed the Atlantic in style. At first Elsie was reluctant to go. Her thoughts were fixed on our families and on our three boys, who, she feared, might be unsettled by having to start again in a new country. All the anxieties of the long-distance traveller preyed on her mind. Conversely, I've always been headstrong. Thinking about it now, I ask myself, 'How did I have the courage to make us do that? I didn't consider anybody.'

Similarly, when my time as England manager ended, I announced unilaterally, 'Elsie, we're going to Eindhoven. Let's pack the bags.'

'Oh, am I going?' Elsie replied.

'What do you mean, "Am I going?"' I said. 'Of course you're going.'

Without Elsie's unstinting support, I wouldn't have been able to make these impulsive decisions. By going to PSV I doubled my England salary. 'We'll go for two years and then come home,' I reassured her. Come home? We ended up going farther afield, travelling south to the Iberian peninsula, to Porto, Lisbon and Barcelona. Even then, Frank Arnesen, the PSV sporting director, sidetracked me just as I was about to come home from Spain, and pleaded, 'Please, I need you for one year. Come back to PSV for twelve months,' and I did. I was like a shark that dare not stop. I was always on the move.

Right at the start of our travels, we emigrated to Vancouver, in essence, because I had signed for three years. I told Elsie straight, 'We might not come back.' All the boys had to be taken out of school and amid tearful farewells on the quayside, Elsie gritted her teeth and walked up the ramp. She didn't want to leave her mother and father. Deep down, I was also tormented to see the coast of England recede. I just thought it would be good for us to try something new. I was more loose in the head than Elsie. I don't regret it now. What an education it was to be meeting new people constantly and to be placed in challenging situations. Travelling of that sort forces you to be confident and to assert yourself. I learned how to face and deal with people from all walks of life. I developed a catholic taste and it enriched me as a man, no doubt about that. Without Canada, I really cannot imagine what I might have done for a living. Gone back to being an electrician? Queued for coaching jobs I was never going to get?

Vancouver was a wonderful experience and salutary. Brigadier Ted Aitkens was the owner of the club. I liked the Brigadier but it turned out that the financing of this new venture was more onerous than he had expected, so he got together with George Flaherty, who owned the franchise in San Francisco, to merge the clubs and their resources. Flaherty hired Ferenc Puskas to run his half of the club and, in theory, I would be taking care of my contingent of players. If it sounds unworkable, that's because it was.

To bolster the squad, I had signed five players – Pat O'Connell and Henry Hill from Fulham, Johnny King from Stoke, a Cypriot goalkeeper and two Chinese brothers I had seen on a tour of Hong Kong, Chung Si Wah and Chung Si Doi. There were 300,000 Chinese people in Vancouver and I reasoned that 10,000 of them might come to see our team if they felt some ethnic connection to the new show in town. It was entirely my idea to court the Chinese vote.

Problems soon started to mount. The first one was that I hadn't been paid. The boys were being set up in school for the start of autumn term and we were trying hard to integrate ourselves but the financial foundations of this brave new world were never strong. Vancouver and San Francisco were 2,000 miles apart, so it was hardly a natural or easy merger. Flaherty bought 51 per cent of the Vancouver franchise – a controlling stake – and before I knew it Puskas and his cronies were moving their tanks on to my lawn.

Flaherty summoned me to his office and delivered some startling news. From now on, I was to be the assistant coach, behind Puskas. 'Oh no I'm not,' I told him. 'Here's a copy of my contract. It says that Bobby Robson is the head coach of Vancouver Royals. H-e-a-d. Head coach.' His response, as I recall it, was, 'Well, we'll see about that.'

In December we were told to take all the players to Spain on a bonding mission. Puskas took his, I took mine. I'd just settled my wife and family in Vancouver and there I was abandoning them for six weeks to take part in this farce with the so-called

Magical Magyar. The idea was that we would fuse the two teams together, like a pantomime horse. I didn't like Puskas and I didn't like the players he'd bought. He had overpaid for some very moderate individuals.

Puskas wasn't a coach at all. He was an old player masquerading as a coach. He took part in the five-a-sides. Despite that huge belly of his, he retained a lot of the talent he had applied so devastatingly for Hungary and Real Madrid. He still had a trick and a turn and could still whack the ball with that left foot of his. It would ping through the air. Heaven knows what he must have been like in his pomp. By this time he was in his mid-forties, but in shooting practice he was still bloody brilliant. He was a player, though, not a tactician or team-builder.

Flaherty wasn't interested in my complaints. I told him I couldn't get on with Puskas. We couldn't work together. He couldn't speak English and I certainly couldn't converse in Hungarian. There was no response from Flaherty, so I ended up taking him to court for breach of contract. I was so happy to see Elsie and the kids when I got back home from Spain. I could have eaten my wife as I went through that front door.

The journey to Vancouver had been sensational – first-class travel through Bermuda, the Panama Canal, Acapulco, San Francisco and Port Everglades – and we had found a lovely house and a good school for the boys, but the problems with Puskas and the general governance of the club were insurmountable. Panic was setting in. I resolved to stay in Vancouver to conduct the legal action but the mood inside the Robson house was deteriorating. I was completely messed up, the kids were unhappy and Elsie was on edge.

Then, in January, Fulham rode to my rescue. They had heard about my troubles and offered to help. By then, unfortunately, Craven Cottage was a troubled place, with a team heading for relegation and a chief investor, Eric Miller, who liked to throw his weight around. I had no hope of saving them from demotion to the old Second Division. It wasn't the ideal homecoming. For my first match, an FA Cup tie against non-league Macclesfield, we were 1–0 down at one point but did manage to come back to win 4–2.

Although my managerial career was heading from bad to worse, I was able to make a couple of creditable entries on my short CV. One was the discovery of a young full-back at non-league Tonbridge who was to turn into a lethal striker for Arsenal, Newcastle and England. Harry Haslam, our chief scout, alerted me to the boy's potential and persuaded me to accompany him to Tonbridge to see this rather bow-legged kid. He had a whammer of a left foot and was a strong type, good in the air, and physically equipped to play at a much higher level. Sold! We paid £1,000 and took Malcolm Macdonald back to Fulham, where we converted him to a striker.

I also made a huge profit on Allan Clarke when we sold him to Leicester for £120,000 cash, plus Frank Large in part-exchange. What a great lad Frank was – not technically gifted but strong and powerful. He could bundle his way through any traffic jam of bodies. Matt Busby was most upset by the arrangement because he thought he'd captured 'Sniffer' Clarke, as he later came to be known. The difference was that Manchester United offered £150,000 up front, whereas we preferred the £120,000 plus Frank Large. United probably assumed we wouldn't sell Allan to Leicester for less cash and so stuck at £150,000 and missed out.

The most salient detail here is that Fulham desperately needed the money. Clubs who sell their best players to cover running costs are always unlikely to find themselves playing Real Madrid in a European Cup final any day soon. First, I was glad to be back in England, buying a house in the Surrey stockbroker belt and getting the boys settled again in English schools. Beyond that, nothing went right. I had played with most of my Fulham team less than a year before and suddenly I was their boss, which created a whole new dynamic. Johnny Haynes was to succeed me, and lasted less than a month, partly for the same reason. Brian Clough lasted forty-four days at Leeds. Johnny lasted twenty-eight at a club where he was a legend. He was a great guy and an illustrious player but he was never manager material. I would advise any young would-be manager not to start at a club where they've been a player. Go somewhere else. I would say that even to Alan Shearer at Newcastle. It's much harder to impose your authority on men who were mates and comrades only a few weeks previously.

We went down, with 27 points, for the simple reason that I didn't have enough good players to save us. We just weren't good enough to be in the top flight and I paid for that with my job at a time, in November, when we were eighth in the Second Division. The board thought eighth place wasn't good enough for Fulham. They gave me no time to regroup but expected us to be in the top three, jockeying to come straight back up.

Driving home along Putney High Street that autumn afternoon, I spotted an *Evening Standard* placard with the headline 'Robson sacked'. I did a double take. Robson sacked? Which Robson could that be? I stopped my car and walked up to Putney High Street station in search of corroborating evidence. In 1968, of course, you could stop your car in Putney High Street and park without worrying about being clamped, or coming back to find a mound of tickets under your windscreen wipers. My mission was to find another of these billboards. The first one might have been a hoax, but there it was, splashed across the evening paper. Read all about it! I'd lost my job.

An hour earlier, I had left Graham Hortop, the Fulham secretary, without any sense of impending disaster. At 4 p.m. I had set off for home. The only hint of trouble had come via a phone call from Bernard Joy, the former Arsenal player who was now a football journalist on the *Standard*. 'Are you all right?' Bernard had asked. 'Yes, of course I am. What do you mean?' I said, and thought no more about it.

All I could do, after reading the reports of my own demise outside Putney station, was race home to ring Chappie D'Amato, one of the few directors whose number I had. I didn't have Tommy Trinder's contact details. As soon as Chappie responded to my 'hello', I knew the *Standard*'s tale was true. It was obvious from his voice.

'Well, Bobby, I think you had better ring Graham Hortop,' he said. Two hours previously I had been sitting with Graham in his office. I can only surmise that he couldn't bring himself to tell me. Finally, on the phone, Graham plucked up the courage to say, 'The board want to see you at ten thirty tomorrow morning. Just leave it till then.'

'What about this stuff in the papers?' I pressed.

'Just leave it until tomorrow,' said Graham.

I felt rough. I felt doomed. The next morning, Eric Miller, who committed suicide some years later, dismissed me. Official explanation – results not good enough, change urgently needed before club's position deteriorates further.

They were very good about my money and my car, which they allowed me to keep. So I left with my wheels and a cheque for £4,000. Neither could assuage my grief or my indignation.

After the sentence was handed down, I left the boardroom and walked up the tunnel of Craven Cottage, across the turf where so much of my footballing life had been played out, and stopped in the centre circle. There wasn't a soul in the ground, only a few seagulls squawking overhead, as there always were beside the Thames. I looked round the old stadium and felt the tears come. I allowed myself to cry. I had been there for twelve years as a player, in two segments of six, and had returned with a three-year contract to be the manager of the club that had given me my big start in life, and here I was, standing alone in the centre circle, devastated and wet-eyed.

The Vancouver episode had turned out badly. Our Canadian period had ended without me taking charge of a match. Within a year, at Fulham, I was back on the street. I felt so embittered. The floor was collapsing beneath me. My life in football was being swept away. How could I go home to my family after this? I uttered a vow: 'I'll never, ever come back to Craven Cottage.'

6

THE LAST CORINTHIANS

Food fights, fist fights, donkeys wandering into the chairman's beautiful house – I saw it all in my thirteen years in charge of Ipswich Town, where my boss, John Cobbold – one of the great eccentrics and Corinthians of English sporting life – would consume one bottle of champagne if we won a game and two if we lost. That was Mr John's civilised way of looking at defeat. The Ipswich chairman was an old Etonian with a stammer, a fondness for strong drink and a brilliant sense of the absurd. I adored him. When results were going against me, in the early years, Mr John would tell the grumblers, 'Our manager's name is not written on a chalkboard with a wet sponge nailed next to it.'

To give you a sense of what life was like at Portman Road in the seventies and eighties, join me on a train back from Middlesbrough following one of my first away trips as Ipswich manager. Naturally, I'm still feeling my way with my new employers as the directors and I take our seats in the dining car, with John and his brother Patrick facing each other across the jug of water, the rolls and pats of butter. Hostilities begin when John picks off a lump of bread and flicks it at Patrick for no discernible reason.

'Bit strange', I think, and assume this is the end of the exchange. Oh, no. Patrick laughs and flicks a second chunk of roll back at his brother. So John pulls off another lump of ammunition and throws it at Patrick, who retaliates. Now the score is two-two. The conflict is escalating. Patrick prods a pat of butter on to the tip of his knife and flicks it at the chairman. Now

Johnny prepares for the end game. He lifts the jug of water off the dining-car table and throws it all over Patrick. The players are watching while they eat their post-match meal. This little scene qualified as outrageous and hilarious at the same time. John and Patrick were lovable naughty schoolboys who never grew up.

How did I come to be in this wonderfully supportive and unpredictable environment? Simply, Ipswich saved me from the dole, the Labour Exchange, the indignity of signing on with large groups of men equally down on their luck. After my dismissal at Fulham I drew state benefits for three months. My legal action against the Vancouver Royals was still in motion but my lawyer was telling me, 'You'll win your case all right, but the club's gone bust so you're wasting your time. All you'll get is a big bill from me. I don't want to take your money. I know you haven't got any. Go home. Forget about it.' What a first year in management. Disastrous. My life story is one of high-profile coaching jobs and glamorous locations, but I had it rough in that first year. I was being eaten alive by the game I so loved.

The festive period was approaching and I was becoming increasingly anxious about fulfilling my duty as a husband and father to provide the family with a proper Christmas. We didn't have a television and I felt embarrassed about that. 'Right, I don't care what it costs, I'm going to make sure my family has a TV for Christmas,' I told myself. Radio Rentals pushed a form in front of me, asking for details of where I worked and how much I earned.

'Unemployed,' I wrote.

'Unemployed? Well, how are you going to pay for a TV?' the shop assistant asked.

'That's my problem,' I replied. He demanded guarantees. The next day a Radio Rentals van deposited an 18-inch TV for the kids for Christmas.

I tried to keep fit and stay positive. Here, at one of my lowest ebbs, one of my favourite people enters the narrative. I've already expressed my affection for Don Howe. Dave Sexton comes into that same special category of trusted and respected friends. Dave's phone call in those dark winter days was a lifeline. He was then managing Chelsea, and wondered whether I would scout for him at an Ipswich Town-Nottingham Forest game. Naturally, I jumped at the chance.

At Portman Road that night, a chap called Murray Sangster approached and introduced himself as one of the Ipswich directors. He was exceptionally friendly and I took an instant shine to him. There was something about that chance encounter that prompted me to apply in writing for the vacant manager's job at Ipswich Town FC, the warm, eccentric, spirited Suffolk club that was to become my domain for the next thirteen years.

Sometimes in life, people are thrown together by chance and a connection is made, electricity flows. This was one of those moments. 'We'll give you the job but we can't offer you a contract,' said Ken Brightwell, Harold Smith and John Cobbold, the three directors I met near Liverpool Street station. That wasn't a problem. There was nothing on my CV to entitle me to any kind of formal deal. They held all the cards. I said, 'I'll come and do whatever I can for you.' That was the last time I had to go for a job on bended knee. I built three great teams at Ipswich – in 1975, 1978 and 1981 – and won the FA Cup (1978) and UEFA Cup (1981) while going agonisingly close on several occasions to winning the League, especially in my final three seasons, when we finished third, second and second again.

Ipswich were a one-off. In the boardroom, the chairman wouldn't let anyone talk about the game they had just watched. 'That's not for us. We know nothing about the game,' he would say. 'The point of being here is to say, "Hello, well played, have a drink and what time's your bus home?" to our guests. The dialogue about the game can be found in the next room along – the manager's room.' I can't recall those words without a chuckle. Can you imagine hearing them at any other British football club? John was great in that respect, every manager's dream. When we spoke of contracts later, John always talked about ten-year deals.

The funny stories are legion. I can remember having lunch with him at the Great Eastern Hotel in London before an away game against West Ham, and joining him in the gents for a pee, after which I couldn't help noticing his failure to wash his hands. As we left the lavatory I remarked, 'Mr John, where I was brought up we were taught to wash our hands after using the toilet.' He studied me for a moment and replied, 'Bobby, where we were brought up we were taught not to piss on our hands in the first place.'

Patrick had a black retriever that he would bring to games. The dog was a friendly creature, very popular with the staff, but the family's love of animals went way beyond the usual limits of owner-pet relations. Not long after we picked up a beautiful crystal bowl for winning a five-a-side tournament in Sweden, I popped into the boardroom and was presented with a glass of sherry – Johnny always tried to get me to take a drink, even though I was virtually teetotal. Scanning the room, I suddenly noticed Patrick's dog slurping tap water from our new crystal trophy, which had been placed on the floor amid the traffic of moving feet. Any of them could have kicked or crushed the bowl we had played so hard to win. According to club legend, Patrick once brought a monkey to a game at Portman Road.

The Cobbolds were incorrigible. At the unveiling of a major sponsorship deal, John told the media, 'It has been suggested that we'll squander the sponsors' money on wine, women and song. That is not true. We don't do a lot of singing here at Portman Road.'

Once, during a particularly important board meeting, while the secretary was launching into the minutes, Johnny suddenly exclaimed, 'Patrick, you shit, you've got Papa's shirt on. I've been looking for that shirt.' Their father, who was universally known as Captain Cobbold, had been killed by a buzz bomb in 1942. The shirt must have had great sentimental value to his sons because John was incensed. We fell about laughing but the chairman was being quite serious.

He knew nothing about football or our players. When I bought Paul Mariner from Plymouth Argyle, he thought I was buying a sailor. 'He's not in the navy, is he?' he asked. At Leicester City one afternoon he patted me on the shoulder when we were 2–0 down.

'The team's playing frightfully well, Bobby. Have you been doing something special in training?' For a moment I was mystified but then it clicked. I thought, 'My God, he thinks we're winning two-nil.'

'Mr John,' I said, 'we're losing two-nil. We're the away side, we've changed to yellow. Leicester are playing in blue.' I swear it's true.

Of course, the Cobbold family were the bedrock of the club. Captain Cobbold had been a keen racing man and great friend of Denis Hill-Wood over at Arsenal. One day Captain Cobbold accepted an invitation from the Hill-Woods to watch a game at Highbury and came away transformed. 'I have to bring this to Ipswich,' he said, and he did. He took charge of the club and made it properly professional in the late-1930s. Scott Duncan was dragged down from Rangers and appointed manager, but he was no pushover, as the captain was about to find out. Away on business, and hearing that results had deteriorated, Captain Cobbold sent Scott Duncan a transatlantic cablegram: 'Buy Rimmer from Sheffield Wednesday.' The response was succinct. 'Will not buy Rimmer of Sheffield Wednesday' Scott fired back.

'As chairman of the club, I insist you buy Rimmer' the Captain replied in the next cablegram. 'As manager of the club, I insist that I do not buy him' came the response. Scott's insubordination had gone too far. 'You are sacked' the Captain's next message read. 'I will not accept the sack' Scott responded, and with that he survived. Sacking a manager was not the done thing at Ipswich. It was the absolute last resort.

Mr John had an enormous place at Kirton in Suffolk with 2000 acres of land, which he rented out to farmers. He never married and lived alone, which prompted people to question his sexuality.

On occasions, especially if we had lost the day before, the phone would ring and John would ask, 'Are you OK, Bobby?' before inviting Elsie and me over for a spot of lunch and a drink. Deep down he was probably lonely. We almost always accepted his invitations. He had a pond with ducks and a family of donkeys that sometimes wandered into the house.

John suffered from digestive problems, probably because he drank so much, and would often belch. To combat this embarrassing affliction he took Alka Seltzer, which gave him an idea when it came to naming his first two donkeys. He decided to call them Alka and Seltzer. Being male and female, they mated and produced a foal, which John called Burp. So he had Alka, Seltzer and Burp. Little Burp grew up and apparently molested his mother, who then produced another foal. John called this one Calamity. Alka, Seltzer, Burp and Calamity – what a gang they were. It was not unusual for one of them to interrupt our Sunday chats by poking his head round the door.

Lady Blanche, the Cobbolds' mother, lived at Glemham Hall, a stately home like Buckingham Palace. She was the president of Ipswich Town – the only lady president in the Football League. Each Sunday during the summer, she would open the house to the public. Glemham Hall had a window for every day of the year, beautiful staircases, big rooms and exquisite furniture. Between three and five tea and scones would be served to visitors and Lady Blanche would sit there taking the money. Sometimes she would serve the teas herself. I even helped out a couple of times. Well, one day, a lady brought her scone back to Patrick, who was on duty, and complained, 'Excuse me, but there's some dirt on my scone.' Patrick took a close look, studied the mark on the scone and said finally, 'I'm sorry madam, but that's not dirt. It's mouse shit.'

John's thirst landed him in all kinds of scrapes. He was fond of the hard stuff until his doctor warned him off spirits, at which point he switched to white wine and champagne. One day he asked my advice about an invitation he had received to become the president of the South East Counties League. Now the South East Counties was a junior league that had been graced by some of the great players of that era – Bobby Moore, Geoff Hurst, Martin Peters, Peter Osgood and Ron 'Chopper' Harris among others. Many of our best young players used it as a step-ping stone – Kevin Beattie, George Burley, Eric Gates, Clive Woods, Trevor Whymark, Mick Lambert and the rest. It was a terrific league for under-18s. 'It would be lovely, John,' I told the chairman. 'They want a figurehead. You should accept it.'

Everything was fine until John's first annual dinner as president. Off we went to one of the leading London hotels, where I joined him on the top table amid a sea of managers, directors and dignitaries. John was due to give his inaugural speech to this large and distinguished gathering – except that he was blotto by the time he came to stand up and address the room. 'He's not going to make this,' I thought, as John gathered his notes and rose unsteadily to his feet. His speech was the shortest in football history. In fact, it never started because John slid under the table before he could utter a word.

Fortunately, laughter swept through the room. The applause

was rapturous. Like undertakers, a couple of us carried him out, unconscious. Most of the audience thought it was hilarious. 'What a great chairman you've got,' they enthused as I struggled to drag John outside where Sydney Wale, the chairman of Tottenham Hotspur, ordered his chauffeur to drive us to Liverpool Street station to catch the train to Ipswich. Back in Suffolk, where his own chauffeur collected him, John could remember nothing of the night's events.

European trips with the team were heaven to John. He was a multi-millionaire but he couldn't resist bringing back bottles of duty free wine. Before he went out in the evenings, he would ask me to write his name on one of the cuffs of his shirt, and the name of the hotel on the other. He took this precaution to avoid getting lost in a strange foreign city. So I would print 'John Cobbold' on one, and 'Hotel Meridian', say, on the other. I wrote on his shirt like that many times.

'Are you going out tonight, Mr John?' I asked him one afternoon in a hotel lobby.

'Why, you're not going to stop me, are you?' he said.

'No, I just wish I could come with you.'

His speech to the youth team in 1975 was a real pearl. Twice we won the FA Youth Cup – in 1974 and again twelve months later. 'I think we should have a banquet to celebrate with the boys. Set it all up, Bobby,' John declared. He knew how to throw a party, did John. He was gentry, you see. He took great pride in his social arrangements. On the night, I suggested, 'Mr John, I think you should just say a few words to thank everybody for coming, say it's been a wonderful night and say how pleased you are to see everybody.' The trouble was, he was half smashed. John made me accompany him on to the floor, where I tapped the microphone and announced, 'Ladies and gentlemen, Mr John would like to say a few words.' In the right circumstances, he was a lovely speaker. I heard him do it sober once or twice and he was amazing. He was a very educated man with an incredibly posh voice. He could swear like a trooper and get away with it because he had that beautiful, polished accent.

I was quite relaxed as he began his oration because I knew how good he could be when the mood was right. He began by saying what a wonderful evening it had been and described how proud he was that the club had produced these wonderful players who'd done so well. Then came the punchline. Addressing the parents, John said he wanted them all to go home that night and have 'a jolly good f***, so the boss can come back here again in eighteen years' time and have another FA Youth Cup to celebrate'. I nearly died but everybody just stood up on their chairs and clapped and cheered. I repeat, John was a truly terrific guy.

He never wavered in his support for me, even in my difficult first three seasons, when we finished twelfth, eighteenth and nineteenth and the crowd chanted 'Robson out' after a home defeat by Manchester United in which George Best featured rather ruinously. The Tommy Carroll-Bill Baxter story amply illustrated the chairman's loyalty, even if I had to acquire a few bruises to discover how far the club would go to back my authority.

During the 1970–71 season we encountered some turbulence with one of our most senior players, Tommy Carroll, who was being a bit obstreperous about his contract. In those days, the manager took care of all the contracts once the terms had been agreed at boardroom level. The chairman never discussed individual deals with the players. Tommy wanted more money. The club offered what they could. 'Not enough,' said Tommy, who then demanded to see Mr John. The chairman, I informed him, would not be setting a precedent for his sake, so his choice was stark – take it or leave it. Tommy still wouldn't sign and I passed that news on to the board. 'Make him sweat,' they told me. Time passed and still Tommy didn't sign. By now he was becoming moody and disobedient on the training ground. This Mexican stand-off lasted about six weeks until the chairman agreed to see the troublemaker face to face.

'The chairman will see you at two tomorrow,' I told Tommy.

Punctual, as ever, the chairman was behind his desk at 1.30 p.m., waiting for Tommy to arrive. I was there, too, but I had no idea what John was going to say.

'So, Tommy, I believe you wanted to see me,' said the chairman.

'Yes, sir, that's right,' responded Tommy.

'Well here I am, have a good look at me.' Then John pointed to me. 'There's the manager, over there. He runs the club, so talk to him. Now I'm sodding off,' and John got up and walked out.

This was not the nadir of my relationship with Tommy Carroll or Bill Baxter, his fellow agent provocateur. Although I'm ashamed to say it, even now, the three of us came to blows in a proper brawl, which was very sad. I've always regretted it. The spiral really started when Bill Baxter challenged my authority on the training ground and left me with no option but to send him off the pitch. I was a young manager. To lose a power struggle with a tough, senior player might have been fatal to my prospects of establishing the respect of my squad.

Bill was the Ipswich captain and had been at the club for years and years. One day we were enacting a man-for-man marking exercise on a small pitch with goals. Man-for-man meant controlling your opponent. If, during the course of a game, you win seven individual contests, you're pretty much guaranteed to win the match. When you have the ball you disengage and 'go'. When they have the ball you defend. I call it engage-and-disengage football. This was too much like hard work for Bill Baxter, who showed no interest in chasing or hustling his counterpart.

'If I make a run, you've got to come with me. If you don't, I've lost you, and you're letting the team down by letting your opponent get free,' I told the players. Whenever Bill allowed this to happen I would shout, 'OK, Bill, you're ten yards away and you've let him go, you haven't contributed, you don't want to run, you're lazy, he's in to score the goal.' He was testing my authority. He was about thirty-two and I was thirty-six. Finally, I sent him off the training ground and I left him out of the team that played West Ham the following day.

If you win those games, you're fine. If you lose, do you survive dropping one of your most important players over a training-ground dispute? Not always. I'm happy to report that we beat West Ham 3–0 in the new luminous yellow away kit I had selected.

In my earliest hours at Ipswich, I had summoned Cyril Lea, who was the caretaker manager, and asked for a full run-down on the players I was about to inherit.

'Bill Baxter, captain, best player in the club, thirty-two years of age,' recited Cyril. I interrupted.

'Cyril, I appreciate what you're saying, and Bill Baxter is a good player, but let me change just one word. He *was* the best player. He's not now because he's losing his pace.'

That explained Bill's reluctance to apply himself on the training ground. Although he was a battler – a tough little Scotsman who was meaty in the tackle and never squirmed – he no longer had the legs to carry him round the pitch. It happens to every footballer in the end.

We were heading for conflict, hand-to-hand combat. My system was to pin the typed teamsheet on the dressing-room notice board each Friday. That piece of paper was sacrosanct. It was not to be touched or interfered with in any way. Bill Baxter and Tommy Carroll saw it differently. Emerging from the shower one Friday afternoon, the two rebels noticed that their names were missing, and ripped my first eleven off the wall.

'Who do you think you are? Don't you dare do that,' I raged. My words were like the opening bell in a prize-fight. The pair of them were on to me, throwing punches. Cyril Lea joined the mêlée on my side. Soon we were on the floor. These two boys were wild, one a rugged Scot and the other a belligerent Irishman. It just so happened that Cyril was Welsh and I, of course, am English, so we had all four components of a music hall joke. Cyril was a good back-up man. He was great – a tenacious little beggar who, in his playing days, loved to put his foot in for a tackle. That fieriness carried over on to the training ground when he started coaching. Cyril loved a little confrontation. Sometimes he would force one, so he was hardly slow to join my team when Carroll and Baxter launched their assault. I replaced Cyril in the end, which is one of my regrets because I let a good man go.

So we had a punch-up. It was disgraceful. I'm not proud of myself and I wish it had never happened. The other players eventually stopped it, pulling the warring factions apart. Significantly, their team-mates, who were deeply upset, thought Baxter and Carroll had disgraced the club and ought to be made to change in the groundsman's shed.

This was perhaps the moment when I imposed my authority on Ipswich Town. The story leaked to the local paper and I gave my report to the chairman.

'Bobby, get them out of the club and don't even worry about the money. Give them away,' John Cobbold declared.

'Mr John, we can't do that because they're good players. We can get good money for them and it's money we can use,' I replied. 'I can put up with them for another couple of weeks. I'll bring them back into the fold,' which I did, but they never played for me again. Carroll went to Birmingham for £20,000 and Baxter fetched £13,000 from Hull City. Good business.

We were toiling near the bottom of the First Division and were short of goals. We needed strikers. Ray Crawford and Frank Brogan had both left the club. We were desperate. We were little Ipswich Town, not Manchester United, so gymnastics were required in the transfer market. With a budget of £100,000, I settled on Arsenal's Jimmy Robertson, who had a pedigree, and Allan Clarke's brother, Frank, a tough, battling player who would get on the end of crosses. Frank cost us £45,000. I did all the negotiations. The board never made a phone call. I did the deals manager to manager, not like it is now.

Johnny's response was priceless – 'Jolly good. I don't want to know who they are because I wouldn't know who they were anyway. Go ahead, do the deal,' and out he walked. He really didn't want to know whom I was buying. He wasn't interested. Back then, spending £100,000 was like unloading £10 million today. Thankfully, Robertson and Clarke got us out of trouble.

At Ipswich, Ron Gray's team of scouts – John Carruthers, George Finlay and Ray Tyrell – came back with an amazing array of talent. Manchester and Liverpool were out of bounds but I retained good contacts in the hotbed of the North East. On a trawl of Carlisle, John found Kevin Beattie. He also spotted Eric Gates, David Geddis, Robin Turner, Tommy Parkin and Paul Gascoigne, who made little impression on me at a trial on account of his rotundity. We sent him back. In Scotland, George unearthed John Wark, Alan Brazil and George Burley. In Derby, my brother Tom happened to come across Russell Osman, who was to form such a fine central-defensive partnership with Terry Butcher.

We scouted Suffolk and Norfolk with a nit-comb. Eleven miles east of Ipswich you hit the sea – no players there, only fish – but wherever local clubs and schoolboy football existed in East Anglia, we spotted the good players. We put Norwich City in the shade. Trevor Whymark, for example, was from Diss, which is halfway between Ipswich and Norwich. We bombarded East Anglia with scouts. Thanks to Ray Tyrell, mainly, Whymark, Brian Talbot, Mick Lambert, Clive Woods, Laurie Sivell, Roger Osborne and Mick Mills were all captured on local football pitches and rewarded with first-class careers.

Schoolteachers who knew the game kept their eyes peeled on our behalf although we couldn't reward them. The English schools FA would have had them removed from the sport for taking money from a professional club, so we had to be very careful. I built up a strong relationship with the schools and local education authorities and often arranged for them to play special school games at Portman Road.

In those early years we were playing in front of crowds of 18,000. We had a little wooden stand that we called the Chicken Run. The club needed to be developed, so over the years we put a bit into the team and a bit into the stadium. We tried to build the stadium and the team at a compatible pace. In my first year we had 1,800 seats. To make decent money we needed far more. We were charging half a crown back then for the fans to stand. That's 12½p. I had the casting vote on whether we redeveloped the stadium or not. Three of the board voted no, arguing that we would never repay the debt, and three called yes.

'Well, it's down to you, Bobby, whether we go ahead or not,' John Cobbold announced.

Taken aback, at first, I said, 'Well, we've got a good team, I can see a bit of daylight. We might not win the championship but we'll be OK.' The brief I had been given was to keep us in the First Division. 'Build,' I said. Once the stand was finished we had 8,000 season-ticket holders, with a waiting list.

I improvised, followed my instincts, tried to build for the future. Ipswich was a galaxy away from the world of Premier League management. I never told my chairman this but one day I hitch-hiked to Old Trafford to see a game. Cyril Lea, who was on his way to Leeds, dropped me at the junction of the M1 and M62, where I thumbed a lift to Manchester from a lorry driver. I was wearing a flat cap and scarf to conceal my identity. John Cobbold would have flipped his lid.

The Cobbolds did everything in style. They were utterly sure of themselves and their place in the world. At Highbury one afternoon, I nipped up to the Arsenal directors' box to see John on a small business matter. The great and the good were just downing their last tipple before the game, and the club chaplain, the Reverend Bone, was saying, 'Come along now, Johnny, may the best team win,' to which John replied, 'F*** that, Reverend, *we* want to win.' Only John could have got away with that.

John understood about losing, too. He was a Corinthian to his marrow. In defeat he would say, 'Bobby, today it wasn't our turn, but we've given the other team the pleasure of winning. That's something.' I would stare at him, horrified, and think, 'Are you for real?' Don't get me wrong. He knew the importance of winning. He could lose and he could win. How many chairmen are there like that today? There will never be another John Cobbold. I still miss him.

7

A TOWN AWAKES

SLEEPY Suffolk they called it, but the county woke up all right when we won the 1978 FA Cup – my first major prize as a manager. It tickles me now to recall the day I took our supporters to task for being too quiet and undemonstrative at Portman Road.

'Look at the crowd, we've got bloody zombies in here,' I remarked to my assistant, Bobby Ferguson, as we were pulling Coventry City to pieces on our home turf. After the game I went public. 'We played well but we've got to get the crowd going,' I told the press. 'We had twenty-five thousand zombies in the ground.' The fans, to their credit, turned the accusation round by having some special badges printed with the words. 'I'm a Robson Zombie'.

The chairman had asked me whether I wished to apologise.

'No, thank you,' I responded. 'We really have got a load of zombies out there. We're playing fantastic football. They need to be behind us. It's the best football this town has seen in its life.'

The 1974–75 season was the start of the great upswing, although we had finished fourth in the League in the two previous seasons. Midway through the seventies we retained the FA Youth Cup and finished third in Division One, the club's highest position since Alf Ramsey's team won the championship in 1962. Our dramatic progress was based on hard work, application, a fine scouting system, good judgement of players and plenty of quality time on the training ground. My passion for coaching players was reflected in the title of a book I wrote, *Time on the Grass*.

Naturally, dexterity in the transfer market was also required. When I sold Brian Talbot to Arsenal for £450,000, I bought two outstanding Dutch midfielders for a total of £350,000, which enabled me to put £100,000 in the club's bank. Arnold Muhren cost £150,000 and Frans Thijssen was £200,000. They were vital components in my UEFA Cup-winning team of 1981, the best I put together in thirteen years. What I'm about to say will amaze the modern reader. The Talbot deal almost broke down because Arsenal could not match the wages he was on at Ipswich. Imagine that now. Terry Neill, the Arsenal manager, could not believe what Brian was earning at Portman Road. For several days Arsenal prevaricated.

The rewards for playing football these days are in another orbit. In my playing career, if you misbehaved, the club would fine you a fiver out of a £20 weekly wage – 25 per cent gone, up in smoke. You couldn't afford that, so you stayed out of trouble. Now the maximum fine is two weeks' wages. If you're on £2 million a season, two weeks' money is not 25 per cent. In 1969, I went to Ipswich on £6,000 a year. Through the seventies and eighties, salaries rose sharply. At Portman Road the players were on £55,000 to £60,000 a year but I was always the best-paid employee. The chairman thought the manager should always earn more than the players.

Most of our stars came through the youth system. Had he been a shade more worldly, the player I consider to be the best British football had produced since George Best might have ended up in a Liverpool shirt. This young lad from Carlisle had been recommended to Anfield but arrived at the city's main train station to find that nobody from the club was there to meet him. Bemused, he climbed on the next train home to Carlisle. When Bill Shankly heard the story he apparently said, 'Fine, if he's daft enough to do that, we don't want him.'

A while later John Carruthers called. 'This boy is a hell of a player,' he said. So after contact was made with the lad's family, I told Ron Gray, 'There's a boy coming down from Carlisle to King's Cross. Be there, meet him and don't lose him.'

Ron met him one Friday. The youngster arrived carrying a brown paper bag containing an old pair of football boots and nothing else – no spare clothes, nothing for an overnight stay. His pockets were empty. Ron took him to a little hotel in King's Cross where they stayed overnight and we gave him some new boots. The youth team were to play Fulham at eleven the next morning. At one o'clock Ron called me. I'll never forget his words: 'Boss, we have got a colossus, wait till you see this boy. He's got a neck like a bull. He can head the ball sixty yards. I've seen the finest thing I've ever seen in my life. For God's sake, you've got to sign him. Don't let him go.'

So that's how we discovered Kevin Beattie in the autumn of 1970. He had everything. What a left foot he had. He could crack a ball sixty yards from a defensive left midfield position to outside-right. A pass like that could change the game. He was a big tackler, and nobody could get near him in the air. At Everton, he once scored from above the crossbar. He jumped so high he could have seen the town clock and told you the time. Nobody, but nobody, could outrun him. He would give opponents a half-yard start on purpose to trick them into thinking they could out-sprint him. He would invite the pass down the gully and then outrun the intended recipient. Kevin and Alan Hunter were a fantastic central-defensive pairing.

George Best aside, I rate Kevin Beattie as the best player these islands produced in twenty-five years. George was special, as were Bobby Charlton and Denis Law from the same era. Duncan Edwards was colossal, strong and a destroyer, but Beattie had pace as well. He just had pure, natural ability.

Talent isn't always easy to handle. Sometimes it brings

complications – part of the package, I suppose. Kevin's speed over the ground was invaluable in matches but it failed to produce the expected bonanza for us in the Powder Hall Sprint in Newcastle, for which the PFA had been invited to enter some professional footballers. Kevin Beattie could run a hundred yards in ten seconds in football boots, never mind spikes, and the farther he ran, the faster he seemed to go. So we entered Beattie for the race, placed our bets and waited for the inevitable payout. We thought he was a 'cert'.

'Get him to the Powder Hall and then bring him straight back. Don't let him go wandering off,' I instructed Charlie Woods, my youth team coach. 'Call me after the race to confirm that Kevin has won.'

About 9.30 p.m. that night the phone rang. It was Charlie.

'So we won, then?' I said.

'No, we didn't,' Charlie replied, followed by a long silence.

'What, Beattie didn't win the race?'

'No, he didn't, and you'll never guess what happened. I got him there, he got changed, got to the starting line, the pistol fired and off he went, but halfway through the race he just started walking.'

'Oh, God. Hamstring?' I asked.

'No, you won't believe this. Kevin wore a pair of tight shorts and didn't put a slip on underneath. He was halfway down the track, way ahead of everyone else, when his penis popped out of his shorts. It just all came out. So he stumbled the last forty yards clutching his shorts and trying to run with one hand free. He got pipped at the post.'

'Give over,' I said, but Charlie was telling the truth.

'Boss, if I never see you again, it happened. I'm sick about it,' he said. We were all sick. We'd all lost our money. That was Beattie all over. All he needed to do was wear a slip underneath his shorts.

My parents, Lillian and Philip, were proud, hard-working people. My father bled the black and white of Newcastle.

A classic Durham mining community – Langley Park in 1935 from the top of Esh Hill.

David Gilliland (at the back), the sports master at Waterhouses Modern Intermediate School, was an inspiration and a keen follower of my career.

Brothers in arms – my brother Ron and me with some early silverware.

No exotic holidays for us but Ron, Tom and I loved our colliery-organised breaks at Whitley Bay.

By fifteen and a half I was toiling underground. First, we were taught the rudiments of mining at the Morrison Training Centre.

Albert Stubbins was my boyhood hero in a Newcastle United shirt.

Jackie Milburn, another of my heroes, was a legend in Newcastle.

Coming up for air – I escaped the pit to sign for Fulham when manager Bill Dodgin enticed me to London, in 1950.

I always had an eye for goal. Here I'm joining the attack with a header against Hull City in Division Two in November 1953.

Here I'm pounding the turf with Bedford Jezzard, Robin Lawler, Johnny Haynes and Joe Stapleton to my left and a greyhound-fit Jimmy Hill on my heels.

Elsie, now Lady Elsie, and I on our wedding day. I almost lost her days into our honeymoon.

At West Brom I became an England regular. Here I'm diving not to gain a penalty but to avoid the Chelsea goalkeeper, Reg Matthews, in 1957.

My days as West Brom captain ended soon after I requested a pay-rise. I finished my playing career back at Fulham.

Above: On the first of my twenty England appearances I scored twice in our victory over France in a friendly at Wembley in November 1957.

Left: Battling with Mazola of Brazil at the 1958 World Cup. Sadly, the great Pele didn't play that day, but I still had my hands full with the little magician, Didi.

Bobby Charlton took my place in the England team against Scotland and we were on opposite sides for our clubs. The rivalry didn't diminish our friendship.

John Charles was one of my great contemporaries. We clashed when an Italian League XI played their English equivalent in Milan in 1960.

Vic Buckingham, who took me to West Brom from Fulham, didn't like too much la-di-da passing. Vic, with chairman Tommy Trinder, is waving to the Craven Cottage crowd after being appointed Fulham manager in 1965.

Meet the new boss. Losing my first manager's job, at Fulham, broke my heart. I received the news of my sacking from a billboard.

Family life – with Elsie and our sons Mark, Andrew and Paul. I'm proud of all our boys.

The reason I had told Charlie to bring Kevin straight back was that he had gone AWOL before his first England call-up. On the day Don Revie's squad were due to assemble in Manchester, Beattie came rushing to the training ground at nine in the morning, searching for his boots.

'What are you doing? You should have taken your boots home with you on Saturday night,' I chided. 'Come on, I'll run you to the train station.' I just about managed to get him on to the platform in time and wished him luck. At one o'clock, Don Revie's voice came down the line.

'Bobby, where is Kevin Beattie?' he asked. I assured Don that I had put him on the train myself.

'Well, he hasn't arrived,' said Don. I asked him to wait another half an hour, in case the train had been delayed. Thirty minutes later, Don rang again.

'He's not here, Bobby. He hasn't arrived. Any idea where he is?'

I was bemused and then worried, really worried. My fingers dialled John Carruthers' number. John had heard nothing. Don kept ringing, repeating the message that Beattie had not arrived for international duty. Eventually, John, a friend of the Beattie family, found him playing dominoes with his dad in the pub. He had changed trains at Crewe and headed home to Carlisle. John managed to persuade him to go to training with England the next day. Beattie's explanation was that he just couldn't face it, and had wanted to be with his dad instead.

Although we struggled to locate him that day, trouble seemed to find him easily enough. One Easter weekend, a caller to my home said, 'I'm Sister so-and-so from the hospital. You're Mr Robson, the manager of Ipswich Town? I have one of your boys here who has been badly burned.'

'Which one of my sons?' I asked, feeling anguish rise in my throat.

'No, not one of your sons, one of your players, Kevin Beattie. He's been admitted to the burns unit with first, second and third degree burns. He got caught in a bonfire at home. You'd better come and see him, but he's not in a very nice condition.'

The story Kevin told me, with some difficulty, was that he had lit a bonfire, and when it didn't catch properly, he'd thrown a can of petrol into the smoke to ignite the flames. The stream of petrol caught fire and travelled backwards towards his neck, which was now a mess. His face was peppered with burns from all the splashes of burning petrol.

'I'll be all right, Boss. I think I'll be able to play tomorrow,' he told me. He didn't play again until the following season. He was out for five months. As I gazed at him in that hospital bed, I thought, 'Kevin, what on earth have you done?'

He was blessed and cursed at the same time – blessed with talent and cursed by bad luck. He sustained a serious knee injury playing for England against Luxembourg in 1977. Five operations in four years told their own story. He scored thirty-two times in 307 appearances for us and won nine England caps, but his physical descent was cruel and rapid. Effectively, he was finished at twenty-eight, although he later turned out for Colchester and Middlesbrough before retiring in 1982. We paid every penny of the one and a half years left on his contract, staged a testimonial for him and got him a job with a building company, but it didn't work out. Kevin was a troubled soul for many years.

Finding accomplished centre-halves was one of our specialities. For Hunter and Beattie, read Russell Osman and Terry Butcher. Terry Butcher is a name that evokes toughness and character. For Ipswich, England and Rangers, Butcher was a really special player who despised losing, relished a conflict and always put the full armoury of his body and soul into the battle. With England, Butcher and Bryan Robson generated a ferocious will to win. 'C'mon, let's welly into them,' Terry might say as he left the dressing room.

No England supporter will ever forget Butcher's grievous head wound in the game against Sweden, when he had a cut in the shape of a V that spewed blood all down his shirt, even after he had been heavily bandaged. He was crimson all over, as if a sniper had picked him off. Whatever his injury, he was heading balls, tough and resolute. Here was a seriously courageous foot-baller. He hated the very concept of defeat. He was wonderful to work with and very reliable. He's one of the best characters I've come across. He would kick the door down in a moment of temper, but was a lovely man beneath that belligerent exterior, kind of Jekyll and Hyde when he pulled on his shirt. He would ruffle opponents on the pitch but he was never a dirty player, just hard and rugged.

He formed an excellent partnership with Osman. Butcher favoured his left foot but you wouldn't know which foot Russell played with, which is a compliment to his technical prowess. Russell was tough in the air and sported a broken nose. My brother Tom spotted him. He rang me from Derbyshire one day to say, 'I've just been to a schoolboy game and seen a fantastic boy. I've met his father, Rex Osman. Take him to Ipswich.' He was great for us, was Russell Osman, a fantastic boy.

As the team grew stronger, and my own reputation was enhanced, I started to receive tempting offers from rival clubs. Derby, Leeds, Manchester United, Barcelona, Bilbao, Sunderland, Saudi Arabia and Everton all tried to entice me away from Suffolk. Technically, I agreed to join Everton in January 1977, after a meeting with Philip Carter and Sir John Moore, the two most powerful men at Goodison Park. We met on a motorway and then proceeded to Sir John's home to clinch the deal. Phil Carter was an extremely nice man and very intelligent. Everton were plainly a bigger club than Ipswich, and had an edge of ambition. To emphasise his desire to have me at the club, Sir John handed me a cheque for £50,000 there and then as a gift. That night I showed it to Elsie, who said, 'Well, you've probably just done the best day's work of your life and you've made our future secure.' It was a fortune, comparable to somebody giving me a £2 million cheque today. It was seven times my Ipswich salary.

Was it bribery? No, it was a golden hello. I knew I had a difficult day ahead at Ipswich but nevertheless I agreed to head north and shook hands on the deal. I laid down one condition. Nothing was to be announced or leaked until I had broken the news to John Cobbold. I woke up the next morning to a shocking newspaper headline: 'Robson goes to Everton'.

I couldn't believe my eyes. I felt nauseous. A thought flashed through my mind – if they could do that to me on the first day, what might happen farther down the line? I raised the receiver to call Johnny. As soon as he answered I could tell he knew.

'Have you seen the papers this morning?' I asked.

'Yes, I have. What's happening, Bobby?'

'Come to the club and meet me straight away. I've got something to tell you,' I said and put down the phone.

I looked at Elsie. 'Do you know what I'm going to do? I'm going to tear that cheque up. I'm going to ask Ipswich if they'll keep me.'

Elsie's reply was succinct. 'If you feel that strongly about it, then that's what you should do.'

I was quite tearful. In fact, tears are welling in my eyes even now, as I recall the taut emotion of my meeting with John.

'Johnny, let me tell you what happened. I was approached by Everton. It's a bigger club, as you know,' I started out. 'I'm ambitious but I love it here and you've been very good to me. I feel ashamed. I should have sought permission from you to speak to these people in the first place but I didn't. I agreed to join them. I shook hands on the deal but there was a condition, which they've failed to meet, so as far as I'm concerned, I'm out of Everton, and if you will still have me, I want to stay here as manager of the club.'

I called Phil Carter, who's one of the nicest men I've met in football, and told him I would not be coming. My relationship with Ipswich was not damaged. In fact, it improved. There were no bad feelings. I was a nobody when Ipswich gave me my chance and I was happy to go on working there, even if losing the chance to manage Everton, at that point in my career, was one of the regrets of my life. I felt I had no choice but to turn that cheque into confetti.

Leeds was another big opportunity I turned down, for different reasons. One morning in 1974 in my office, Pat Godbold, my secretary, called out, 'Bobby, the Welsh FA are on the line.' In fact, it was a chap called Tony Collins from Leeds United.

'Don Revie has asked me to ring you. He's leaving us, you know,' Tony announced. 'He's proposed that you take over from him. Leeds United want you to come. You have to do it. We've got great players, and money to spend. You can just step in and carry on Don's good work. You'd be a fool not to take it. It's a fabulous opportunity.'

It was, but by this time I had my own high-calibre team and a good quality of life. Nobody at the club earned more than me. I had the best employment conditions. I was the king of my domain. So I turned it down, and instead Brian Clough took charge at Leeds for all of forty-four days.

Clough was one of my nearest adversaries through much of the 1970s. What a character. He was dogmatic, autocratic, powerful. He ran the show. He deferred to no one. He got under people's skin. I had one unforgettable encounter with him.

Cut to the City Ground, where we had just drawn 3–3 with

Brian's Nottingham Forest in the FA Cup sixth round, in a week when we had already beaten Coventry 4–0 and won 4–1 at St Etienne in the UEFA Cup. A Tuesday replay would mean us playing four games in ten days. I had injury problems. So had Clough. I knew that. I wanted an extra day to recover. So after my press conference I made my way down the corridor to find Brian, knocked on the door and heard a muffled sound, which I took to be 'come in'.

Inside, it's pitch black. 'Wrong room,' I say to myself. 'I've just entered the broom cupboard.' Click. A table light comes on. Clough is framed, like the villain in a Bond movie, sitting with his feet up on his desk, wearing his familiar green tracksuit. Peter Taylor is lounging in an armchair. Larry Lloyd, the big centre-half, is there, too, still in his kit. All three of them have been sitting in the pitch black.

'What do you effin' want?' says Brian.

'I'll tell you what I want. I've come to ask you to play us on Wednesday instead of Tuesday to give the lads an extra day to recuperate. I know you've got a couple of injuries and so have I.' There was no ambiguity in Brian's response.

'Eff off, you. I want to play you tomorrow, so I'm doing you no favours. I'd play you on Felixstowe beach.'

'Thanks very much, Brian,' I said, and walked out.

In the event we beat them 1–0, with an Arnold Muhren volley, in a pulsating match, a real seesaw of a game.

Clough lived on that border between arrogance and self-confidence, between popularity and unpopularity. He was brash, honest, brutally direct, a complete maverick. He rejected the norm at every opportunity. It's astonishing to think he won two European Cups with a club from Nottingham. Trevor Francis was no ordinary player, but generally Clough had a knack of picking out apparently ordinary players and improving them out of all recognition – John McGovern, Garry Birtles and Peter

Withe are examples. Players who left Forest to join other clubs were often never the same again.

Forest's football was lovely on the eye. I used to like watching them because they played carpet football, all on the ground with no high or long balls or scrapping for knockdowns. It was constructive football. John Robertson, Clough's best winger, was not quick but he would dummy and feint and drag the ball back to give him an advantage. After the trickery his final ball was always good.

Trevor Francis, the first £1 million player, was the final piece in Clough's jigsaw. I'm told that Brian made Trevor wait ages before he would see him on his first day at the club. In his first week he made him make the tea. Typical Clough. He pulled those stunts on purpose. He was arrogant, no doubt about that, not like Jose Mourinho, who's simply self-confident. Clough was properly arrogant. He frightened people. I'm not sure he would manage it now. In those days players weren't on big money. If you were fined, it hurt you. Now, it doesn't.

Our FA Cup-winning year, 1978, was our worst season since 1971. We were constantly battling with injury problems. Relegation was a threat all season and yet we finished the campaign in raptures, beating Arsenal 1–0 at Wembley and returning to a huge heroes' welcome in Suffolk, the entire population of which appeared to be lining the route back into Ipswich.

The whole day seemed to have been shaped by some celestial hand. Even the obligatory FA Cup selection dilemma that all managers face went my way. We had a South African midfielder called Colin Viljoen, who, when naturalised, was good enough to play twice for England. He was quick, an astute passer and a good finisher. The choice on the day was between Colin and Roger Osborne, a whole-hearted worker who lacked Viljoen's ability but was more popular with his team-mates.

At Aston Villa the week before, I left Roger out and played

Viljoen, who was coming back from injury. We were awful. The only decent performance was by our eighteen-year-old goal-keeper. For that reason I chose Roger ahead of Colin at Wembley. Thus another indelible image was added to the history of the FA Cup. The winning goal that Roger scored for us drained him emotionally. The moment suffocated him. The whole sequence of scoring the goal, the excitement, the adrenalin were too much. After the greatest act of his career he just collapsed. Sunstroke also played a part. I had to substitute him before the restart. Roger was a lovely boy. If, in the dressing room before the kick-off, we had been asked to choose the player we wanted to score the winning goal, everybody at the club would have voted for Roger ahead of even Paul Mariner or John Wark.

Winning the Cup was just sublime. With the bookmakers we were 5:2 against in a two-dog race, yet we knew we had a big chance. George Burley and Mick Mills were our two excellent full-backs. Our goalkeeper, Paul Cooper, was brilliant. Across the midfield we had Osborne, Talbot and Wark. Talbot and Osborne were hard workers and Wark could score goals. That team was built on hard-working players who would run for ninety minutes, men who would track and mark and tackle, recover the ball and never let people free.

My assistant Bobby Ferguson's report told us that Arsenal's left-side was the stronger. On that flank they had Sammy Nelson, Liam Brady and Graham Rix. Instead of playing Clive Woods and Mariner up front in a 4–4–2 formation, we brought in David Geddis on the right-hand side to stop Nelson making runs. Our three midfielders worked like pistons to help the defenders while also getting forward to support Mariner on crosses. We were dominant, easily the best side. That morning, we had read in the papers how Malcolm Macdonald was going to do this and that to us. About eight seconds into the match, the ball was played up the channel for him, and Hunter, who had passed a late fitness test, tackled him so hard they almost ended up in Row 8.

Needless to say, the spirit of the Cobbolds made its presence felt in the Royal Box. During the build-up, I had called Ted Croker at the FA with a special request – 'Ted, our chairman Patrick Cobbold will sit in the front row next to the Queen when she presents the Cup, but Johnny has been the chairman of the club for years and only recently handed over to his brother. Can you get them both in the front row?'

Ted pulled it off but he was in for a shock when he asked Lady Blanche whether she might like to meet Jim Callaghan, the Labour Prime Minister. Lady Blanche was a daughter of the Duke of Devonshire. Her blood ran blue. One of her sisters was Harold Macmillan's wife, Lady Dorothy. With the Cobbolds it was all upper crust. Johnny had photos of himself as a little boy with his father, Captain Cobbold, shooting grouse with the King at Sandringham. So Lady Blanche's answer to Ted's inquiry was hardly surprising.

'No,' she said. 'Actually, I wouldn't. I'd much rather have a gin and tonic.'

That night we stayed in London at the Royal Gardens hotel and set off for home at eleven the next morning, after the boys had had a lie in and some breakfast. With blue and white ribbons streaming from the coach, we were cheered and serenaded from the moment we entered East Anglia. Well-wishers hailed us from every bridge and junction on the A12 and people lined the road for sixty miles. Thousands upon thousands of people were toasting us and shouting. Each time we passed under a bridge I called to the driver, 'Slow down, slow down, let them see the Cup.' We had one hell of a homecoming. The landlord of a little pub near Chelmsford was dumbstruck when we rolled in for refreshments. Johnny ordered wine and champagne. We drank to our victory and re-boarded the bus to continue the pageant.

In Ipswich, supporters had climbed on to rooftops and up trees. How the bus made it through the crush I'll never know.

I had a good team in 1975 and a trophy-winning side in 1978, but my best was the class of '81, a mixture of continental talent and some really high-quality home-grown players. In that UEFA Cup-winning season we had Mariner, Wark, Burley, Alan Brazil, Eric Gates and, of course, Muhren and Thijssen. We played without wingers but the two Dutch boys knew the value of width. They were happy to do their bit in wide positions, tucked in slightly. We played with two strikers, Mariner and Brazil and Gates just behind the front two. It was actually a midfield diamond, which was way ahead of its time. It was very fluent, very cohesive, and every player gelled. The system ran like clockwork, fantastic.

These days it's almost unthinkable that a top Premier League club would go shopping at Plymouth Argyle for an international-class centre-forward, but that's where we found Paul Mariner. We watched him several times and pounced when Ron Greenwood's West Ham started to take a keen interest. Paul was good with his back to goal and prolific in the air from crosses. He scored plenty but he probably should have scored even more. He ought to have been an Alan Shearer. He was more silky on the ball than Shearer but his finishing was not as good. Shearer is as clean as a whistle – a crisp striker of the ball, with good timing and technique, who shoots with his body over the ball. Paul could always have a run at you and beat you with the ball at his toes.

The two Dutch boys were classy individuals. I could be in Amsterdam quicker than I could be in Leicester, so watching them play in Holland was no logistical challenge. I could easily watch, say, Ajax play on a Sunday afternoon. Throughout my time at Ipswich I never stopped moving. I did a tremendous amount of scouting with Ron Gray.

Alan Brazil, who was a terrific finisher, had a nice arrangement with Muhren and Thijssen. 'You pass it and I'll get on the end of it,' he would say, much as Jimmy Greaves used to some years earlier. He crashed in plenty of goals from threaded passes by our Dutch stars.

Our European campaign pitted us against Salonika, Bohemians of Prague, Widzew Lodz, Saint-Etienne, Cologne and finally AZ 67 from Alkmaar in Holland. Our 4–1 quarter-final victory at Saint-Etienne deserves to be remembered as one of the finest by an English club in European competition. In the previous round, the Polish coach of Widzew Lodz, who had just knocked out Manchester United; had approached me with a proposition.

'You want to bet on your team?' he asked. I was bemused, and stalled for time.

'What do you mean, for money?'

'Yes,' he said. 'I want to bet against you. I want to bet my team wins. You want to bet?'

'No, I don't bet,' I said, incredulous. You meet all sorts in football.

I had never known such brutal cold. It was like playing in a deep freeze. In essence, we played on ice, after the UEFA delegate had told me, 'Mr Robson, this game is unplayable. You have my authority not to play. The conditions are too serious. But Widzew Lodz wants to play.' We led 5–0 from the first leg. Had we been one up, I would have accepted the UEFA man's offer to postpone. We played in silk stockings, gloves and vests – except Kevin Beattie, who wore short sleeves, no gloves and no tights – and lost 1–0 on a treacherous, unstable surface but went through 5–1 on aggregate to face the mighty Saint-Etienne of Platini, Battiston, Rep, Janvion, Larios and Castenada. The away leg was to produce undoubtedly the greatest single performance by any of my Ipswich teams. We beat them 4–1 away and 3–1 at home. We were just magnificent.

With the players jumping and singing in the dressing room in

France, a knock came on our door, and the Saint-Etienne president's face appeared. 'Lads, let's have some hush,' I shouted, not knowing what he might be about to say. He said he wanted to congratulate the players on the way they had played and told us we had a fantastic side. His club hadn't lost a match at home in European competition for twenty-six years. 'We have never, ever played a team like this,' he said.

Later, I added my own plaudit when I told the directors, 'We're not Liverpool or Manchester United, but you have just witnessed one of the greatest performances you will ever see by an English team on foreign soil.' I was enraptured by our lads that night – Muhren, Thijssen, Mariner, Gates, Wark, Butcher, Osman and our captain Mick Mills.

Before the semi-final against Cologne, we played on the Saturday against Birmingham, then again on Easter Monday against Norwich. Straight after the East Anglia derby we jumped on a plane to Germany, where I decided to abandon the normal training routine in favour of a day out and a laugh. We invaded the local fun park, where the lads went on the water shoots and swings. We'd had a tough few days and had lost to Norwich. It was time to take some pressure off. I wandered round the park, discreetly checking to make sure the players didn't do anything daft, and sent my staff to do the same. 'Anything to report?' I asked, intermittently.

'No, Bobby.'

'Good, as long as they've enjoyed themselves, that's the main thing.'

Cologne were tough opponents but we won 1–0 both home and away. AZ 67 Alkmaar may sound like a computer programme but they were pretty formidable opponents for us in the final. The core of their team was Peters, Metgod, Spelbos, Hovenkamp, Nygard, Jonker and Kist. Metgod and Spelbos were first-class. After a thumping 3–0 win in the home leg, we extended the aggregate lead to four in Holland before Alkmaar threw caution to the wind and left two defenders to mark our strikers. The two full-backs just went hunting and helped to conjure some amazing attacking football. The two-on-two defensive scenario ought to have suited us, because both their full-backs were being redeployed way up field, but the hard part was regaining possession of the ball to sweep it to Brazil and Mariner. The aggregate score was 5–4, which, given that we had started 3–0 up, was a shade close for comfort. What a ding-dong that second leg was.

For me, winning a European competition surpassed our FA Cup victory. The supporters, the directors and some of the players took the opposite view. They thought the FA Cup was the business but I placed a higher currency on the fact that we had knocked out Saint-Etienne and had travelled through Poland, Germany, Greece and Czechoslovakia, facing good teams along the way. A lack of squad strength, of numbers, explains our narrow failure to win the League Championship in those years. When injuries struck, our only option was to call on youth. We shuffled and re-shuffled but came up short. We had perhaps fourteen championship-calibre players when we needed nineteen. The closest we came was the season after the UEFA Cup win when we were runners-up with 83 points.

Not winning the League with Ipswich remains the biggest regret of my career in club management. In 1981 we were voted the best team in Europe by sportswriters across the Continent. When my time at Portman Road was drawing to a close, Murray Sangster, one of our directors, slipped his hand in mine and said, 'I'm really sorry to see you go, Bobby. I know you have to and you're right to leave but I'd like to thank you because we have seen a decade of football here at Ipswich the likes of which we will never see again.' I will never forget Murray saying those words to me.

When my country called, Patrick Cobbold took me for a very nice lunch on the outskirts of Ipswich and told me the club would extend my contract for another ten years if I was willing to decline the England job. Security, contentment, happiness – all the things that people generally aspire to in life – I had in my hands. I was completely and utterly in command of a big club, the board never interfered with my work and were constantly telling me how much they loved me. In 1982, when we finished second in the table again, we had a squad stuffed with budding stars. There was always enough money in the kitty to finance the odd foray into the transfer market for a Thijssen, Muhren, Mariner or David Johnson, and a wide path had been established from youth academy to first team. Sporting principles governed life at Portman Road. The chairman had the old Corinthian spirit – happy when you win, smile when you lose but try to win.

All this was swirling through my mind as I approached the most difficult decision of my career. I was facing giving up a quality of life that most managers would have killed for. I had it in the palm of my hand but I knew that if I said no to England, regret would come hunting for me later in life. It would chase me down. Already I had turned down Leeds, Manchester United, Barcelona and Bilbao, among others, but this was different. I visualised sitting in a rocking chair at eighty years old, mumbling to myself, 'Well, Bobby, they gave you a chance to be England manager and you turned them away.'

On 16 July 2002, a statue of me was unveiled outside Portman Road. It was a joint venture between the club, the council and the supporters' club, who, together, contributed a sum measuring tens of thousands of pounds. It's a very nice statue, quite big, just outside the main stand. Quite a few of my family were there, and David Sheepshanks, the Ipswich chairman, made a speech, to which I replied before we all went off for lunch. It was a major civic event.

Alf Ramsey had been at Ipswich before me, of course, and Alf had his own memorial, so I suppose it made sense to erect one of his successor as Ipswich and England manager. Alf won a World Cup and I reached a semi-final. We both won trophies at Portman Road, so we were indelibly linked. The difference was that they put up Alf's monument after he died, whereas I was able to look mine in the eye. People tease me that it's the ultimate honour to be turned into a statue before you've met your maker.

8

SLINGS AND ARROWS

QUIET years, the England years. Oh, yes. Not much to report beyond Diego Maradona's 'Hand of God' outrage in '86, an epic World Cup semi-final against West Germany four years later, Gazza's tears, two resignation attempts, supporters spitting and throwing lager at me, hooliganism, racism, a press circulation war with me as piggy in the middle and a scurrilous charge of treachery to round off eight seasons of national service.

Somehow, I say all this with a smile. Despite the turbulence of those eight years, I didn't emerge embittered, mistrustful or traumatised. People are kind enough to praise me for not turning sour or harbouring grudges against the journalists who tried to barbecue me in print, or the supporters who spat at me at Wembley and even St James' Park. No level of abuse could alter the fact that I considered it an honour to be England manager, which is why I accepted a pay–cut when I finally said goodbye to the Cobbolds and Ipswich, and parked myself behind a desk at the Football Association's London headquarters as Ron Greenwood's successor. I was forty-nine years old.

On 7 July 1982, when I arrived at Lancaster Gate on a five-year contract, my salary for managing the England team and working simultaneously as head of coaching for the whole of English football was £65,000. At Ipswich I had been on £72,000. I was the second Ipswich manager in nineteen years to take charge of the national team, following Alf Ramsey. According to the newspapers, Sven-Goran Eriksson was appointed two decades later on an annual salary of £3–4 million. Sven might feel some days as if he has been round several cycles in a spin dryer, but I hope he won't mind me pointing out that the upheavals in his reign have been minor compared to the craziness of my England years.

By virtue of the fact that we reached the semi-final of Italia '90, mine was the most successful England record since Alf Ramsey raised the 1966 World Cup. For that reason, and others, I'm proud of my contribution, although the near-miss of our penalty shoot-out in Turin in the summer of 1990 haunts me to this day. We won forty-seven of my ninety-five games and lost only eighteen. I was defeated in one qualifying match in four campaigns, or twenty-eight matches – against Denmark in 1983, when Phil Neal tried to breast a ball down in the penalty area but touched it with his hand. Little Allan Simonsen strode up and knocked the cherry in.

The world of the England manager then is unrecognisable compared to the one that greets Sven these days when he slips into his FA limo. Graham Taylor, I gather, was met by an FA car when he took over from me, but in the 1980s I travelled by train and tube from Ipswich, or drove myself if I had a game to go to that evening. Working my way through London from the east would consume an hour and a half.

Twenty years later, Sven doubtless stays at home and goes to his match in the evening, but I did a day's work first because I was also director of coaching, working with Charles Hughes, who is often caricatured as the father of the long-ball game, on the residential school, the centre of excellence and so on. I worked hard and banged the drum for the English game. One of my battles was with the schools to gain greater control over the country's best boys. I was a member of the international technical committee and was charged with producing a blueprint for élite football. All this was new to me and daunting, at first.

In retrospect, my energies were probably diluted by my bureaucratic responsibilities, but I had plenty of zest in those days and was deeply interested in the science of football coaching. Charles was cast by many as a Luddite, an obstacle to progress, but I had a high opinion of him. He was an educated man, a fine speaker with some sound ideas. He was no caveman. His lectures on direct football were so academically sound that they were extremely hard to knock down. He more or less argued that the way Brazil played football was not the way to play. His philosophy was this – play it early, get forward, play in behind defenders. Those were his three tenets. In some respects they made sense. If you can play it early, rather than square or short, then great, but Charles was telling his audience to follow that route every time, which you can't. Sometimes you'll knock the ball forward and lose it.

'Two passes are better than one, if you retain possession,' I would argue. We'd knock it around.

'Goals are not scored from nine or ten or eleven or twelve consecutive passes,' Charles would assert. 'They're scored from one, two or three. So why fanny around with twelve passes when they're not going to get you a goal anyway?'

Charles and I had endless debates. He would deconstruct a game into phases and could always support, with evidence, his case for direct football. He believed passionately in set plays and crosses into the box.

Like most doctrines, the theory of direct play was taken to extremes. Jack Charlton's Ireland team were among those who pushed the idea to its limits. From the kick-off, the extreme long-ball proponent would send the ball out of play by the corner flag, and then press to stop the opposition escaping the siege. They were like half-backs in rugby, kicking for field position. It wasn't my way of playing. I liked the beautiful game, the passing game. On the other hand, I see Premier League players pass the ball square, without looking, and I think, 'Hang on, the idea is to play the ball forward. If you can't play it forward, pass it square, but otherwise be positive. Look for the best option.'

Many of my contemporaries regarded Charles as an amateur, a boffin, a charlatan, and yet on the coaching courses we organised he was terrific. In the middle of a pitch for a defensive session or a midfield session or a free-kicks session, there were few better coaches in England. Don Howe or Jim Smith would back me up. His organisational skills were outstanding, so I stuck up for him.

One day he came up with a new phrase – POMO, or position of maximum opportunity. He was an educationalist, so he was bound to come up with an academic term for what I would have described as 'sticking a player on the back post'.

'What's POMO, Charles?' I asked him. His answer, paraphrased, was, 'Get your crosses in, and you must – I repeat, must – have a player in line with the back post because, whatever the spread of players, he is in the position of maximum opportunity. That player will score more goals than any other.'

In training sometimes, the lads would take the mickey, shouting, 'Quick, POMO, POMO!' but Charles deserved better than that. Charles Hughes and I got along.

Although the workload was sometimes onerous, I would have hated Sven-Goran Eriksson's routine – leaving the house for Premiership games at 6 p.m., beating the traffic ten minutes before the end, getting the squad together now and then, playing matches. I would have been bored rigid, but what a struggle it was to modernise the post of England manager. My first request to have Don Howe appointed as my full-time number two was rejected on the grounds that there was insufficient work for two of us.

Don Howe was a top-notch coach, one of England's best. People made a lazy assumption that he was a defensive coach, which was not true. He was extremely good at tutoring defenders but on top of that he was bright and inventive in his approach to forward play. I couldn't have had a better ally. He was supportive, he had footballing intelligence and a good tactical knowledge. Don had everything. At the time when some newspapers were rummaging through my personal life, I rang Don and told him, 'There's going to be an article in tomorrow's paper. You won't like it, I don't like it, but I can't stop it.'

'Why don't you come and stay with me for a few days so they can't find you?' Don answered.

When my employers said Don could not come on board, I had to exclaim, 'Insufficient work? Do you know how many teams we run?' We ran Under-15, Under-17, Under-19 and Under-21 teams as well as the seniors. We ran more teams than Manchester United. For his freelance contributions, the FA were paying Don peanuts. With no team of scouts, I drove all over the country to watch games. Just finding the stadiums was hard enough. At Ipswich, I would sit on the coach until I heard the hiss of the handbrake, look up and there we were at Anfield or The Dell. Now I had to locate these places by myself. Needless to say there was no satellite navigation in 1982.

It didn't take long for me to realise that I had entered a jungle. Finding and coaching England's best players was the easy bit. The hard parts were dealing with the hysterical expectations of some England fans and trying to keep the press off my back. My first disadvantage was that I had been chosen ahead of Brian Clough, supposedly the populist hero. At times, there was no haven, no refuge. For omitting Kevin Keegan from my squad to face Denmark in September 1982, I was showered with phlegm by my own people, the Newcastle supporters. The rift with Keegan hurt us both. But now we get on extremely well. I was spat at again and sprayed with beer at Wembley on 2 June 1984, after we lost 2–0 to Russia. If an invisible critic empties the contents of his mouth on you, there's really not much you can do except wipe it off.

A contributing factor was that the circulation war between the *Sun* and the *Daily Mirror* was turning medieval. The office of the England manager was one of their battlegrounds. I tried not to take the abuse I was attracting personally, but the headlines, the barbs, the dismissive remarks from former England players and managers did play on my mind like a recurring bad dream. I can't pretend that I was always able to shut them out. 'How do I react to this?' I would ask myself in quiet moments. 'Do I resign, do I get out of it, should I change my life? What do you do, how do you solve it?'

I was denounced as a 'plonker' and a 'prat' in headlines. 'In the name of Allah, go' was another little beauty, after our 1–1 draw against Saudi Arabia in 1988. I was lampooned and vilified. The implication was that England would conquer the world if only I would stand aside.

Work was the only escape, hard work. In later years I forgot without ever fully forgiving. At the time I hoped my tormentors would catch a glimpse of themselves in the mirror and reflect, feel remorse, comprehend what they were doing to me. The most vivid memory, of course, is of the *Mirror*'s Nigel Clarke getting off a plane in Greece and telling the TV cameras, 'I'm here to fry Bobby Robson.' I heard him say those words and I thought, 'What? What do you want to fry me for?' I suppose you could say he was sent on a special assignment, hoping England would lose so he could nail me to the cross. We won the game 2–1, but when we went 1–0 down I joked to Don on the bench, 'Nigel Clarke is going to fry me now.'

Alf Ramsey was also giving me grief through a newspaper column. To this day I've no idea what Alf had against me. When I took the Ipswich job and we began our ascent, I wrote to him inviting him to be our special guest at Portman Road. We sent him two tickets for the directors' box. 'These are for you and your wife, come whenever you want, the seats will always be free for you,' I wrote. He never came, never even acknowledged the letter. A bizarre fellow, Alf. One day after a match at Chelsea, I spotted Alf and offered him a lift.

'I'm going home now. I've got my car outside. Why don't you come home with me?' I said. His reply was icy.

'Thank you, but I came by train and I'll go home by train.'

I found it odd because I had always been very respectful towards Alf. For God's sake, he won us the World Cup. Also, he had special status in Ipswich. I respected his position and his reputation but he was always either hostile, in print, or unfriendly, in person. The mystery will have to stay unsolved.

The late Emlyn Hughes was another who laid into me. So I had a former England manager and a former England captain burying me. Each time we lost a match I was back in the stocks to be pelted. Emlyn, God rest his soul, was a great player but I had to ask what did he achieve as a manager? When his playing days were over, he went off to manage Rotherham, found it bewildering and resigned. He couldn't cut it as a manager, but there he was telling me what I was doing wrong with the England team.

Although I was defiant and stoical for the most part, I did offer to resign, twice, on the grounds that the public had apparently turned irrevocably against me. The first time was after Simonsen's penalty for Denmark in September 1983, which ultimately cost us a place in the 1984 European Championship. We had a terrific goal tally in qualifying but missed out by a single point. At that time Brian Clough's name was constantly being touted as England manager. The theory was that a genius was ready to ride to England's rescue if only the FA would see the light. To Bert Millichip, the FA chairman, I said, 'I'm enjoying my job and I'm doing the best I can. If you want to lift the pressure off yourselves and give Clough the job, I'll resign. If he succeeds, you're happy, he's happy, the country's happy and even I'm happy, because England are winning.

'If he fails, that's the end of the Brian Clough legend and you won't have the problem again. Forget about me. I'll go back to club management. I'll find a job. If he's too much of a maverick, or upsets people, or the results aren't good, he's off my back and maybe I can step back in.'

'Oh, no, we're not going to do that. You've got the job. We had a list and your name came out top. So you soldier on,' Bert said. Resignation rejected.

The following European Championship in 1988 also unleashed a crisis. This time we qualified, but lost all three group games – to the Republic of Ireland, Holland and the USSR. We had been superb in qualifying and had travelled to West Germany as one of the tournament favourites. My forward line was going to be Chris Waddle, Gary Lineker, Peter Beardsley and John Barnes. I considered that to be the best front four in Europe. Waddle was excelling at Tottenham, Lineker had proved himself at Barcelona and Barnes and Beardsley had been brilliant together for Liverpool. What great buys they were. I really rated all our attacking players. I felt we were more mature, more confident than in the 1986 World Cup in Mexico. My conviction was that we had a major chance of bringing the trophy home.

Barnes and Beardsley were running on empty. They had expended every drop of fuel for Liverpool that season. They were gone, absolutely bushed, and could hardly raise a gallop. John Barnes barely went past an opponent in any of our three games. Waddle, meanwhile, had undergone a double hernia operation in March and had only just recovered by the end of the season. I assumed he would be OK but he, too, was devoid of energy and spark. His legs were empty. There was no foundation of fitness on which he could perform his work.

As if that wasn't enough, Lineker was very subdued and ended up in hospital with hepatitis a week after we returned from the tournament. Hepatitis is in your system for several weeks before it emerges and it makes you feel poorly, lethargic. Later, the doctor called to say, 'Well, now you know why Gary was so listless. He would have been about sixty-five per cent fit.'

So while I went there believing I had the best forward line in Europe, what I really had was four dead men at the front of the team. We played Jack Charlton's Ireland team and lost 1–0, despite having eighteen chances to their four. At 1–1 with twelve minutes to go against Holland, in our next match, Lineker and Hoddle both struck the post while Marco Van Basten completed a hat-trick to secure a Dutch victory, 3–1. The Soviet Union beat us by the same score. Holland, of course, finished up winning the competition in style. They were a marvellous team, with Van Basten, Ruud Gullit, Frank Rijkaard, Ronald Koeman and the rest.

While the brimstone cascaded on my head, I again tried to quit. 'I've had enough, it's time for a change,' I instructed myself. Back I went to Bert, who stuck to his line of five years earlier.

'There's nobody better than you. You've been in the job since 'eighty-two, six years, and nobody knows it better than you. If you can handle the heat in the kitchen, so can I,' he said.

He caught me off guard. I thought my time was up. I thought that by offering myself at the guillotine I was giving them the chance to let me go, but they were as solid as teak. I found them to be great people. Bert was a special, supportive employer. I didn't want to surrender the job but I thought it right to offer my resignation. I thought I'd test them out. Had they said yes, I would have walked out of Lancaster Gate feeling I had fulfilled my duty to the country. I'd been unlucky in the 1986 World Cup and we'd performed with real promise to qualify for the European Championship. I would leave the FA through the front door, not the back.

'Are you sure?' I asked, to which Bert replied, 'We're absolutely sure. We don't want you to go but it's up to you.'

The 1980s were the decade of the Heysel, Hillsborough and Bradford City disasters. Bloodshed and tragedy pursued our national game. There were repercussions, of course, for the England team, and for me. After Heysel, English clubs were banned from European club competitions. We were in the wilderness, detached from mainstream continental action and ideas. I'm sure this hampered the tactical and technical development of our players.

A few days after thirty-nine Juventus fans lost their lives at the Heysel Stadium in Belgium as the result of the actions of some Liverpool supporters, we were due to play Italy in Mexico, in a pre-World Cup friendly. *El Sol*, the Mexican version of the *Sun*, blasted a chilling headline across their front page: 'THE ANIMALS ARE COMING'. The game went ahead but the atmosphere, predictably, was funereal. This was the backdrop to our efforts to make English football respected and successful once more. The 1988 European Championship was marred by violence between English, German and Dutch fans, which led to hundreds of arrests.

The virus of racism infected our trips abroad. Sometimes it even boarded our plane. Everyone can recall John Barnes' sublime solo goal against Brazil at the Maracana, in Rio de Janeiro, in June 1984, but fewer will know that the National Front managed to book seats on our subsequent flight to Uruguay. We had beaten Brazil 2–0, England's first victory in the spiritual home of modern football. John gathered the ball on the left and ran half the length of the pitch to score in front of 56,000 mostly Brazilian spectators. One English newspaper remarked, 'Pele would have been proud of it.' The victory brought me some much-needed respite after our defeats by Wales, in the Home Nations Championship, and the USSR. The wolves had been circling the camp.

For that expedition to South America, around eighteen players were unavailable to me on account of injury or burn-out. After the Soviet Union game, Jimmy Hill had interviewed me on TV and said, 'You've just lost two nil to Russia. What are you going to Brazil for? You're going to get a hiding. The crowd are shouting "Robson out". Can't you persuade the FA to pull out?' I've always been a fan of Jimmy's and I think he likes me, too. That day I told him straight.

'If we don't go, we'll never know what might have happened. I know I'm without a lot of my senior players, but it's an opportunity to test some youngsters. If we lose, we lose. I'm not scared, and we might learn something. It would be stupid to pull out. People will think we're afraid of Brazil.'

We had Peter Shilton, Kenny Sansom, Ray Wilkins, Tony Woodcock and Bryan Robson. That was our hardcore. The rest were young and inexperienced – Clive Allen, Mark Hateley, Mark Chamberlain and Mike Duxbury. The two centre-halves were Dave Watson and Terry Fenwick. Barnes, Chamberlain and Hateley would all play up front. I would deploy a 4–2–4 attacking formation. The Brazilian press split their sides. 'There's no alternative,' I said. The locals predicted a massacre.

Shilton, Sansom, Wilkins and Robson were stupendous. What a performance those four gave. Sansom played against a typically elusive outside-right who ought to have buried him but Kenny never let him pass, not once. He jockeyed, turned, sped over the ground and got his tackles in. He was brilliant. Robson was equally influential. Wilkins steadied the ship, Shilton was safe on crosses and his handling was impeccable. It was as if we had two goalkeepers.

When John set off on that meandering run, I muttered, 'Pass

it, pass it,' but he just kept going, beating four players and then the goalkeeper. These people on our plane, though, wouldn't accept John's brilliant goal as legitimate. They tried to wipe it from the slate. 'One-nil, one-nil' they chanted, and subjected Barnes and Chamberlain to boos and monkey chants. It was utterly disgraceful. Disgusting. Imagine that now – a horde of racists on an England flight, taunting the team's black players.

I don't want to portray my time as England manager as one long struggle against adversity. I worked with great players, saw the world, made new friends. I'll give you an example. On a trip to Israel in 1988 I acquired a lifelong pal in Joe Mirimovic, who was managing our hosts. We drew 0–0, after the pitch had been turned into a swamp by torrential rain, but that's not why the trip left such an impression on me. It was Joe who provided the real entertainment when he asked me whether he could come to watch us train.

'No, Joe, you can't do that,' I told him, trying to sound severe.

'Oh, go on,' he protested but I was adamant. The next day, we went to practise in the rain and, blow me, Joe was there, standing under an umbrella. I marched over.

'Joe, what on earth are you doing?' I demanded. He was busy writing down everything we were doing on a notepad, while an assistant held the brolly. I did my best to give him a rocket, while trying to suppress my mirth.

Joe's motto was 'Only one goal more'. He would explain, 'If they score one, you score two. If they score two, you score three. Only one goal more, Bobby.'

The next day, before the match, Joe approached me and said, 'You know I wrote everything down when you were training yesterday?'

'Yes, Joe,' I sighed.

'Well, it got all wet and I can't read it,' he said. 'Can you tell me what you did?'

9

A LEFT HOOK

I T WASN'T the hand of God. It was the hand of a rascal. God had nothing to do with it. The world bought in to Diego Maradona's poetic description of the 'goal' that put us out of the 1986 World Cup but I didn't. That day, Maradona was diminished in my eyes for ever.

Funny how time can soften an outrage. In the heat of Mexico, of course, no sane witness to the deed actually applauded the world's best footballer for punching the ball past Peter Shilton five minutes into the second half of our World Cup quarter-final against Argentina. Later, when the perpetrator went into steep physical and moral decline, a tendency emerged to rewrite this blatant act of cheating as the work of a loveable Jack the lad. Maradona was a product of the street, his apologists pointed out, and so brilliance and craftiness were bound to come together in the little bundle of talent we faced in Mexico City on 22 June 1986.

Maybe so, but I keep returning to the fact that our nemesis had the chance, in my opinion, to be not only the finest footballer in the world but also the best sportsman. In his blindness, his willingness to pursue victory at any price, he let that opportunity slip. So he'll always be marked down in history as a cheat. However idealistic this sounds, he could have run over to the referee to tell him, 'No, no, I'm sorry, that wasn't a goal.' Pele, Johan Cruyff or Marco Van Basten wouldn't have taken a goal that way. Maradona wasn't from that school. He grew up in a shack. He was a street urchin who grabbed what he could.

I do not seek to dismiss the brilliance and audacity of his second, legitimate, goal against us in a game weighed down by the legacy of the Falklands War. In his autobiography, Maradona claimed that the fist he applied to a cross too high for him to head was for all the young Argentine soldiers who had died when Britain had reclaimed the Falkland Islands from his government. A combination of cheating and incompetent refereeing sent us home from the tournament just as we were coming into bloom.

The locals had called ours the 'Group of the Sleeping', such was the shortage of excitement as we plotted our way past Portugal, Morocco and Poland, but even in the heat of Monterrey, where we played all our three group games, I knew we were amply endowed with match-winning talent. We had Lineker, Hoddle, Barnes and Waddle. We had little Peter Beardsley and the mighty Bryan Robson (or at least we hoped we did). We had Peter Shilton in goal and the marvellous Terry Butcher to protect him. I can't think of a single year since 1966 when England have lacked authentic talent. Producing good players has never been our problem.

Hoddle is a fine example. Glenn played more regularly for me than he did for Ron Greenwood, who, I suspect, doubted him – not as a player but as a tough, competitive international star. In all, Hoddle appeared fifty-three times for England, and most of those caps were awarded by me. I saw him as a purveyor of the ball, a specialist passer. He would hit the long diagonal pass or keep it short when he considered that more appropriate. Glenn was not a recoverer of the ball in any shape or form. Forget about that. He'd wait in space for a team-mate to dig it out and give it to him to use in a constructive manner. You were wasting your time if you waited for Glenn to go sliding in or crunch an opponent for a fifty-fifty ball.

His primary assets were a good brain and extraordinary vision.

He had two lovely feet. He could swivel with his left foot and send it one way, then swivel with his right and send it on the opposite path. He could penetrate both with his passing and his running. He knew when to gamble and when to play safe. He had all that and should have scored more international goals than he did. Perhaps he needed to spend more of his time in the penalty area. Eight goals in fifty-three matches was a mediocre return for a player of his capabilities. In that sense he reminded me of Johnny Haynes.

Johnny was also a great passer who should have scored more frequently. At Fulham, he would strike a beautiful thirty-yard pass to Tosh Chamberlain but had a mental block about deploying that skill in shots on goal. One day I said to him, 'Johnny, you can hit thirty-yarders to Tosh's toe, so hit thirty-yarders into the back of the net.' It was a psychological obstacle he struggled to overcome. Johnny was frightened of missing or hitting the crowd. I would tell him, 'If it means putting it over the bar once or twice to get one in, then put a few over the bar.'

The other England players knew how good Hoddle was.

'What do you think of him?' I asked Peter Reid in training one day. Well, with Peter every other word was unprintable.

'Effin' hell, what an effin' player, I wish I had his effin' ability,' Peter replied. After another session, Reid came off and said, 'He's in a different class to me, Boss, I just can't believe my eyes. No wonder I can't get in the side when you've got him.'

Peter was a competitive little bugger. His game was about nudges, tackles, putting his foot in, winning it, giving it five yards. Occasionally he might stroke the ball twenty yards to the outside-right, but essentially he was a clever nudger. Peter had a lot of quality.

Hoddle was often highly influential in games but he never single-handedly won us a match. If I had the choice, in a fantasy football game, between Hoddle and Paul Gascoigne, Gazza at his best would take my vote. Hoddle was a better all-round passer but Gazza worked harder, running from box to box and carrying the ball through midfield. He gave you the hard yards. Hoddle would turn and pass. Gazza, a skilful dribbler, would run the ball through midfield if the pass wasn't on. Glenn's method of beating an opponent was early collection, early touch, ball in stride, deliver. Gascoigne would beat people in a duel. He could run along the touchline and jink past a challenger. Hoddle never did that.

Paul also offered more of a goal threat. Glenn could set the chance up for a team-mate. He would swing wide, chip it on to the back post or drag it back. He had the full artist's repertoire but he didn't have the physical presence of Gazza, who would crunch in to the tackle like Bryan Robson. Gazza would break your leg. He was mean.

Gazza's debut, of course, was still three years away when we stepped into the oven of the Mexico World Cup. I remember our team doctor, Vernon Edwards, poking his thermometer into the ground the day before we played Morocco and coming up with a 40 degree reading. 'Well, don't tell the players. Keep it to yourself,' I told him. The last thing I wanted was an alarmist doctor on the loose. Imagine the effect on the players if they had heard a senior member of the medical profession worrying out loud, 'My God, it's hot – nobody can play in these conditions.' I was with Dr Edwards when he had a heart attack at high altitude in these suffocating conditions.

Portugal were our first opponents, and although the match statistics show seven shots on goal for us and only two for them, we lost 1–0 on the back of a stifled performance. A rare defensive error by Kenny Sansom let Portugal's Carlos Manuel in to score.

Bryan Robson had developed a history of dislocating his shoulder and was not fully sound when we touched down in Mexico. Long before the tournament, I had pressed Ron Atkinson, his manager at Manchester United, to deal with Bryan's affliction. My hope was that the club would send him for an operation three months before the World Cup but, of course, Ron wanted him available for the remainder of the club's own campaign.

'I know what you're saying, Bob, but Bryan's a very important and influential player for me. We're going to keep him playing and hope his shoulder doesn't pop out,' Ron responded. I didn't fall out with him about it. I felt it was the wrong decision for Bryan Robson but I also understood the demands of club management.

From the beginning Dr Edwards was quite clear. It was a risk to take Bryan to the World Cup. He needed an operation. The more his shoulder popped out the more susceptible he was. He reached the point where he was vulnerable just taking his jacket off. A wrong move could cause another dislocation. Sure enough, in our first match, Bryan was very cagey, very tentative, not the real Bryan Robson. The real Bryan Robson went into everything like a locomotive. He was, in my opinion, the best player in the country but he was only half present against Portugal. After seventy-five minutes I replaced him with Steve Hodge to protect his shoulder. Worse was to follow.

Morocco were next, three days later, in equally savage heat. This time, in the space of five minutes, Robson was carried off with a dislocated shoulder and Ray Wilkins, of all people, was sent off. The referee had given a lousy offside decision and Ray had gently rolled the ball towards him. It would have been easy for the official to step aside but instead he remained motionless and allowed the ball to bump his shin. Up went his finger. So we were down to ten men in 40 degree heat. At half-time, I swear the players were sizzling, as if they'd just rolled off a barbecue. A tin bath full of ice and some wet towels were waiting for them in the dressing room. It was like giving a team talk in a Turkish bath.

We did well in testing circumstances thanks largely to Hoddle, whose cleverness with the ball came into play. Glenn understood that, in those conditions, possession of the ball was vital – give it, get it back, give it, get it back. In the circumstances we coped admirably and came away with a 0–0 draw. In their next match, Morocco defeated Portugal, so they were no fools. That was all very well, but after two matches in Group F we had one point and had scored no goals. We faced Poland needing to win.

By now Bryan Robson was on his way home and Wilkins was suspended, so I revamped my team. Reid and Hodge came into midfield and Peter Beardsley replaced Mark Hateley in a 4–2–4 formation. Within thirty-five minutes, Lineker had scored a hat-trick. At half-time, as Reid lay on the floor with his feet up on the bench and cold towels sucking the heat from his baked body, his Liverpudlian voice piped up, 'Well, we're winning three nil at half-time and some effer must be playing well because I haven't touched the effin' ball yet.'

The Poland game was one of Hoddle's finest moments. We won 3–0 and he put the stamp of his ability on the midfield play. He had a little tugboat beside him in Reid, who scrapped and fought and dug and whacked, and then gave it to Hoddle. With Hodge and Trevor Steven we had real width to complement the marauding qualities of Lineker and Beardsley.

Hodge, Lineker and Beardsley were all small men, and Steven was only 5ft 10in. We must have had one of the smallest forward line-ups in the tournament. With Beardsley (5ft 8in) and Lineker (5ft 10in) in tandem, crosses had to be pulled back across the penalty area. It was no use floating high balls into the box for those two because they were not tall enough, as a partnership, to play any kind of aerial game. We had to play ground football, or carpet football as I used to call it. They were clever in pos-session, those two, specialising in little one-twos. Peter played deeper than Gary. He could turn and dribble into the box, yet when balls were played into the area by other players, Peter was seldom there. Hence he scored only nine times in fifty-nine appearances. When he hit the target, it was by being clever with the ball, beating players by himself. He was brilliant at that. He had a little twitch that would enable him to fake a pass, go by the defender and take the ball on again.

Peter and Gary loved playing together. Peter was adept at threading balls between the centre-halves for Gary to make runs. He was hard working, too. It was second nature to him to chase an opposition midfielder from behind to recover the ball. Mostly, though, Gary and Peter spent their international careers torturing centre-halves. As a partnership, it was one of England's best.

Relieved to have beaten Poland with such authority, Don Howe and I went off to watch Spain in Monterrey. Ten minutes before the kick-off, Don and I climbed the steps of the stand to tumultuous applause. I assumed the Spanish were clapping us after watching us destroy the Poles 3–0; so I puffed out my chest and felt the warm glow of acclaim. What I didn't realise was that Placido Domingo, the great opera singer, was coming up the steps behind me. The Spanish VIPs didn't know me from Adam. Luckily, I had resisted the temptation to wave back at them like a conquering emperor.

Lineker's hat-trick helped him win the Golden Boot for the tournament's top scorer and, with it, a move to Barcelona, for £2.5 million. One of the distinguishing features of my coaching career is how lucky I've been to work with great strikers from all over the world – Mariner and David Johnson at Ipswich, Lineker, Romario, Ronaldo, van Nistelrooy, Alan Shearer, Figo and so on. It's quite a catalogue. Lineker was a goalscorer to his bones and was unlucky not to surpass Bobby Charlton's England record of forty-nine career goals. Gary scored four against both Spain and Malaysia and two hat-tricks against Turkey, as well as his one against Poland. He was twice voted Footballer of the Year. Simplicity was at the core of his art. His domain was the penalty area. Gary was a one-touch finisher, quite adept in the air for his height, perceptive in his positioning, good on the turn and exemplary in the six-yard box.

Gary left the dressing room believing that he could get on the end of any decent pass into the danger zone. A predatory instinct was backed up by the confidence to hit first-time shots. He was quick as well, although sprinting on to passes took more out of him than would have been evident to the untrained eye. If he played on the Saturday, often he would be too stiff to train on the Monday.

Part of Gary's appeal was that he went through an eighty-game international career without being booked. He was not a spiteful tackler and was never argumentative with referees. He just got on with the game. He chased opponents and tackled them but always legitimately. Conversely, he caused plenty of defenders to be cautioned because he was swift on the turn and tempted opponents to bring him down. He had the thighs of an Olympic sprinter.

With Gary flying, and our hopes boosted by the Poland result, we advanced to the last sixteen to play Paraguay at altitude. The fitness of our players was a decisive factor in another 3–0 win, in which Lineker scored two more, but this was a minor Anglo-South American skirmish compared to what was about to hit us – a quarter-final against the favourites, who had the world's best player, against the backdrop of the Falklands War.

At the 1982 World Cup in Spain, I had scouted for Ron Greenwood. The locals were pro-Argentina and the enmity was palpable – it still was. There was an odour about England against Argentina that I tried to disperse by refusing to answer questions about the war in the south Atlantic. Instinct told me to steer clear of this huge and emotive political issue and I decided to be aggressive with the press. 'If you want to talk about the

Falklands, I'm going to walk out of the room, and there'll be no press conference – so please yourselves,' I told them. 'I'm here for football. If you want to take that tack then fine, but do it without me, I'm walking out.'

In private, our dilemma was what to do about Maradona, this elusive, darting wizard from the wrong side of the tracks. It would have been suicidal to go into the match without devising some kind of scheme to nullify his threat. It was our professional duty to come up with a plan to put genius back in its box without compromising our own style of play. Argentina also had Burrachaga and Valdano and some tough, competitive defenders, including Jose Luis Brown, who owed his surname to some Irish ancestors, but Maradona was the one who might demolish us with a single act.

His position on the field was hard to define. He was neither a striker nor a midfielder but something in between. He was a classic No. 10, a conductor. The Italians call them 'trequartistas' – 'three-quarters' players. Maradona played in the 'hole' close to Valdano. He was a free spirit, loose on the field, with a mandate to conjure and destroy. The choice was stark – do we assign an England player to do nothing but mark Maradona or find some other way?

In the event we decided against man-marking. Taking one player out of his normal role and planting him on Maradona would have forced us to alter our system and unbalanced our team, which was: Shilton; Stevens, Fenwick, Butcher, Sansom; Reid, Hoddle; Steven, Lineker, Beardsley, Hodge. We approached the Argentina game emboldened by two 3–0 victories, cohesive and confident. Plainly, Hoddle was not qualified to be Maradona's shadow. Peter Reid would have stuck to him like flypaper but he had other vital duties to fulfil. If we took Reid out of the loop so he could man-mark Maradona, we would lose the services he was providing for the rest of the team.

The whole starting eleven was in on our final discussions about the Maradona problem and we were unanimous that the best way to tackle him was to ask the nearest man to intervene whenever he received the ball in a threatening position. Each player had the responsibility to respond to the red alert. That way we would retain our shape and purpose. We needed to play our own game, not be dictated to by one gifted opponent.

'If we change the team and we lose, people will criticise us for changing the system. There's no point,' I remarked to Don Howe.

For the most part the policy worked, but you can't legislate for genius. Sometimes in sport an opponent is simply unplayable – nor is there adequate response to bad refereeing or cheating that goes unpunished. Maradona's legal goal was a solo effort from the gods, which left Peter Reid and Terry Fenwick for dead. His final flourish was to go past Butcher and slide the ball past Shilton. Let's be clear – Maradona scored one of the greatest goals of any World Cup. As the ball bobbled over the line, we looked at each other on the England bench in disbelief. My train of thought was: 'Well, he's done it. He's just scored a mesmerising goal.'

He was a bewitching player, quick over the ground, with a lethal ability to sidestep and feint. His two feet functioned equally well. Like Tom Finney, Stanley Matthews, George Best or Ronaldo, he simply sliced through anyone who stood in his path. Sometimes you just have to bow to a master craftsman, which Maradona undoubtedly was, especially in 1986, when he was at the summit of his powers – and yet . . .

The 'Hand of God' was as clear as a bell to me because I was at pitch height and at the perfect angle. As a high back-pass from Hodge sailed towards Shilton, Maradona nipped in, opportunistically, and leapt with his elbow bent and fist clenched. I saw the ball strike the side of his fist and veer towards the goal. Then I watched Maradona spin and run towards the crowd, skipping and bouncing as he went. To anyone forty or fifty feet up in the stands, the offence might not have been so clear but I saw it in forensic detail. In bright light, I saw the rascal's hand above his head and saw him knock the damn ball in.

For a moment nothing happened in my head, or my heart or my body. I didn't have the usual agonised reaction that I would expect when the other team scores. The reason was simple. I knew it wasn't really a goal. My emotions kicked into life only when I noticed the linesman galloping back to the halfway line with his flag down, and the referee striding in the same direction.

'Bloody hell, I think he's given it, he's given a goal,' I muttered to Don. 'He hasn't seen it. He hasn't seen the hand ball.'

Shilton, Fenwick, Butcher and Reid all chased the referee, who was Tunisian. Nothing wrong with that, of course, but in those days officials from such minor footballing nations did not have the experience to be refereeing World Cup quarter-finals. How the hell they came to give England against Argentina to an obscure referee I'll never know. He was simply not qualified to handle such an emotionally charged occasion. The linesman who failed to spot the hand ball was from a Caribbean island where a low grade of football was played. We needed hardened experts from Germany or Sweden or Italy or Holland. It was an accident waiting to happen.

We were powerless. The goal had been given. The protests of Shilton, who had travelled thirty-five yards to admonish the referee, Butcher, Fenwick and Reid were all waved away. Later, Butcher tried to get at Maradona in the dressing room. 'You cheating little . . .' was about as far as he got before being hauled away.

Trailing 2–0 after a crime against sport and then a wonder goal, we brought on Barnes and Waddle in place of Reid and Steven, who had done their bit. My thinking was that John and Chris could jink and dribble and disorientate.

Oddly, John sometimes didn't quite perform at international level the way he did for Liverpool. I don't know why. He certainly had the arsenal. He was a high-calibre player, and well educated. He picked up seventy-nine caps but scored only eleven goals in an England shirt. John had some fine games for us, no question about that, but other times he just didn't turn it on the way he did for his club. He could torment full-backs, feint and double feint and turn a fellow dizzy. A beautiful crosser of the ball with a cultured left foot, he was also good in the air around the back post, but he should have scored more often, and it's fair to conclude that he never really fulfilled his international potential. Even so, he was usually in my teams, which, I suppose, is a measure of his talent. Ironically, England are looking for a John Barnes right now – a magician with a good left foot and the dexterity that John brought to his job. He had the full range of crosses. It was just that sometimes he would be subdued, and I would sit on the bench thinking, 'John, you haven't played the way you should and the way you can. You haven't ripped the full-back apart like you know you can.' Bryan Robson or I would shout at him, 'Go on, John, have a go, get at him, get by him.' Then John would half-attack his opponent, stop and cut the ball square to a colleague. Something would hold him back.

Still, I like to remember John Barnes as a sometimes dazzling talent and the one who sent in a terrific cross for Lineker's goal against Argentina, and then almost set up a second to bring us level. Gary says he will never quite comprehend how the equaliser slipped from his grasp. Late in the game, as Lineker was about to meet a Barnes cross, Brown, who started out on the wrong side of Gary, nipped in front and leaned on him just hard enough to make Gary's head duck slightly. With that, the ball hit him on the shoulder and flew over the bar instead of into the corner of the net. It was an obvious foul, not least because Lineker ended up in the goal. Later, he told me, 'I was looking for the ball in the back of the net. I couldn't believe it wasn't in there with me.'

After the game I remained calm and philosophical in the press conference, even though I was deeply aggrieved. I couldn't alter the result. I couldn't get the game replayed. I knew that was never a possibility. I just put it down to rotten luck and a bad decision that hadn't gone our way, but I was quite clear about my feelings towards Maradona. 'It's not the hand of a god, it's the hand of a rascal. He's cheated the game,' I declared. It never occurred to me to suspect dishonesty on the part of the match officials. We were the victims of mendacity and incompetence. In those days, I believed that people in positions of power at that high level were straight, and that a cheating referee would always be exposed. Since then I've changed that optimistic opinion.

In our absence, Argentina went on to beat West Germany 3–2 in the final, with Maradona again the inspiration, but football was to be in denial for many months. In the July issue of *FIFA News*, our nemesis was exonerated in an article that concluded: 'Diego Maradona's football in Mexico was honest,' as if the 'Hand of God' could be conveniently expunged from the story of the 1986 finals. Not in the Robson household, it couldn't.

10
ZEROES TO HEROES

IN FORTY days, in the summer of 1990, I went from being a 'traitor', who had declared he was bailing out to manage PSV Eindhoven after the World Cup, to the most acclaimed England manager since Alf Ramsey. During Italia '90, my players were informed by one newspaper that they ought to be sent home in disgrace after drawing with the Republic of Ireland at the start of our campaign, and then returned, some twenty-five days later, to a heroes' welcome, with the same paper lauding them as 'England's lionhearts'.

There is a lesson there. Emotion, more than reason, determines the public's attitude to our England teams. Logic comes a remote second to passion and patriotism. Within days, the most damning verdict can be reversed by a good result. The beauty of being a non-combatant, I suppose, is that you can condemn one minute and praise the next. This is not unique to English football. Ours is a game of the heart, as well as the head.

Italia '90 was a turning point for the English game. The revival of football in these islands is often traced to England's near miss at the World Cup in Italy. Somehow, the country was reunited with their team. There were other catalysts, of course, but it's gratifying to know that my last season as England manager coincided with an upturn in the national mood.

The allegation of treachery was easily dispelled, although it hurt me deeply when it was laid at my door. The reason I agreed, before the World Cup, to join PSV in time for the start of the following season was that the Football Association had informed me they would be looking for a new coach once the tournament was over. I was a free agent. I needed work. The change was imposed on me from above.

Against that backdrop, I had received an approach from PSV, and asked Bert Millichip whether he would permit me to meet emissaries from the club, in secret, to explore their offer. Bert gave me his consent. I had the FA's permission to listen to offers. My meeting with Jack Rutts and Kees Ploesgma took place in April, after they had flown into a small airport in Cambridge. Their offer was attractive. Bert and I agreed that we would announce the new arrangement once the World Cup had passed. The problem was that the story leaked, and a certain broadsheet journalist wrote that I had been seen giving a brown paper envelope to every member of the international committee, explaining my resignation. What a load of codswallop that was. 'If you can find one of those envelopes,' I told the press, 'I will give you a million pounds.'

As long as I live, I will never forget the day I went to the FA to defend myself against that spurious allegation. That scarred me. I walked into bedlam. You should have seen the journalists and photographers fighting for position as I tried to open my press conference. Finally, I barked at them, 'I thought hooliganism was supposed to be caused by fans who don't know how to behave. Look how you people are behaving.' They were disgraceful – like sharks after a lump of meat in the sea. The following morning, I was belted by the press. Some of my fiercest critics were writers who had been trying for two years to lever me out of the job. Now I was leaving and granting their wish, suddenly I was a 'traitor' who had no right to exercise the freedom the FA had decided I should have.

I flew to Italy with a stigma attached to my reputation – not among the players, I might add. They told me, to a man, that I was justified in seeking alternative employment.

'The FA aren't renewing your contract, and you've been offered another job,' said Don Howe, kindly. 'You're only doing what anyone would do.'

'Good luck,' the players said. 'You're doing the right thing.'

Incensed by the reaction of some newspapers, I sued *Today* for calling me a turncoat and settled out of court.

My final expedition as England manager got off to a shaky start – a 1–1 draw with the Republic of Ireland that was portrayed, by the *Sun* in particular, as just about the end of English civilisation. The match, played on a slippery pitch in Cagliari on 11 June, was an almost medieval struggle against the Republic's long-ball game. Jack Charlton, one of the heroes of 1966, but now the Republic's manager, had his way of playing and it didn't involve much action on the ground.

I warned our lads, especially Butcher and Des Walker, our two centre-halves, that the ball would be arriving in our box like a projectile fired out of a cannon. Jack instructed his players to conduct an aerial bombardment of Peter Shilton. Crosses weren't aimed towards the penalty spot. They were directed down Peter's throat. Tony Cascarino and John Aldridge were under orders to contest the incoming cross while Butcher tried to provide some measure of personal protection for our keeper.

There was a bloody dog-fight in our penalty area that night. Four Irish players ran at Shilton like rugby forwards on a driving maul. Butcher, Des Walker and Gary Stevens were in a constant state of anxiety. The aerial threat was unrelenting. Although it was a scrap, we tried to play constructive football. In a route-one game on a bad surface, Lineker had put us a goal in front but then Steve McMahon lost control of a ball that slid straight to Kevin Sheedy, who struck it first time across Shilton and into the net.

The *Sun*'s headline the next day was: 'Send them home'. I've still got a copy of that day's paper. They said we were a disgrace because we couldn't beat the Republic of Ireland, we had no chance of qualifying for the knock-out rounds, we might as well come home to save the country from more humiliation. The sky had fallen in on the English game. As a footnote, I should say that the authors of that editorial sent each of us a medal when we returned to Britain three and a half weeks later.

Holland were next. Two years earlier in the European Championship, I had made the mistake of taking on Gullit and Van Basten with only two central defenders, Tony Adams and Mark Wright. That day, the Dutch strikers ripped us to shreds. In a two v. two match-up, Gullit and Van Basten were too good for most centre-half combinations. So, for our second game in the group in Italy, I decided to add a sweeper to our defensive structure, to play three defenders against two attackers, which brings me to the great myth of that World Cup, one of the great fairy stories of my career, in fact – the players' revolt. If you believe the whisperers, we switched to a sweeper system at Italia '90 at the request of the senior players. A delegation approached me, apparently, and demanded the change. Allow me to place this story where it belongs – in the realms of fiction.

I was never dictated to by my England players. In all my time in management I've never had to ask a team to make decisions on my behalf. It's a ludicrous concept. The manager who allows his players to determine the shape or composition of his team is dead in the water. He surrenders his authority. That's not to say that we, as a group of professionals, did not discuss tactical ideas that originated with me, the manager, but the sweeper system was my initiative. Sure, I bounced the idea off the players who would be asked to apply the formation five days after our draw against Ireland, but I made the switch, not them. I had no intention of allowing Van Basten and Gullit to rip holes in us the way they had in Dusseldorf in June 1988. That day, Van Basten had wrecked Shilton's one hundredth international appearance with a hat-trick and Gullit had tied Adams and Wright in knots.

So Mark Wright, Terry Butcher and Des Walker would be our three centre-halves, with Paul Parker on the right and Stuart Pearce to the left. Nowadays they call those two positions 'wing-backs'. Robson, Waddle and Gascoigne were to be my three central midfielders, with Lineker and Barnes up front.

I saw that Mark Wright had the attributes to play as a sweeper. He was tall, he could pass, he was good in the air, clever in possession and not a bad marker. The so-called 'libero' role was perfect for him. Mark was a sufficiently accomplished footballer to be able to carry the ball out of defence and support his midfield. He was ideally equipped to work the two sectors of the pitch.

I can remember saying to Don Howe, 'Let's modify the team to give us a bit of strength through the middle.' Then, on the training ground, I shared my thoughts with the players and asked them to practise in a 3–5–2 formation. Pearce and Parker were given licence to 'bomb on', provided we always kept three-on-two at the back.

'This is what I intend us to do. What do you think?' I asked Gary Lineker.

'Yeah, I think it'll work.'

'What do you think, Mark?'

'Yeah, I can handle that.'

'Terry, what do you think?'

'Yeah, that'll suit me.'

'I don't want to put you into a situation you don't fancy, or you don't believe in. What do you feel? I'm telling you that this is how I think we should play against Holland. Can you handle what I'm saying to you?' This is how I remember our discussion before the Holland game, mature and sensible. It hardly adds up to a mutiny. All I was really asking them was, if we get in to this plane, can you fly it? The answer was a resounding yes. I would stake my whole reputation on this version of events.

Don Howe and I discussed it one last time.

'Bob, you're the manager. If you think that's the way to play against Holland, I'll support you,' he said. 'If you win, you'll get the credit.'

Don was the ideal man to help refine the system on the training pitch. I was in my element, devising a strategy to beat an opponent and then making it work on the practice ground – time on the grass, the great love of my career.

I suppose there was no chance of keeping it from the press, but still I was peeved when the news crept out that we had shifted to a new system and the artillery started coming in. I was accused of taking orders from my players – not a cat in hell's chance. By then, the media needed no second invitation to take a swipe at me, but the game would not be played on newspaper pages. These were noises off stage. I knew we were going to be defensively sound against Holland. Equally, I was sure that Mark Wright would provide an extra attacking presence because his runs out of defence would disrupt the whole Dutch formation.

'Get the ball, Mark, and use it,' I told him. 'Gullit and Van Basten won't like you doing that. They like the two versus two confrontation because they think they can always win it. Let's give them what they don't like and give them plenty.'

We should have won that match in Cagliari on 16 June. Our performance in a 0–0 draw was described in some quarters as genuinely world class. In the last minute, a Stuart Pearce free-kick fizzed past Hans van Breukelen, the Dutch keeper, but was cancelled out by the referee, who insisted he had awarded an indirect free-kick. We were fluent and threatening throughout, and David Platt emerged as a real World Cup player, after coming on as a replacement for Bryan Robson, who had made his last contribution of the tournament. Platt's winning goal against Belgium from a Gascoigne free-kick, in the second round, was one of the best by an England player for many years, but first we needed to win our last group game. We abandoned the sweeper system against Egypt, beating them 1–0 with a goal from Wright, but went back to 3–5–2 for the remainder of our matches, against Belgium, Cameroon and West Germany.

Here, Paul Gascoigne enters the narrative as a player of world repute. The Holland game was his coming of age as an international footballer. His skill and dynamism in that game announced him to a global audience. What an item, what a package, we had in this eccentric, loveable Geordie lad who had the game at his feet. It was my job to allow his talent to flourish while trying to keep him out of trouble, which was never far away.

Let's start at the beginning. In his early Tottenham days, following his move south from Newcastle, I must have received twenty detailed scouting reports about this slightly pudgy but sublimely gifted lad from the North East. I sent Don Howe, Dave Sexton and several other scouts to study him in action. I probably saw him eight times myself in 1989, the year of his international debut. He was thriving at Spurs, no doubt about that, but he was indisciplined. He would try to nutmeg a fellow outside his own penalty area. Some of his passing was careless. When his little conjuring tricks came off he was sensational, when they didn't, he was a liability. It wasn't simply a case of inviting a genius to bestow his gifts on the England team.

The challenge to us all was the World Cup. There's no higher plane to play on. The best players in the best countries in the world converge in one tournament. It's no giggle, no excursion. You can have a laugh and some fun in the hotel, playing ping-pong and cards, but when it comes to training and playing matches, it's a deadly serious business. The brain needs to be fully engaged.

Gazza's potential was obvious but I still needed to be sure he could channel his talent for the benefit of the team. There was no room for a sideshow. The performance that persuaded me he was ready to graduate to World Cup football was our 4–2 victory over Czechoslovakia at Wembley in the April before Italia '90. Paul already had seven England caps but this was the one that made him an obligatory choice for my World Cup squad. He was sensible and disciplined. He laid on two goals and scored the fourth. He was in his element. The bigger the game, the more Paul loved it. In England colours, he was like a dog with a bone.

My mind was made up. Bryan Robson, I figured, would help keep him in line. He would be the stalwart for Paul to look up to. Bryan would encourage him on the field but also restrain him when he was losing sight of the needs of the team. He would loosen or tighten the leash. I had no idea, of course, that Bryan would play just a game and a half in Italy. The theory was sound.

In Gazza, for whom Newcastle had received a British record fee of £2 million, we had a jewel of a player – hyper-active, constantly up to pranks, in need of slowing down, not revving up. After the Czechoslovakia game I called Paul in.

'Well done, son, you scored yourself and made two more,' I said.

'Three,' replied Gazza.

'Paul, I'm the England manager, I've just seen you play and I know what I've seen. You made two goals.'

'I made three,' he said.

'All right. Tell me how you made three.'

So off he goes. 'Remember the corner?' he asked. I told him we hadn't scored from a corner. 'Yeah,' he said, 'but when we had this particular corner, it got headed out to Stuart Pearce, who played the ball to Shilton, who kicked it upfield to Trevor Steven, who crossed the ball to Steve Bull, who put it in with a flashing header.'

'Yeah?' I said, not catching his drift.

A camel ride in Egypt before England played in Cairo, 1986. I did manage to have some fun in the 'impossible job'.

My old pal Jimmy Hill interviews me at the 1982 World Cup after my appointment as England manager is confirmed.

Coaching is my great passion. John Barnes, Glenn Hoddle and Peter Beardsley were among my England students. My right-hand man, Don Howe, looks on.

My mother and father – always watching, always there.

Ron Greenwood was an old friend and regular visitor to Portman Road. I succeeded him as England manager.

Goodbye to all that. My captain Mick Mills leads the farewells as I leave Ipswich Town for Lancaster Gate.

Sleepy Suffolk comes alive. My finest Ipswich team – UEFA Cup winners, 1981. Bobby Ferguson and I show the fans the trophy.

Double Dutch – Arnold Muhren (*left*) and Frans Thijssen were two of my best buys.

Home-grown talent was my religion at Portman Road. Terry Butcher (*right*) was a colossus and Russell Osman (*left*) was a defensive star.

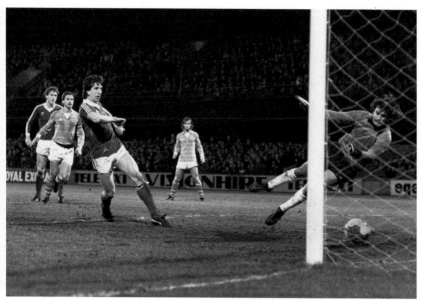

Beating the brilliant St Etienne in the UEFA Cup quarter-finals brought us rave reviews across Europe. Paul Mariner scores.

My famous jig in Cologne as we win our semi-final. The UEFA Cup is within reach.

John Wark connects with a flying header in the first leg of the final against AZ67 Alkmaar.

Victory over the mighty Arsenal in the FA Cup final.

My father and brothers hold the trophy on a proud day for the Robson family.

'Love the game more than the prize' was Ipswich chairman John Cobbold's great advice.

I managed most aspects of life at Ipswich Town. Most important was building a winning team.

On our way to Wembley – Alan Hunter, Kevin Beattie and Paul Mariner celebrate our FA Cup semi-final win in 1978.

'Well, I took the corner,' Gazza said. There was no answer to that.

I have lots of precious memories of Paul. I vividly remember him, before one match, fidgeting with his shorts and grumbling to himself.

'What's the matter, lad?' I asked.

'It's these shorts, I'm not happy with them,' he replied.

'Well change them. You want to be right, don't you, son?'

I called Norman Medhurst, our kitman, over.

'Norman, Paul's shorts are a bit tight. Can you get him some new ones?' Norman nodded and took Gazza's shorts from him. I followed Norman behind a partition, took the original pair of shorts and put them back in their cellophane wrapping. Then I strode back over to where Gazza was standing, half-dressed.

'Try these, they'll be better,' I said.

'Wow,' Gazza said, slapping his thighs. 'These are just the ticket.'

He was wearing the original pair. The explanation? Nervous energy. He couldn't bear the idea of running out at Wembley unless he felt perfect in every respect. A lot of strange impulses and insecurities were crashing around his head.

The lads adored him. He was a laugh a minute. How Chris Waddle put up with him as a room-mate, though, I'll never know. Paul would talk until two or three in the morning. One night in Sardinia, when they were billeted next door to me, I decided to give them a knock to make sure they were OK. It was about 11.45 p.m. No answer. So I decided to take a quick tour of the hotel to see what they were up to. No sign.

An old story about Alf Ramsey went through my mind. It concerned two players who went walkabout and returned to find a note pushed under their door. 'Get your passports ready. You're going home tomorrow,' the message said. I followed Alf's example. Mine read: 'Called to see you. You're not in your beds.

You might be going home tomorrow. Bobby.' Then I went to sleep.

The next morning, Chris Waddle knocked on my door.

'So what happened?' I asked coldly.

'Well, you know what he's like,' said Chris. 'He just talked and talked and talked, and in the end, about eleven thirty, I took him outside for a walk. We walked for an hour.'

My anger subsided. I understood Chris's predicament.

'Just let me know next time,' I told him.

Gazza, as I said, was hyper-active. I'd be chatting to somebody in the hotel and he would be there, right on my shoulder. I would stroll down to the pool, get settled, open a book and Paul would be next to me again. I'd think, 'I've just left you a hundred yards away.' Like an anxious boy, he would follow me around.

In the build-up to the 1990 World Cup, we were carrying a number of niggling injuries. Robson had hurt himself, Parker had a thigh problem and Shilton was struggling. Medical bulletins were flying around. David Seaman fractured a finger and had to be replaced by Dave Beasant. Three days before the tournament kicked off, after a rigorous training session, Don Howe and I were having a cup of coffee and reflecting on the absence of any new injury issues that day. The lads were in their room resting and avoiding the sun. All was well with the world when our peace was disturbed by a terrible groan, a sound of agony, of acute human distress.

'What the eff is that?' said Don, wide-eyed.

Suddenly, Gascoigne staggered round the corner, and I mumbled to myself, 'Ee, my God, what's happened to him?'

'Don, he's fallen off the bloody balcony,' I said.

Gazza's arm was in a sling and his head was heavily bandaged, with spots of blood on the dressing. Our eyes were trying to register these details from twenty yards away. Around one thigh there was padding and strapping and as he dragged his body towards us, blood-curdling noises were coming from his throat. I honestly thought he'd fallen off his balcony.

'What – on earth – has happened – to you?' I called, despairingly.

'Have you seen the doctor?' Gazza asked, but then started running and he dived into the pool with bandages flapping.

Golf was one activity we thought might keep him calm but the etiquette of golf was way outside Paul's social compass. I used to have to chase him round the course, explaining the conventions of the game. In the searing heat, he would pull off his top. 'For Christ's sake, Paul,' I'd say, 'you're not allowed to play golf with your shirt off.' In a buggy, he was murder. He would chase the ball as if he was on the dodgems, driving straight across the greens. 'Paul, we're guests of the club, you can't behave like this,' I would groan. 'Leave your buggy on the side. Play your shot and then go back to it. Don't take it over the greens and in the bunkers. It's against the rules,' and so on.

Tennis was another potential disaster area – yes, tennis, that most innocent of pursuits.

'Where's Paul?' I asked one afternoon before the Belgium game as we sat in the shade. Shoulders shrugged. Eventually someone pointed sheepishly beyond the swimming pool to the tennis courts. I strode over to find Gazza playing tennis, in blistering heat, at 3.30 p.m., with some American guy. We had trained that morning, and were playing the next day. Gazza was drenched in sweat.

'Paul, you've got to be more professional,' I would say to him. 'You don't see Bryan doing that, do you, or Gary? Ask yourself – "Is what I'm doing right? Could it affect me? Is the boss going to be happy?" If the answers are no, don't do it.'

In that World Cup squad, he was the focal point of everything, a bonny lad who trained like a demon as though his life depended on it. He'd be the last off the training pitch, complaining as he went, 'One more shot, Boss, please, just one more.' It was impossible to exhaust him. He was like a Labrador pup. I loved him but, oh dear, did he tire me out.

On the pitch he shone throughout the tournament. Really, he became a world star. Against Cameroon, in the quarter-finals, Paul slid two excellent passes in for Gary Lineker, who was brought down both times for penalties. This has a special resonance for me. When Gary stepped up to take the winning penalty against Cameroon, I was thinking of my dad. The promise from the FA was that if we reached the semi-final, our families would be flown out to watch us play. So, on the bench, I was thinking, 'Come on, Gary, please score so my father can come out to Italy. I'd love my father to come out to this. Come on, Gary, knock it in.'

After the match, funnily enough, I asked him what had been racing through his mind when he struck the ball.

'You know what, I was thinking about my brother,' Gary replied. 'I knew he'd be thinking about me, and would come to the semi-final if we got through.'

During that game, Gazza had chased the ball too much, in torrid heat. He was like a cat pursuing a bird. What happens when the cat reaches the bird? It flies away. This was happening to Paul and it took him out of position too many times, opening space for the opposition to exploit. So before the semi-final, against Germany, I pulled him aside.

'Paul, listen, you were all right against Cameroon. Two fantastic passes for the two penalties. High energy – you did very well, son, but you were all over the place. You've got to develop a greater positional awareness. Ask yourself, what are my responsibilities? What is my area? You can go outside that area, of course, but against Cameroon you ran too far and left gaps for people to get through. Tomorrow you're playing against Lothar Matthaus. He's a great player and the captain of Germany. Already in this competition he's run twenty-five yards and smashed in great goals. If you give him that opportunity tomorrow, he'll do that against us. You have to play with more discipline.'

You know what he said? 'I tell you what, Boss. You just smoke your cigars and leave Matthaus to me. I'll look after him for you.'

This comment, delivered with a classic Gazza grin, had a context. When we progressed to the semi-finals, Ted Croker's son Andrew asked me to endorse an advert for a small-cigar company. The theme was 'Relax, be calm'. I told him I didn't smoke but the offer was £10,000, which was half the bonus the FA were going to pay me for winning the World Cup. All I had to do was allow my name to be attached to the advert. The players must have found out. Hence Gazza's advice to me to 'smoke my cigars' while he took care of the German captain. In the game, I should say, he was true to his word.

With Rudi Voeller and Jurgen Klinsmann posing such a potent threat, we again decided to play with three centre-halves. With their World Cup pedigree, and those two fine strikers, the Germans were marginal favourites to reach the final. Matthaus was top-class and Andreas Brehme was a formidable left-back. By this stage of the tournament, however, we had matured into a really accomplished side – confident, improving and with high morale. Platt had filled the void left by Bryan Robson, Gascoigne was flying, Waddle was in full song and in Beardsley and Lineker we had two bright strikers working in harmony. The defence looked good and we had just won two hard games in extra time. If this epic encounter with our old rivals was to go into extra time, we thought we would win again, because we had done so twice before. We felt we were within touching distance of immortality.

No England supporter will ever forget the drama of Turin. It's one of those games that is imprinted on the memory for life. We all remember the agony but we can also recall how well England played. Gallant failure is not a language I like to adopt but I also know that the margin between victory and defeat that night was painfully thin. The prize, of course, was huge – a place in a World Cup final against Argentina, our nemesis of four years earlier. The musical motif of Italia '90 was opera and this game was surely one, with a savage reckoning to round it off.

We were unlucky with Germany's goal from a fifty-ninth minute free-kick by Brehme. The ball hit Paul Parker in the wall and deviated in the air past Shilton. On the bench we felt disbelief, but not despair. A deflection had put us a goal down. Pot luck. We weren't going to surrender to a random accident. Our equaliser, in the eightieth minute, came when Lineker, in full stride, fired a shot across the keeper and into the corner of the net. Thereafter, in extra time, both Waddle and Guido Buchwald struck the post. We were the superior team. I consider ours to have been one of England's best performances in the last twenty-five years – and yes, we had practised penalties, so in principle the denouement held no terrors for us.

Before the tournament, Gary Lineker had approached me, asking, 'Do you mind if I take the penalties?' I didn't, even though Stuart Pearce was our regular penalty taker. Gary had won the Golden Boot in Mexico four years earlier and I assumed he wanted to win it again. I admired him for asking. Not for a moment did I think him big-headed. A manager is hardly likely to find negative connotations in his senior striker asking to be given the penalty-taking duties at a World Cup. Stuart Pearce, who I thought was our best penalty taker, was not remotely offended.

By then, Gazza's tears had watered the pitch. I don't know anybody who dislikes Paul Gascoigne. The affection we all felt for him added to the poignancy of his booking in extra time, which meant that he would have missed the final had we prevailed in that infernal penalty shoot-out. Gary Lineker's gesture to the bench has gone down in English folklore. Gary pointed to his eyes and then grimaced at me, as if to say, 'He's just been booked, he's going to miss the final, he could go berserk now, so we need to watch him.' The game wasn't over. We needed Paul to control his emotions.

As we went into the second period of extra time, I had said to Paul, 'Look, I know you can't play in the final but what you can do is make sure all the other lads can. Just concentrate on that. You can help us win the game.' This was in the heat of battle. Now, I can appreciate how crushed Paul would have felt had we beaten the Germans that night in Turin.

Neither country could break the deadlock. Chris Waddle fired a shot that was going in, deviated at the last minute and bounced off the post at slightly the wrong angle for Lineker, who couldn't quite make the necessary contact. Such is the margin between failure and success. So I found myself asking for volunteers, like a First World War general, as the clock ticked towards the endgame of five penalties per team. Gascoigne's hand went up but we decided to look elsewhere for the top five, choosing Lineker one, Beardsley two, Platt three, Pearce four, Waddle five. The fourth penalty is often crucial and for that reason I wanted my best penalty taker to go fourth. In training, they knocked them in like cherries. Chris Waddle could walk up to the penalty spot, close his eyes and score, but in front of 70,000 people, with millions watching on TV, with all that tension and pressure, it's a different story.

At three-three, Stuart walked towards the spot. 'This'll be four three,' I told myself. Pearce was a strong character and tough. He had the moral fibre. I had no worries about him. 'I know he'll bloody well hit it, that's for sure,' I thought. 'He won't try and be clever and do something he's never done before. Oh no, he'll whack it.' Well, he did, but he whacked it just a little bit straight. The keeper went one way, stretched out his leg and redirected the ball over the bar. Olaf Thon took another cracking penalty for the Germans, so now it was all up to Chris.

'Come on, Chris, knock it in, put pressure on them to score the fifth,' I muttered.

Chris ran up, lost his shape, leaned back and whacked it over the bar. The players were inconsolable. I laid a hand on each one's back and said, 'You did your best. You didn't do it on purpose,' but while these words left my lips I was distraught. If only – 'if' is the biggest word I've known in football. In the aftermath, Franz Beckenbauer was extremely kind. He said to me, 'You know what, you've played so well. At this level there should never be a loser after a performance like that. You have a nice team, Bobby.'

On the team bus, the curtain fell on my career in international management, although there was still the relatively small matter of the third-place play-off with Italy, which we lost 2–1. Later, when the smoke had cleared, I wrote to Bert Millichip to say that we could hold our heads high. I felt that the performance of the England team at Italia '90 had restored our credibility and pride in world football.

After the press conference, I boarded the bus, desolate. As both sets of players waited to come out together, I got on to an empty vehicle with no one around it, not a soul. Surrounding the German coach in Turin were perhaps 150 people – arc-lights illuminating journalists and well-wishers, laughing and celebrating – and we stepped into silence, oblivion, depression. That really hurt. In our world that night there was no glow, no warmth, only the solitude of defeat.

---| | |---

ON THE ROAD

ALL parents know that there's no greater achievement in life than to produce fine children – sons and daughters who are kind, sympathetic, loving, caring, disciplined. It's not how much you have that counts, it's who you are.

I can still hear myself saying to Elsie, back in the summer of 1990, 'Come on, we'll go to Holland for a couple of years. Then we'll go home to retire.' Her willingness to keep moving from home to home, country to country, was vital to me. It sustained my addiction to football management. I'm not sure a modern wife would have been so accommodating. Different upbringing, I suppose. Different decades.

Looking back, I do feel that football took too much of my family time away from me, away from all of us. I don't remember playing with my kids much in the evenings, or spending time with them playing football on the lawn, reading to them, telling them stories. Those pleasures and duties fell mostly to Elsie, who has been a wonderful mother to our boys, Paul, Andrew and Mark. During the core years of their childhood, I would often be out watching games, or attending some social event at Ipswich Town. In my defence, I felt I was creating a good life for our family. Our homes were always comfortable, attractive, cosy, and we didn't waste our money. I didn't drink or smoke or change my car every six months. We were ordinary people from the North East who understood the value of saving a little money for a rainy day.

On one side, I wasn't seeing my kids enough. On the other, I was building a strong platform of financial security for our futures, and I did spend money on the boys' education. When it came to paying three lots of school fees, three times a year, I would say to Elsie, 'Is this really the right way to do it?' and she would reply, with firmness in her voice, 'Just sign the cheques, and put them in the envelopes. I'll post them.'

The boys have turned out to be nice people. I'm proud of them. I could go to any event in any place in the world and feel honoured to have my three sons standing alongside me. They would be interesting, they would be engaging, they could converse, they would be courteous – everything a father could want from his children. Like all parents, I reflect sometimes that my kids could have finished up as drug addicts or drunks or burglars, and I thank God every day that they've turned out the way they have. Every time we leave after visiting any one of them, I say to Elsie in the car, 'They're great, aren't they?'

'Yes, they are,' she says.

After Italia '90, we really hit the road, travelling to Holland, Portugal, Spain and back to Eindhoven for twelve more months before finally coming home for good. Throughout this Grand Tour of Europe, the family was right behind me. There was no formal farewell from the England job, although Jack Wiseman, Jovial Jack of the FA's international committee, bought me an extremely nice original painting, while the players clubbed together to buy me some porcelain. When the goodbyes were said, I came home, packed, loaded my car with clothes, training gear and other belongings, and boarded the ferry from Harwich to the Hook of Holland. I was semi-emigrating, so I needed a hefty cargo of possessions. From the port I found my way to Eindhoven to earn twice the salary I'd been paid for managing England.

What a culture shock it was, moving from England to PSV, a big Dutch club but hardly the goldfish bowl I had just left.

My new job had a lower profile and I wasn't unhappy to see England's shore recede. I felt a sense of adventure, a sense of release. With Elsie, one day, I had mused, 'Where do you go when you've been England manager?' Most people either retire or take over a big domestic club, but I just fancied going abroad. I'd travelled a lot with Ipswich and England, but had never lived overseas for any appreciable length of time. I regarded PSV as a nice club in a pleasant city. Every home game was sold out in a 32,000-seat arena. I'd been told that the people who ran the club were decent folk. Financial muscle and good business sense were provided by the sponsors, Philips, the electrical giant.

I didn't know a soul in the town that was to be our home. I walked in blind. My assistant was a chap called Hans Dorjee, who spoke good English. He was reliable and trustworthy and didn't seem to want my job. Frank Arnesen, who was to become director of football at Spurs, was on the staff on the commerical side. He was the liaison between the club and Philips. Frank and I got to know each other well. In my second season, I made him my assistant after Hans had suffered a heart attack. Frank had been a very fine player with Ajax, Anderlecht and PSV. We were peas in a pod.

In a large pool of good players, we had one tropical fish. Romario, the little jinking Brazilian striker, was as brilliant as he was unmanageable. Nobody could bring Romario to heel. He was a fantastic player, a match-winner, but his indiscipline was a constant cause for concern. He would train only when he chose to. When it came to one of our brisk five kilometre runs, for example, he would lose all interest in the job. He didn't like the heart and leg work that came with being a professional athlete. He only liked the ball. So his back or some other part of his anatomy would give way when the strenuous work began.

Not surprisingly, the other PSV players began to resent his slacking. 'Aah, not again, get him out of here. If he's not going to do it, we're not either,' they would say when the little demon peeled away from the group. They knew the star of the team was earning far more than they were because his talent marked him out as a lethal weapon, a special case. In return, however, his colleagues expected him to train as hard as they did, be on the coach on time and observe the basic disciplines of a professional footballer.

In some matches he would be scintillating. In others he would be lethargic, distracted. The players soon recognised Romario's off days. In defeat one day, I overheard Eric Gerets jabbering away to him aggressively. Eric was a formidable guy, the captain of Belgium, who later became a coach. Frank translated for me. Eric was saying, 'Listen, you effing this or that, I know you get more than me. I understand that and I don't quibble with it because you're a better player than I am. I might save a match, but you can win one. What I quibble about is that on Saturday afternoon we all share a bonus, and I'm trying my balls off to get that bonus, and you ain't. Together, we fight.'

When he'd finished this little rallying cry I went to Eric Gerets and told him, 'I like what you said.' Eric and I got along well. He was one tough hombre, dead straight.

The Romarios of the world don't realise how much they can undermine the fabric of a team. On the whole, the lads liked him. He was a classic Brazilian, bubbly and full of life. They respected him as a player, too. Thirty yards from goal, he was mustard. He could take anyone on. He was a great finisher, a good hold-up player and was dangerous in the air, despite his modest size. Some mornings he would be phenomenal in training. Other days, you'd take one look at him and know he'd left his energy and his legs at home, or in a nightclub.

There was no controlling his private life. To Romario, Friday night was party night, even if we had a game the next day. Alcohol was not the problem – he was a Coca-Cola guy – but he'd stay out until four in the morning and sleep all day before a 7.30 p.m. kick-off. We would take calls from people saying, 'Romario's been out all night. He left here at four.' He would dance, chat, meet a local lady, carouse with her and then sleep all day to be 'fresh' for the game.

One day, we were playing eight versus eight in a positioning exercise, as the Dutch called it. The object was for both teams to keep possession of the ball in a 40m × 40m space. One team seemed to be struggling. There was an imbalance somewhere on the pitch. So I counted the bodies – one two three four five six seven eight, then one two three four five six seven. Someone was missing. Just then I turned to see Romario disappearing into the dressing room. From sixty yards away, I shouted, 'Hey! Romario! What are you doing?' He pointed to his lower back, made a dismissive gesture and carried on walking in.

One of the problems I had with him was that he knew no English and I spoke no Portuguese. Frank Arnesen could speak a little Spanish and so, after a discussion about our growing problem with our star player, it was decided that Frank would act as translator and peacemaker. For the big showdown, we'd get by somehow in Spanish.

The three of us convened in a room at the training ground. Through Frank, I said, 'Romario, you've got to stop walking off the training ground. Romario, you've got to stop going out on a Friday night,' and so on and so on.

Let me tell you, Romario didn't say a word. All he did was stare, like a cobra, into Frank Arnesen's eyes, quite aggressively. Frank was getting edgy. He was being defied. He was beginning to feel humiliated. 'Comprehendo?' we would ask, as our mini summit wore on, but still Romario wouldn't speak.

Frank was getting riled. The peacemaker was losing his cool. On the table sat a thick Dutch telephone directory, and when Frank finally snapped, he picked up this book, slammed it down in front of Romario and roared, 'You son of a bitch!' in Spanish. In that language, apparently, it's the rudest thing you can say to a man's face. Then Frank stomped out, leaving me alone with Romario.

'Thanks for bringing Frank in to help me with Romario. He ended up having a row with him!' I laughed when I gave my report to Kees Ploegsma, the club's general manager.

In essence, Romario was telling us, through his silence, 'I don't care what you're saying. It means nothing to me. I've got no response for you.' Players don't change their spots. Some, you can't transform with a sit-down and a few home truths.

As a footballer, he was in Ronaldo's class, although undeniably he was lazy. He didn't believe in chasing a centre-half to regain possession. He conserved his energy for bursts of speed and diagonal runs. The ball would be superglued to his feet. He had a good repertoire of Brazilian tricks of the sort Ronaldinho performs. If Romario hadn't been such a brilliant player, you would have run him out of town. The bottom line was that he could win matches for you. That was his insurance policy against the sack.

We won the Dutch title in both my first two seasons at PSV. After so many near-misses with Ipswich, it was deeply satisfying to win, and then retain, a domestic championship. Equally, after coaching the England players for perhaps ten games a year, I loved being back on the training ground each morning. Abroad, you're the trainer, not the manager. If you can't coach, you won't survive. At Newcastle, later, I would finish coaching and then be back in the office until six o'clock at night. Ipswich was the same. There would be board meetings and scouting and youth policies and admin to attend to. In Europe, the chairman didn't really expect to see you in the afternoons, provided you were happy with the fitness of the players. Some days, in Holland, early in the week, I even found myself having a game of golf.

Working at PSV for two years made me a better coach. It was very fulfilling. The reward for all that patient teaching came on the last day of the season, when we finished ahead of Ajax in a race that went right to the wire, the reverse of what had happened to me in my last two years at Ipswich.

PSV let me go after two years and two championships because we hadn't made the expected headway in European competition. In my second year, I contracted cancer for the first time, and maybe that shook the club's owners. Perhaps they thought I wouldn't be strong enough to go on for a third campaign. My second brush with that often fatal condition, in the summer of 1995, was the more serious of the two. The first was hardly a walk in the park, either, although that's how I started the recovery process.

I noticed I was passing a little blood and thought, 'That's strange,' but then allowed it to slip from my mind. This went on for two or three weeks. I felt fine with not a murmur of ill-health. I was on the pitch every day. If I thought about it at all, I assumed it might be piles, but as a precaution I mentioned it to the club physician, Artur Woolf, who arranged for me to have a consultation at St Anne's hospital in Geldorf. A camera was inserted into my rectum and on the monitor I could see large deposits of blood.

'Get dressed,' said Artur. 'You need an operation – yesterday. You've got a bit of cancer in your colon and must have it removed. I'm afraid you're going to be out of football for at least three months. I'm going to have to tell the chairman that you need surgery. It's very fortunate you've brought this to my attention.'

I was shaken, I admit. There was no evading the seriousness of what the doctor was saying to me. However great my physical resilience, however vast my love for the game, I had to face this enemy inside my body.

'Bobby, this is your life. Don't worry about us, we'll be OK,' Jacques Rutts, the chairman, reassured me. The reserve coach, Huub Stevens, took over, with Frank Arnesen as his assistant. I was to be on the sidelines from November to January.

On the operating table, they removed a section of my colon and then re-connected the two ends. The statement issued by the club said that I had been in hospital for a stomach operation. Nobody twigged and I didn't broadcast the real story. After the procedure, I felt truly awful. They had cut me open from side to side and the immediate aftermath was excruciatingly painful. Morphine helped. For a week, I took it three times a day and it eased the searing pain in my stomach, but I was stiff, sore and bruised. To reach the diseased area they had cut through my stomach muscles. In bed, another strange pain was nagging away at me, one that didn't fit with all the others.

'I have to tell you, Artur, that I've got an ache in my chest,' I told the club physician during one of his frequent visits. I assumed I'd pulled a muscle hauling myself upright via the metal bar that was suspended above the bed, but on top of everything else, I had an embolism in one of my arteries, and it was dangerous. That detained me for another week while they thinned my blood.

At home, Elsie looked after me and pulled me round. For exercise, later, I would walk Frank Arnesen's five-year-old daughter, Rebecca, around the park next to our flat. Frank's wife, Kate, would chat to Elsie while I took little Rebecca for a stroll. Walking was about as much as I could do. For the final month, I went to watch PSV, sitting next to Jacques Rutts at games.

The club were just exemplary in the way they treated me. Unlike at Newcastle, I was told in absolutely the right way that I would be leaving at the end of the 1991–92 campaign. Jacques Rutts invited me to his house to tell me, 'Bobby, you've had two wonderful years, but we're not going to renew your contract.'

This was a couple of months before I won the second league title.

'Jacques, are you unhappy with me?' I asked.

'Not at all,' he said. 'This is the way it is on the Continent. We tend to change every two or three years.' I took it on the chin. It was all very civilised and amicable.

Towards the end of that season, Jacques strode into the dressing room to address the players, after asking my permission. He announced that I would be leaving and said, 'I hope that between now and the end of the season you will strive to give Bobby your full support and be champions yet again.'

I was a free agent once more. Again, I confess that I didn't ask Elsie when the chance came to join Sporting Lisbon, in July 1992.

'I've accepted an offer to go to Lisbon. It'll be great for us,' I told her.

'What?' Elsie said.

'It'll be different, it'll be warm, we'll have a nice life there for a year or two, then we'll come home.'

'Do we have to?' said my wife.

The idea had been first put to me by Dennis Roach, the football agent, who called me to say, 'Sporting Lisbon are looking for a coach, preferably English. You're ideal.' There I met an unknown young man who was to have a stunning impact on the European game. My initial encounter with the future Chelsea manager was at Lisbon airport, where he was standing beside Sousa Sintra, the Sporting chairman. Sintra couldn't speak one word of English and so had brought with him this young, good-looking ex-schoolteacher who spoke very good English and had a minor Portuguese coaching certificate. The interpreter introduced himself as Jose Mourinho and told me his father had been a goalkeeper. He also declared a strong interest in the game. How they chose him, or where they got him from, I had no idea, but I did discover than Jose was a good friend of Manuel Fernandes, a former Sporting player whom I would be employing as my assistant.

In essence, Jose was a translator with a knowledge of football. He was bright, alert and willing. We got on famously and our wives became friends. At half-time, full-time, at press conferences and on the training ground, Jose would get my message across to the players. He grew up with me. I had him under my wing for six years. He was exceptionally loyal and watched my back. 'Tell me what they're saying, Jose. I want to know everything they say,' I would insist. Each time I went to see the president, Jose would be with me. I soon picked up enough Portuguese football terminology to get me by on the pitch. Jose would write down phrases for me to learn.

The club were in a terrible state, although we did manage to finish third in my first season in charge. The president, I soon discovered, was a loose cannon, extremely emotional and vola-tile. To strengthen the squad I bought my old ally Stan Valckx from PSV and Sergei Cherbakov from the Ukraine. Jorge Cadete, Krasimir Balakov, Fernando Nelson and Luis Figo were already there. The president fancied himself as something of a talent spotter. He signed Antonio Pacheco and Paulo Sousa from Benfica, probably because he thought he could damage our biggest rival by snatching two of their top players. When those two joined, 15,000 fans turned up at Sporting to greet them. They were presidential signings but I knew they were good players.

That one season and the start of another was a strange and turbulent phase on our tour, and the ending was spectacular. It came when the president grabbed hold of the tannoy on the flight back from a game against Casino Salzburg and announced, in effect, that the coach would be removed the following day. Jose translated for me as I sat in my aeroplane seat, flabbergasted. The next morning I was called in and dismissed. We were top of the Portuguese league, for the first time in fifteen years and here

I was being sacked. Jose was with me when the bullet was fired. This loopy president was jabbering away, 'We're out of Europe, it's a disaster for the club, you have to go!'

The game that brought about my dismissal was vintage farce. The first thing to say is that the president had signed an inexperienced goalkeeper called Costinha, who played in that fatal game. We'd won the first leg of this UEFA Cup tie at home 2–0 and should have won the return by at least five. It was savagely cold in Salzburg in December. In the dressing room, Paulo Sousa was wrapping brown paper round his feet to provide an extra layer of warmth.

In the game, we were losing 1–0 with about ten seconds to go when Manuel Fernandes stepped on to the touchline, waving his arms to tell the players the game was over.

A Salzburg player gathered the ball thirty-five yards out and hit a shot that flew through Costinha's fingers – 2–0, 2–2 on aggregate, extra time. In the last minute of the thirty added, Costinha mishandled a corner and dropped the ball in front of an Austrian, who gratefully tapped it in. By then, Figo had missed a penalty for us. When Cristiano Ronaldo of Manchester United realises that football is a passing as well as a dribbling game, he's going to be a great player. Figo, who was then eighteen, was the Cristiano Ronaldo of his time. He could go inside or outside, put good balls into the box and was immensely strong. He was a good guy to have around, very ambitious.

I should have known what to expect from Sousa Sintra after that calamity in Salzburg. One week, we were due to play Benfica at the Alvalade Stadium. We hadn't beaten them home or away for years and the rivalry was so intense that the president tried to ban me from going there beforehand to see them play.

'You don't go there. We hate them. You are our trainer and you are not to be seen at Benfica football club. I forbid you to go,' he told me.

'Are you serious?' I responded. Imagine a Liverpool manager not going to a game at Manchester United for that reason. Portugal had a different culture entirely.

The president offered me the chance to take the players to a small island we used to train and relax. On the Friday before the match, Jose informed me, 'Bobby, the president wants to come down to see the players.' When he arrived he delivered a rant, full of passion and gesticulation. I didn't understand a single word of what was being said to my players. He then drank a cup of coffee and left.

'What was that all about?' I asked Jose.

'Well,' he said, 'he's put the boys on a special bonus.'

Sintra had doubled the special bonus that was always paid when Sporting beat Porto or Benfica. The players were understandably chuffed. Within twelve seconds, Balakov, who was a great player – as good as Figo – had put the ball in the back of the net from thirty-five yards. Twelve seconds against Benfica and we're one up.

Not long afterwards, Stan Valckx, my trusty centre-half, took an elbow in the face. From the dug-out, I studied Stan's face and said to the doctor, 'Stan has a broken cheekbone. He's got an indentation in his cheek.' At half-time, while we were trying to sort this out, the president appeared in the dressing room, waving his arms, yelling, exhorting the players to put our old enemy to the sword. The players were responding in kind. 'Yeah! Yeah!' they were hollering. I'd never had a president or chairman in my dressing room at half-time and I didn't like it. In that fifteen-minute break, I believe in being calm and methodical. In this mayhem, with a madman on the loose, I couldn't get a sensible word in.

'He's doubled the bonus again,' Jose explained.

'Again?'

We won the game 2–0 and Stan Valckx played on to the end.

He refused point blank to remove his shirt. Now there was a tough man. Manuel Fernandes confided in me, 'Boss, we have never had a player like Stan Valckx at this club, someone with his character, his demeanour on the training ground.' Stan and I have remained great friends. He was devastated when I was sacked, as were all the players. They threw a party for me down in Cascais on the sad night Sergei Cherbakov was paralysed in a road accident. I saw him recently on a trip to Russia for a Champions League tie. After some publicity in the local press, they found him and brought him to my hotel in his wheelchair to say hello.

Sergei's terrible accident was not the only tragedy to darken my four seasons in Portugal. At Porto, where I went in 1994, I had a young player called Rui Felipe. One Friday night, he went out with his family and was involved in a dreadful motoring accident. On the morning of the match, I came down for breakfast to be told by the secretary, Luis Cesar, who was a wonderful guy, 'I have some very bad news for you. Rui Felipe is dead.' My blood ran cold. In the impact, Rui had been thrown from the car and had landed a hundred yards away on his face, dead. He was such a lovely boy.

I hadn't been to a Portuguese funeral before but I went to this one. Along with hundreds of other mourners, I filed past his body, trying not to dwell on the appalling injuries to his face. All funerals are sad but this one was the most melancholic I have attended. People were wailing. Not long afterwards, they erected a Rui Felipe monument in a courtyard at the club. More or less every day, as I left the club to walk to my car, I would touch the hand of Rui's statue and say a few words of remembrance.

When it ended for me at Sporting, eighteen months into my stay, I persuaded Elsie that we should spend the rest of the winter in Portugal and wait for Sousa Sintra to honour my contract. I was in no doubt what would happen if I went back to England.

The debt would not be paid. My intention was to play some golf, sit on the beach, and go home to see the kids once or twice. A cricket tour to the West Indies was another enticing prospect. I had it all arranged with my friend Bob Harris when FC Porto came on the line. Pinto Da Costa, the Porto president, ordered his chauffeur to drive him south to my house, where he tried to persuade me that we could make the third biggest club in Portugal the king of the hill.

'Tell me about Porto,' I said to Jose over the phone.

'Big tough city in the north. Big club. Very ambitious, with a strong president,' Jose replied. Where Lisbon was cosmopolitan and multi-national, Porto was distinctly Portuguese.

To Jose, I said, 'I can take over up there if I want to. Shall I go? And will you come with me?'

'Oh yes, Mister, I'd love to come there with you.'

Jose was unemployed. He and Manuel Fernandes had stayed on at Sporting for a while but were ousted when Carlos Queiroz assumed command. Later, Queiroz was to become Sir Alex Ferguson's assistant at Manchester United. He had his own assistant and Sporting decided that they no longer needed an interpreter. So I took Jose to Porto with me, and after that to Barcelona in 1996. He stood at my shoulder on the training ground throughout those six years and we travelled to matches together. From time to time, we would also socialise.

At Porto, where the team was in a poor state and the crowds had dwindled to 10,000, we followed the same pattern every day on the training pitch. The more time we spent together the more we liked one another. At the end of my contract, when I moved to Catalonia, with Porto owing me quite a substantial sum of money, I asked him, 'Jose, I'm going to Barcelona. Do you want to come?'

'Not half,' he said.

'Right, well, if I can arrange a deal for you, let's go together.'

I made it a condition of my employment at Barcelona that Jose would come too.

'I'll pick up Catalan from Portuguese in two months,' he promised, and he did. He was the world's best-paid interpreter and he settled in fast. He had a nice attitude on the training ground and the players accepted him into their group. With his language skills he could communicate with them better than I could. He became indispensable to me. He picked up my methods, my coaching style, even my sayings. I had no doubt Jose was working his way towards becoming a very fine coach and every now and then I would test him.

'Jose, I don't know what to do at training today. Any ideas?' I'd ask and Jose would always have a suggestion.

He didn't take coaching sessions in my time at the Nou Camp but when Louis Van Gaal took over he was given more responsibility. At the end of my second year in Barcelona, when I was director of signings, I advised Jose to stay on with Louis, coaching the first-team squad. Before I knew it, Jose was being offered a job by a small Portuguese club, and then by Benfica, where he lasted just a few months before returning to Porto, where, clearly, they remembered him from our successful time together. When Porto took a chance on him, his CV as a head coach ran to one year and three months, and most of that had been served with a minor Portuguese club. So what he has achieved since then is sensational. I'm really proud of him.

Where does his talent stem from? Well, he served a good apprenticeship, working with me for six years and with Louis for one. He was a student of the game and he was working at the top of the tree. I was open with him and he had a thirst for knowledge. Somehow our talents and personalities interlocked. 'Arrogant' is not a label I would attach to him. He was never flash with me. He was always very respectful of the man he called Mister. What he had was self-belief. At Porto, he was liked by everybody – players, media, fans. For him to win the UEFA Cup and the Champions League in successive seasons took my breath away.

I confess it surprised me that Chelsea didn't call me to ask about Jose before they offered him the contract to succeed Claudio Ranieri. I thought Peter Kenyon, the chief executive at Stamford Bridge, might want to find out more about the man they were bringing in. I found that astonishing but maybe they had no need of reassurance. Perhaps it became an obvious choice after Jose raised the European Cup. Jose didn't ring me, either. I thought he might call to ask, 'What's Chelsea like? What can I expect?' although I met him once the deal was confirmed.

Back in Porto in 1994, we won so many games 5–0 that I became known to the locals as 'Bobby Five-O'. My predecessor's five best players were all centre-halves and he liked to play them all, with two of them in midfield, so 5–0 victories for Porto were understandably rare. If there was ever a result in club football I've truly loved, it was the 2–1 win over Sporting Lisbon in the final of the Portuguese Cup. The following season, we also won the Portuguese title at Sporting's expense and the players threw me up in the air in the middle of the pitch. Sweet triumphs.

My popularity in Porto was expanding by the day. After winning the league championship in 1994–95, I re-signed on the verbal understanding that if a big club in England came in for me, I would be allowed to return home. 'Not a problem,' said the president and we shook hands on it, but nothing was added to the contract. When an offer did come in, from Arsenal via David Dein, the vice-chairman, who flew over to see me, I said yes pretty quickly and went to England to meet Peter Hill-Wood. I met the whole board of Arsenal directors at a house in South Kensington and resolved to tell my president face to face on a scouting trip to Switzerland that I was leaving to go to Highbury. The president went wild.

'How can you leave us? You've done so well, I've just given you a contract, I've just bought a couple of players on your recommendation,' which was true. 'I can't let you leave this club.' I referred him to our verbal agreement. 'I'll take you to dinner tomorrow night and we will solve this problem,' he said.

So the following night, Jose and I sat down to eat with Pinto Da Costa. On the table sat a present, a gold pen. He was turning on the charm but I was churned up and didn't enjoy the evening. I wanted to leave to manage Arsenal. As the mood at the table deteriorated, the president threatened to take the case to UEFA to have my contract enforced. I had been there for fifteen months, taking the club from fifth to second to start with and then winning the title in my first full season in charge. However, no apparently meant no.

Arsenal would have been a fantastic job for me. To think I turned down Manchester United, in 1981, and here I was about to reject Arsenal as well. I called them.

'Look,' I said, 'the president's being very unpleasant. He won't let me go. He's not interested in compensation, so I'm going to have to stay for another year.' Still, it was a nice gold pen.

In the light of what happened to me next, my disappointment seems trivial now. I turned Arsenal down in May and by August I was fighting for my life.

12

AN ANGEL AT MY SIDE

THE score so far is Me 2, Cancer 0. Without my wife's nagging, though, it wouldn't have been a home win. Without Elsie's love, persistence and good sense, you wouldn't be reading this book. My story would be found on the obituaries page.

In the summer of 1995, my Porto team came to England to play a Saturday benefit match for Paul Elliott, the Chelsea centre-half whose career had been ended after a tackle by Dean Saunders of Liverpool. My intention was to stay in England on the Monday and Tuesday and then go back to Portugal, while the lads were going home immediately after the game. In my stomach I could feel the familiar tension of pre-season. Time was short, the list of jobs was long.

On the Monday, at our home in Ipswich, Elsie suddenly announced, 'I've got an appointment for you.'

'What? An appointment? What for?' I asked tetchily.

'Your sinuses.'

'Elsie, my sinuses are all right. I'm OK.'

'You're not all right. You're always complaining about them. I've made the appointment. It'll be embarrassing if I have to cancel it. Please, do it for me.'

'Oh, all right, I'll go,' I huffed.

I had no pain, no headaches and no swelling. All I had was a constantly blocked nose. At Ipswich many years previously, Bobby Bell had swung his arm quite accidentally while I was standing behind him and hit me on the nose. The force of the blow put me on the floor. I could feel my nose all over my face and the blood was gushing. From that moment on my sinuses were never right. I was constantly bunged up, especially on flights. The firms who make inhalant sticks have never had a better customer. I always had one handy to use when the congestion got too bad. Summer was usually OK, but winter time was a pest.

So I turned up, as instructed by Elsie, to be told by our GP, Dr Keeble, that he needed to refer me to an ear, nose and throat specialist. There was no cause for alarm at that point. It was simply that our doctor felt the problem was best handled by an expert in the field. That resulted in more tension at home.

'Elsie, please, I really haven't got time for this. I've got to get back to Porto,' I complained, but again I relented. The appointment with the specialist, Mr Ian Lord, was made for that evening, with fortuitous speed, as it turned out. Ian remembered me well from my Ipswich days.

'All I can do is clean out your sinuses. You'll be in and out in a day,' he promised. I'd been here before. A couple of years earlier, they had gone up through the roof of my mouth and washed out all the muck, but it hadn't really worked. Ian was as good as his word, rushing me through the ward. The next morning he gave me an update.

'There was a lot of debris up there. Some of it was like black pudding. Awful. You'll feel a lot better now. We'll send some of it for a biopsy, and we should have the results back in two or three weeks.'

I was grateful to him, and after asking if he could get a reading on the biopsy as soon as possible, I left the hospital at about eleven to prepare for the flight back to Porto the next day. That afternoon, meanwhile, Elsie travelled down to Dorset to stay with some friends for a few days. Later, in the evening the phone rang. It was Ian Lord.

'Bobby, we pushed that biopsy through even quicker than you wanted,' he said. 'In fact, we did it today. I have to come and see you. I know where you live. Just sit tight. You're not going out, are you?'

'No,' I replied, 'but I'm going back to Porto tomorrow.'

'Well, I don't think so, but I'll see you shortly,' he said, and hung up. Odd.

Ten minutes later he was standing in my front room. I remember the precise details and inflexions of that conversation to this day. This is what Ian said.

'I have some very grave news for you. The results of the biopsy are disturbing. You have a malignant melanoma in your face and we don't know how long it's been there.'

A lone thought shot through my mind – 'What the hell is a malignant melanoma?' It was the first time I'd heard that expression. I found out soon enough. I had cancer in my head, behind my face, below my eye. Even then, I imagined a small incision to remove the growth, but Ian used the same expression as the physician in Holland had used a couple of years earlier.

'You need an operation yesterday. I've already arranged for the consultant surgeon to come and see you tomorrow.'

'But I'm going back to Porto tomorrow,' I protested.

'You're not,' Ian said quietly. 'I'm afraid it's life-threatening. The surgeon will tell you more tomorrow.'

This was a private consultation, speeded up by private health care. Had I been an NHS patient, would my biopsy have been rushed through so fast? I can't know the answer to that question but without private care, I suspect I might be dead. Early diagnosis and swift action saved me from oblivion.

Now my life was hurtling towards a confrontation with death. True to his word, Ian Lord came back the next day with Huw Davies, a consultant surgeon for four hospitals in the area and a cancer expert. Huw reiterated that I had a very serious and rare form of cancer inside my head. It was malignant. Without the operation, he told me, I would be gone in six months.

'Are you serious?' I exclaimed.

'I understand you're a football manager,' Huw replied. 'Well, you will not see this season out, Mr Robson. By January, this thing will have gone into your eye and then into your brain.'

Incredulity was still winning the battle for my thoughts.

'Look at me, I'm fit and strong. I feel fine.'

'We know. But you've got a malignant tumour inside your head, and we're going to have to go through your head to get it. We're going to have to cut you open, take your teeth out, go through the roof of your mouth and remove a fair proportion of the inside of your head to make sure we get it all out.'

Huw gave me the name of a world expert in this field of surgery and promised that he would be leading the surgical team – Dan Archer. People accuse me of mixing up names but this is one I'll never forget. Dan was a Liverpudlian who had performed coming on for three hundred of these complex operations. This one would take place at the Royal Marsden in London, and it would be under way within forty-eight hours. The total cost to me would be £14,000.

They cut me from the corner of my eye, round the contour of my nostril and through the lip, which they completely severed. Then they pinned the flap of my face almost to my ear, took my teeth out and went through the roof of my mouth, just as Huw had said. They needed twenty-eight stitches to put the outside of my face back together. I was on the slab for nine hours, so long that the surgeons even went off for lunch.

'You didn't, did you?' I asked when they told me they'd gone for a sandwich and a cup of tea.

'We did. We can't work for nine hours,' they chorused. 'We were gone for an hour.'

'You buggers. I thought you were my friends.'

'We are. We saved your life, didn't we?'

They saved me from the evil grip of cancer and left me with a permanent legacy – a hole in the roof of my mouth that I have to fill with a bespoke, pink rubber plug, which itself cost £2,000. I've had hundreds of letters from people who have had terrible problems finding the right shape, the right fitting, for the holes in their own heads. I was lucky enough to be able to go to the very best. The plug has clasps, which secure it to the roof of my mouth, and a rubber extension to which are fitted false teeth to replace the ones I lost. If I take it out, the inside of my mouth collapses and I can't speak intelligibly. I have one regular and one spare. If I travelled abroad without the spare and dropped the original one, breaking one of the clasps, I just couldn't function. Normal life would implode.

Each time I eat, I have to take the plug out and clean it with brushes and hot water. Otherwise all sorts of food becomes congealed in the gaps. Morning, noon and night I have to do that. I also have to suck hot water up my nostrils to flush out the detritus. Otherwise, I'd be horribly bunged up. My God, it was hard to learn how to use the contraption properly. Getting it back in once I'd removed it for cleaning was a nightmare. It's a tight fit, for obvious reasons, and the flesh around the hole was horribly sensitive and sore.

In those traumatic early days Elsie was marvellous. 'Look, just go in the bathroom and lock the door,' she would say. 'Sit on the floor and just practise, in private, in peace.' She was so positive, so helpful, but there were times when I locked that bathroom door and cried. 'I'll never be able to get this thing in and out,' I wept. 'I'll never survive, never be able to live.' Ten years later, I take it in and out in a second. I can do it in the click of a finger.

Radiotherapy was another, brutal stage of the post-operative treatment. First, I had to lie down while they poured wax over my face to create a mask.

'This is going to be extremely unpleasant. A lot of people can't stand this. They jump up and run away,' the chap who did the procedure warned me, 'and they don't come back.'

The wax freezes, they pull it off and then cut a hole to direct the radiotherapy rays through. In my case, the tumour was about one inch below my left eye. I was strapped to a bench and told to remain absolutely still. Four bolts held me down, and a pipe ran into my mouth for me to breathe. I lay like that for eight sessions of radiotherapy.

The first couple were fine, a piece of cake, but I'd been warned that it might get unpleasant later on and it did. Radiotherapy burns the rogue cells but it also burns healthy ones. My tongue became swollen and sore. I couldn't eat. I couldn't talk. I could only drink through a straw. I just had to get through it somehow. I had to keep my spirits up by dreaming of better days, imagining a life without pain, fighting the fight. Waiting up ahead was the awkward question of whether I would ever go back to work. All I knew was that I wanted to be back on the training ground.

'Well, most people don't go back to work after this operation,' warned Huw Davies, who became a great family friend, 'and your occupation is full of stress. Cancer can be stress related. No one really knows, but tension doesn't help. So Bobby, why don't you pack it in?' There was no chance of that. I couldn't do it.

The club, meanwhile, was in good hands. Jose, Pinto Da Costa and his wife, Philomena, and the club doctor all came over to see me before and after the operation. Like PSV, they all treated me with humanity and respect. I had the operation in August and was back at work at Porto towards the end of October. The following summer we retained our league title.

I went back on the pitch. I needed to be back in football. I didn't feel too well, I admit, but I just had to be back at work. It was my way of reaffirming to myself that I was still alive. Long walks in the park and other retirement rituals were not going to do it for me. Elsie, bless her, understood that compulsion. After Christmas, we moved down to Foz, the seaside area of Portugal, to a beautiful apartment next to the beach, and I had a good few more months as Porto manager, assuming that I would be there for a fourth and even a fifth campaign, but then the club's finances began to unravel.

With the players not receiving their bonuses, as that season wore on, I had to implore them not to mutiny, to keep fighting to win the title. Embarrassed, the president stopped coming to the training ground. Sometimes the salaries would be a month late. At a civic reception at the end of the season, I noticed that the Brazilian, Emerson, was missing. I assumed he had opted out of the party, but on the Monday morning, when we made enquiries, Jose informed me that the player was now in Middlesbrough, having been signed by Bryan Robson. He was sold for £6 million without a word from the president to me.

'Well, at least we might get our bonuses now,' I joked to Jose.

Out of the blue, I received a call from Joan Gaspart, the anglophile vice-president of Barcelona, who had previously asked for my advice on whether the club should buy Luis Figo.

'Is he a Barcelona player?' asked Joan.

'Yes, he is. Trust me. Buy him,' I replied.

This latest conversation floated round to my own predicament, and I explained the verbal agreement I'd had with Porto, how it had been broken, and the problems with our bonuses and salaries. When curiosity turned to firm interest from Barcelona's side, I told them I would walk out on Porto to be their manager. This time, I felt I had the moral justification to resign, and would take the case to UEFA if Porto continued to stand in my way. After turning them down twice – once during my Ipswich years, and then with England when I was preparing the team to play Scotland – I was in no mood to miss out this time.

Long after my health had recovered, I paid a visit to Huw

Bryan Robson's troublesome shoulder is about to 'go' against Morocco in the 1986 World Cup.

Glenn Hoddle displaying his usual skill and athleticism in our game against Portugal in Monterrey.

Gary Lineker's hat-trick against Poland brought our campaign to life.

The hand of a rascal. I can't forgive Diego Maradona for punching the ball past Peter Shilton.

My departure as England manager was ugly. Disgraceful behaviour by the media marred my final press conference.

Paul Gascoigne was the new star of the 1990 World Cup. The hyper-active Gazza was never far from my side.

David Platt's brilliant winning goal against Belgium.

Gary Lineker steers us past Cameroon with the first of two penalties. A semi-final against Germany awaits.

'Don't worry, I'll take care of Lothar Matthaus for you.' Gazza delivers on his pre-match promise.

High noon – the Germans win an epic penalty shoot-out and we're going home.
Physio Norman Medhurst offers support.

Post mortem – Jim Rosenthal asks the questions, Gary Lineker looks serene.

My tour of Europe begins – PSV Eindhoven was the first stop in my happy exile.

Frank Arnesen was my assistant at PSV. Frank went on to the become director of football at Spurs.

The Brazilian Romario was a match-winner for PSV but a law unto himself when it came to training and curfews.

Luis Figo stands behind me on the pitch at Sporting Lisbon and an ambitious young coach is to my right. Jose Mourinho was my trusted lieutenant in Portugal and Spain.

Stan Valckx was one of the toughest men I've known in football. Here he is contesting a ball with Joao Pinto, as Sporting Lisbon take on Benfica.

Left: Porto were my second employers in Portugal. Behind me is the president, Jorge Nuno Pinto da Costa.

Above: Jose Mourinho was a great ally and a brilliant student. He could talk the language of the players.

Below: Celebrating after Porto win the Portuguese League Championship in Sporting Lisbon's Alvalade stadium.

Davies, who persuaded me to take part in a cancer awareness programme in Ipswich, with great success. Huw confided, 'I'll tell you something now, Bobby, now that you've survived, now that five years have passed. Dan Archer and I thought you might live about a year and a half after the operation. We thought the cancer might come back.'

Without my wife's love and concern for me, I would be dead. I can so vividly recall her insisting that I see the doctor and then the specialist, and my own irritation at her throwing obstacles in my path back to Porto. If I hadn't come home that weekend, if I hadn't given in to my wife's demands, I would have flown back to Porto and carried on pushing a Vick's inhaler stick up my nose. I had an angel watching over me. Her name was Elsie.

13

THE HOUSE OF FUN

FROM where I'm standing, the two biggest football clubs in the world are both to be found in Spain – Real Madrid and Barcelona. Manchester United comes third. One summer's day in July 1996 I walked into the cauldron of the Nou Camp with a chance to manage Catalonia's team, in a great city that has everything you could ever want in a metropolis. I was in heaven.

Barcelona had history and culture, the coast, the weather, all wrapped round a wonderful football club that was the spiritual headquarters of a nation. From my visits with Ipswich, and on scouting missions, I had smelt the intoxicating air of Barcelona Football Club. Barça are more than a mere sporting institution. They are the nation. They represent the Catalan tribe in their long conflict with Spain. That's the first thing you need to understand. The city of Barcelona is not like Cardiff is to Wales. It's much bigger than that. It's the cultural army of Catalonia, and when they cross the 'border' into Spain to play football, they regard it as a battle, a foreign adventure, especially when the destination is Madrid, the capital of Castile and the fortress of royal Spain.

To a young, inexperienced coach, striding into that vast amphitheatre would be terrifying, but by this stage I had been a club and international coach at the highest levels for two decades, and had plenty of honours to protect me against the kind of creeping insecurity that might have afflicted a manager with a less rounded CV. Although I couldn't speak much Spanish, Jose was alongside me to build verbal bridges. To walk into a dressing room where none of the players speak your language is quite daunting, but anxiety was a distant second to excitement on my list of emotions.

On this high peak of management, I would be working with Ronaldo, Stoichkov, Pizzi, Guardiola, Blanc, Popescu, De La Pena and Giovanni. Just for a moment, when you walk into these places, it's like a wild west saloon when the gunslinger comes through the doors. Can he command the respect of the room? Again, my record smoothed the way. They knew I'd been England manager for eight years. They knew I'd won two league titles at PSV and two more with Porto in the previous six years. Equally, they knew I could handle great players. I was an England international myself. It all helped.

So the welcome was warm. I learned how to say 'I'm very happy to be here' in Spanish. That phrase was in my head as I first explained that I didn't speak the language very well. Again, Jose supplied the words. I introduced him to the players and explained that he would be my conduit. 'Proud' is another word I emphasised. I was proud to be their manager. Hard work is the basis of any successful football club, I told them. Together, we would do great things.

Johan Cruyff was the ghost in the machine. He haunted my early days. My predecessor was one of the world's greatest players and a hero to many Barcelona fans, even though his success as a manager had run dry. For many in the city, he embodied the artistic spirit of the club. In my opening address, I made reference to Johan, and said I hoped they would give me the commitment they had shown to him.

My biggest asset was my coaching record. My work on the training ground would fully establish my credibility with the players. That would be my passport to success, and so to work. Most mornings, I would go through my training programme on a flip-board – twenty minutes of this, fifteen minutes of that. 'Todos comprehendos?' I would ask, and off we'd go, but I couldn't do anything to alter the fact that Barcelona were a deeply divided club. A pro-Cruyff faction sniped at an anti-Cruyff clique. The president, Josep Luis Nunez, was fighting to hold on to his power. It was a highly political environment and I wasn't a political animal.

Cruyff had been there for eight years, in various capacities, but had won nothing for two seasons. A strong personality, who liked to impose his will, Johan was being tipped by some to run for president one day. My sense was that the people who ran the club felt they ought to get him out before he became too powerful and turned himself into a political opponent. The lack of a major trophy for two seasons gave them an excuse to bring him down.

I knew nothing of this background when I first arrived. I was just excited to be managing Barcelona. I didn't look for hidden agendas. The city, however, was divided, too. Some supporters thought Johan should have been sacrosanct. In truth, I walked into a city where half the spectators didn't want me.

Unfortunately, the media split along the same lines. Every day I faced fifty accredited journalists, all watching training, except on Fridays, all desperate for a story. One faction was willing to give me a chance, the other was against me from the start. This gave rise to some cracking comedies in the local press. Take, for example, the time in January 1997 when we were lambasted by some papers after beating Rayo Vallecano 6–0. Not only that, we had been 5–0 up by half-time. 'Barcelona win 6–0 but play no football' was one headline. It was surreal. I couldn't believe my eyes.

Like most Barcelona coaches, I also received the white hankie treatment at times. In Spanish football, the flicking of white hankies is a withering expression of displeasure. The worst example was a game against Atletico Madrid. We were 3–0 down but won 5–4 in the most incredible match I've been involved in. I thought it was snowing inside the stadium.

If they do it at the team, or you, it's unpleasant but not terminal, but if the fans swivel in their seats and wave their hankies at the president, that's it, anno domini. That's when you're dead. The president doesn't mind the coach getting the white hankie treatment but if it happens to him, he'll have you out, because then it's you or him. Under the electoral system at Spanish clubs, the president needs the votes of club members to stay in his job, which gives the fans amazing power.

Atletico were despised by our supporters almost as much as Real Madrid – hence the anger when we fell 3–0 behind against the smaller of the two clubs from the Spanish capital. I found out later that the directors had held a meeting at half-time and decided, 'If the score stays like this, Bobby will have to go.' Crazy. The volatility of the club was mind-blowing. Hysteria would sweep round the ground at the smallest invitation. I've always found it bewildering that when the public's mood shifts a certain way, only the coach has to go. The players stay, the coach goes. I've always thought that sad.

Nothing beat a Barcelona-Real Madrid 'derby' for intensity, hostility and passion. That was the most fervent environment I've encountered in more than fifty years in the game. It gets to the players. There's malice in the match as well. You can feel the adrenaline and see the spite in the eyes of the players. I was quite aware of the importance of these clashes. These were games you dare not lose. In my year as manager, we played them four times. In the League, we lost at the Bernabeu but beat them in Barcelona. In the Spanish Cup, we drew in Madrid and then beat them at home. So I came out on top, which helped, believe me.

These are magnificent football matches, played at blinding pace. You can't slow them down. They're like high-tempo tennis matches – one long rally, with a high fitness level and exemplary technique. What an experience! Spain is hardly a docile country, and in football the two giants arouse immense hostility at the smaller clubs. I recall us having to be shepherded out of Real Zaragoza after coming back from 3–1 down to win 5–4. Ronaldo turned the match and then the public turned on us. After being pelted with projectiles as we left the pitch, we were confined to the dressing room for more than an hour. With a mob of hundreds waiting for us outside, we escaped through the back and sped away through the side streets, avoiding the hail of bricks that would have peppered our windows had we dared to leave through the front.

As an added complication, in my early days I had Johan's son, Jordi, on the books. Johan would be up in the stands each week, watching his son, who, at that time, was a first-team player. Inevitably, Jordi would go home and tell his dad what I had said in the dressing room, what type of coach I was, how we trained, what sort of person I was. It didn't take long to work out that this was an intolerable situation for all of us. However nice Jordi was, he was cast in the role of dressing-room mole. I was advised by the board to let him go and I agreed. He was very much in love with Barcelona and had no desire to leave, but Joan Gaspart rang Martin Edwards, the Manchester United chairman, and arranged a move for him to Old Trafford. We felt we'd looked after Jordi by selling him to an almost equally big club. It would have been unfair to move him down the food chain.

The playing squad were not immune from the politics of the club and, again, the media played a large role in poking the beehive. On the night we came from 3–0 down to beat Atletico Madrid, some newspapers claimed the players had put things right at half-time – hence, they alleged, the improved perform-ance in the second half. This really got my goat. Did Gica Popescu and Laurent Blanc substitute themselves in the interval? Did my captain voluntarily walk off the pitch? The truth is that I withdrew two defensive players and sent on two attackers. That night I had to tell the captains of France and Romania that they wouldn't be going out for the second half. To his great credit, Josep Guardiola issued a statement the next day dispelling the myth of the half-time rebellion.

I liked 'Pepe', as we called him. He was a great player. He knew the game and knew how to conduct himself. Some footballers wouldn't stand up for anything. They can't see beyond themselves. You'd have no chance of engaging them in any kind of sensible debate, but Pepe had class. He had bearing. He always had a contribution to make at half-time – 'Their number seven's getting the ball too much,' that sort of thing. I also liked Popescu, whom I'd managed at PSV. Stoichkov was a real character. He and Jose got on famously. Although he had a reputation for being difficult, he was straight and respectful – the very opposite of what I'd expected. He was the one guy I had picked out as a potential troublemaker but he turned out to be a top professional, who accepted, with good grace, being left out of the side or being used in a cameo role as a substitute.

When players moaned about not being in the team, I would call a meeting and tell them, 'Look, we've all got great jobs and good salaries, but we're in this together. If you're not in the team, it's because I've made a choice between twenty excellent players. If you're not picked, you have to say nothing, because to object via the media is disrespectful to the players who have been picked. When it turns round and you're in the team instead of the guy sitting next to you, he will then feel a duty to keep his mouth shut, because that's what you did when he was picked ahead of you. Respect has to flow both ways. That's how we're going to be at this club.'

One of my legacies from the year I was in charge of the first team was to bring Ronaldo to the great Catalan circus. It took me four weeks to buy Brazil's best young striker.

'Bobby, we need a top striker, someone to excite the supporters, someone to score goals. Do you know anybody?' Nunez asked one day.

'Yes, I do. There's a boy in England I like very much. He's called Alan Shearer. He'll get goals wherever he is. Put him in a decent side, provide good service, which Guardiola and Stoichkov can do, and he'll score goals off the top of his head. He'll get thirty a season, guaranteed – and he's got good character, too.' To reassure themselves, the club sent Joan Gaspart over to Wembley to watch Shearer play Spain in the European Championship.

Incidentally, another recommendation, when I was still England coach, was Terry Venables, whose name was unfamiliar to Joan Gaspart back in 1986. 'He's a young, thinking, English coach,' I told them. Not long afterwards, Terry was in charge of the club.

With my president's backing and money to spend, I called the late Ray Harford, by then the manager at Blackburn Rovers.

'Ray, I just have to tell you, we'd like to buy Alan Shearer,' I said.

'Not a chance. Not for sale,' Ray replied. 'The chairman won't sell him at any price.'

'We've got big money to spend,' I went on.

'Bobby, he's not for sale, and I don't want you to disturb him, so I don't want to see anything in the papers. If he knows you're interested, I'll know you've gone round the back door and I don't expect that from you.'

When I reported this back to the president, he asked if there was anyone else. I told him about Ronaldo, a boy with incredible potential. He was only twenty and had a better dribbling technique than Shearer, but not the strong, mature personality that Alan had.

'How much do you think?' asked Nunez.

'Well, I know the club, and I think they'll take ten million dollars.'

PSV had a history of selling to big clubs. In the meantime, I should point out, Blackburn sold Alan Shearer to Newcastle for £15 million not long after telling me he wasn't for sale. Never mind. Our bid for Ronaldo went in and was rejected.

'What do we do now?' asked Nunez.

'Offer them eleven,' I said, which elicited the same response, and then the same question.

'Offer twelve,' I said. That was rejected too.

At one point, Nunez wagged his finger at me and warned, 'Bobby, you know your job depends on this?' At that stage, I hadn't taken charge of a single game, yet here I was being threatened with the sack. Up and up we went, to $18 million.

'Right, that's enough,' declared Nunez.

'I agree, and we'll make them sweat because I know PSV want the money,' I told him. 'I also know they'll be panicking. They'll be worried that they've been a bit too clever. They'll come back,' but they didn't. Five or six days went by. Despite the publicity, no other clubs had joined the race, which I found odd, and I began to question my own judgement. 'Do I see something in him that nobody else sees,' I thought, 'or is there something wrong with him that everybody else can see but I can't?'

Most of our conversations were conducted through Jose because Nunez spoke no English, and my grasp of Spanish was nowhere near strong enough to conduct such complex business discussions in a foreign language. I had an idea.

'Do you mind if I ring the PSV president?' I asked. Nunez gave his permission and I dialled Harry Van Raay's number.

'Harry, you keep turning us down on Ronaldo, so can I ask what is the figure in your mind? I'm not saying the president is going to pay, but we'd like to know what this magic figure is.'

'Well,' replied Harry, 'we may take twenty.'

'Does that mean "may" or "will"?' I asked. He thought for a while and said, 'Yes, we'd take twenty.'

I went back to Nunez.

'Twenty million dollars? You said ten!' he kept saying. Over and over, he kept repeating those three words, 'You said ten!'

'Yeah, but I don't control this,' I told him, trying to get myself off the hook.

The bottom line was that Ronaldo was twenty years old, sublimely talented and Brazilian, which made him ideal for the Barcelona culture. It was a gamble, but a good one. I urged Nunez to pay. Had Ronaldo been a flop, I'm sure it would have cost me my job. In triumph, we tied him into an eight-year contract. Eight months later, he was sold to Inter Milan for $38 million. Why? Agents. Ronaldo was so good for us that at the end of his first and only season in a Barça shirt his three agents flooded in wanting to renegotiate his contract. In the Spanish legal tradition, he had a release clause specifying that if another club came in and offered a certain price he could go. Three months into his time with us, I asked Joan Gaspart, 'This kid's amazing. Is the club protected?'

When his agents pounced, Ronaldo just carried on playing football, and left the exhausting palaver of his contract talks to his three representatives. A new deal was hammered out, but when the three agents asked the club for a fee for their part in the negotiations, Nunez flipped, tore up the replacement contract and sold Ronaldo to Inter Milan.

This sad story notwithstanding, I reflect with pride on my role in his emergence as a player of world repute. Quite simply, he was a phenomenon, even though we lost him in April to the Copa America, where he was representing Brazil in South America's mini-World Cup. We played a Spanish Cup final without him and Giovanni, another major signing for us that year. At least we had Ronaldo in our ranks for the European Cup Winners' Cup final, in which he scored the winner from a penalty.

He was a great boy, a real enthusiast, full of respect for me, the manager, and the senior players. 'Buenas dias, Mister,' he would say to me as he breezed into the training ground, where he had an excellent attitude to his work. 'Una mas, Mister,' he would say when I tried to call a halt to his shooting practice. Then I would have to roll another ball to him, and another. He used to wear me out. When he stripped, he looked like a boxer. He had wonderful biceps and shoulders with terrific definition. He was so strong and so quick.

Unlike Romario, who would poach high up the pitch, Ronaldo could collect the ball on the halfway line, turn and take off. Whatever was ahead of him, he would clear a path. I watched him go thirty, thirty-five, forty yards, taking people on, fizzing in the way Wayne Rooney does now. Jermain Defoe also does it, a little further up the field. Ronaldo could start from that halfway line and the whole stadium would ignite, a current would course round the stands.

I remember him scoring a goal against Valencia after dropping deep to escape the attentions of two rugged centre-halves. He gathered the ball and ran at these two monsters, who both went for him. In their minds the ball was an irrelevance. Their only objective was to knock him over, but Ronaldo stayed on his feet, evaded the first one, skinned the second and struck the ball past the goalkeeper. Our whole bench erupted.

'Look at that, Jose. Just look,' I exclaimed. What a goal! What an incredible goal!

I was really sad to see him go. He was so popular with the other players and the fans. I used to say to him, 'Ronaldo, don't ever leave this place.' He had the whole of Catalonia in his pocket, the whole nation. The girls adored him. Every day there would be 250 people outside the training ground just to see him leave. The girls would run in front of his car and blow kisses. I once made the mistake of following him out of the training ground and it took me half an hour to get through the gates. I used to say to Jose, 'Make sure we don't try to leave this training ground at the same time as Ronaldo.'

We kept him on the rails. At that point in his life he wasn't inclined to adopt the playboy life, although he did buy an island on one trip home to Brazil. The press broke the news to me.

'Really?' I said. 'I went out shopping yesterday as well. I bought a silk tie.' Everybody laughed.

On the whole, it was all football with Ronaldo in those eight months. That was the best season he's had in his whole career. He was scintillating on the pitch, and injury-free.

While covetous looks were being aimed his way, I was also being sized-up on the jobs market. In January of 1997, six months into the season, a delegation headed to Barcelona with a tempting offer. The team was Freddie Fletcher, Freddy Shepherd, Douglas Hall and his father, Sir John Hall, who came up from Marbella – an impressive cast. We convened in my house in Sitges. 'Kevin Keegan's leaving, we want you to come home to manage Newcastle,' they chorused.

Terrible anguish took hold of me. This was Newcastle United – not even Arsenal or Manchester United could have engaged my heart in such a way – but the truth was that I was happy, the team were doing well and we had a great life in Sitges, one street back from the promenade. I discussed Newcastle's offer with Nunez, and explained to him how enticing it was for me to be offered the manager's job at the club I had worshipped as a boy.

'Impossible,' he said. 'Nobody leaves Barcelona. We sack people, but people don't sack us.'

With those words they made my decision for me. However strong the pull of Newcastle and the North East, I had waited eighteen years for my chance to manage Barcelona and I wanted to see it through. Of course, I had no way of knowing that Louis Van Gaal was being lined up to replace me in the summer.

According to my terms of employment, the club had the right to move me from head coach to director of football after one season. Barcelona had one other hold over me. Also in my contract was a clause that said I would have to give the club twice what they were paying me in wages if I chose to leave. In my excitement, during the Newcastle talks, I'd forgotten that clause was there.

Elsie had a great saying: 'Everybody should either see the sea or see a mountain or walk in the woods every day of their lives.' It's a lovely saying. I saw the blue Mediterranean sea every day of my life. I used to drive along the promenade, making a conscious effort to look at the ocean on my right, and then hit the motorway to Barcelona, which was thirty minutes away. In the two years we were in Sitges, we had seventy-two house guests – seventy-two. My sons came, their friends came, my surgeon, Huw Davies, came with his wife Helen and their kids.

Although the rumours started circulating in February, I found out for sure that Louis Van Gaal was taking my job right at the end of the campaign.

The president and his men were quite unaware that Jose had picked up Catalan, and I instructed my assistant not to tell them, so he could eavesdrop on their conversations.

As the end of the campaign approached, they kept saying to me, 'You're doing a great job – there's nothing to worry about, we'll honour your contract,' which of course they did, but the crux was they'd signed Louis on a pre-contract and had to honour it, which was bad news for me.

Louis Van Gaal had announced that he was leaving Ajax to pursue other interests. He had such an impressive CV that Barcelona had approached him and offered him a delayed contract, which cut into my two-year deal. They didn't want him going to Bayern Munich or Lazio, so they struck the arrangement in advance. Louis must have asked them, 'What about Bobby Robson?' and I can only assume they told him, 'Don't worry about that. You will come in after the first year of Bobby's two-season contract.' Johan Cruyff hadn't won a sausage for two years and I suppose that from that lowly start they assumed I wouldn't do well. It would be easy to remove me after one campaign.

In fact, I won the Spanish Cup, the European Cup Winners' Cup and the Super Cup, and I finished second in the League, two points behind Real Madrid, who played fourteen fewer games than we did because they weren't so heavily involved in Europe. I had a phenomenal year. I embarrassed the president and his men. They didn't know what to do. The supporters had swung my way, as well. Eventually, Joan Gaspart said to me rather sheepishly, 'What can we do? We've got Louis Van Gaal coming in here as first-team coach.'

'I'll tell you what you can do,' I said. 'Get rid of him. I'm on a two-year contract. I want the job.' Imagine saying that to Joan Gaspart! But as the legal complexity of the club's predicament became apparent I decided to be a gentleman. We convened a meeting at which Louis announced, 'If it's going to be a huge problem, let Bobby have his final year and I'll sit on the fringe doing other jobs, scouting, looking after the youth teams and so on.' I could see that he was making the offer reluctantly, with a touch of bitterness. The president rejected his proposal and I could see which way the wind was blowing.

'Look, Louis,' I said, 'you're going to be the future, so you have the job and I'll walk away. Let's shake hands and do it nicely. I'll scout for you. You tell me which players you want watched and I'll go and see them. I won't undermine you, I'll get out of your way. I won't even come to the club.' I ought to say that Louis was totally respectful towards me.

So I went scouting for a year, had a sabbatical. My official title was Director of Signings. I went to the Africa Nations Cup. I'd never done that before. The club paid for first-class hotels and first-class flights and paid my salary as well. I was the world's best-rewarded scout. I never once appeared on the training ground. I tried to be honourable with Louis. I loved the life I had that year. I would sit at home in Sitges for three or four days, deciding where to go next, and then jump on another plane. I went to France, Italy, Holland and Germany, though not to England much. I went to Brazil and Argentina, and to Egypt to see the FIFA World Youth Championship. A driver would pick me up from my beautiful hotel and take me to Port Said and Alexandria. Money seemed to be no object. I sat by the pool in the afternoons, walked, shopped, read lots of books and mixed with a lot of football people. In Argentina, Louis called one day.

'I want you to do something on my behalf. Will you go to Rio de Janeiro for me?' he said.

'Only if it's for three months,' I laughed.

I found myself at the Rio derby with 100,000 other people, watching a left-back.

I was diligent in my work, filing dozens of reports, which my Spanish secretary typed up for me. I was disappointed to be sidelined but not bitchy, and I still felt part of the club and the decision-making process. In the August of Louis's first year, he informed me he was going to buy Steve McManaman from Liverpool.

'Are you sure?' I asked. 'He's not the one for me.'

'Why?' said Louis.

'Two reasons. One, his final ball's not good enough, and two, he might score three goals for you in a season.'

I offered to watch McManaman play against Coventry in Liverpool's first match of the season. I asked George Burley at Ipswich to give Charlie Woods a day off to come with me. Charlie picked me up at the airport and drove us both to Merseyside. I watched McManaman play and still thought, 'Not for me.' I called Louis to give him my report.

'Listen,' I said, 'do yourself a favour and go and sign Rivaldo from Deportivo La Coruna. He's a Brazilian with a left foot who can go wide. He'll get you seventeen goals – ten from free-kicks alone. He'll bend it over the wall. He's the one you want.'

I was quite proud of that. After Ronaldo, I'd recommended Rivaldo – the two best Brazilians of their era. When I ran into Rivaldo later, I teased him, 'Hey, muchas gracias para mi.' He gave them two or three sensational years. In the meantime, I attracted a lot of sympathy from the people of Barcelona, where I'd be greeted with cries of 'Bobby, Bobby!'

The Belgrade derby had been another of my stops, and this one was to delay my homecoming still further. At the Partizan-Red Star match, which is Yugoslavia's answer to Boca Juniors versus River Plate, or Manchester United–Liverpool, I ran into Frank Arnesen.

'You're just the guy I was hoping to see,' he said. 'I was going to come looking for you next week, and here you are in Belgrade. Will you come to PSV for one season?'

'Frank, I'm going home,' I said wearily.

'Can't you break your journey for one year?' he responded.

Eric Gerets was to be the future of the club but he didn't have his Dutch coaching qualifications. Frank wanted me to look after the team while Eric acquired his certificates. Financially, the offer was extremely generous and reflected the fairly thankless nature of the task. I asked for a couple of days to think about it before saying yes. My accommodation was to be Ronaldo's old apartment in the heart of the city.

That summer, PSV sold Stam to Manchester United, Cocu and Zenden to Barcelona, Jonk to Sheffield Wednesday and Numan to Rangers. All five were serving Dutch internationals.

'Frank, if you'd told me you were going to sell five international players I wouldn't have come,' I complained.

'Yes, but we have plenty of other players,' he said. One was Ruud van Nistelrooy, with whom I was able to work for a year before his eventual move to Manchester United. We finished third and qualified for the Champions League on the last day of the season, which was a miracle.

At an airport in Holland, during my Newcastle years, I ran into Martin Ferguson, Sir Alex's brother, who does some scouting for Manchester United. I knew where he'd been.

'Tell your brother to buy him,' I said. 'I worked with him for a year and the boy will be great. Loves training, great character, and I think he'll do very well in English football. Tell your brother – buy him.'

Strikers – boy, I've seen some good ones. Think of Shearer at his best, Romario at his best, Ronaldo at his best, van Nistelrooy, Gary Lineker, Paul Mariner at Ipswich – just don't ask me to pick my all-time number one.

— 14 —
GOING HOME

WHEN the call came, a passer-by might have mistaken me for a contented pensioner, smashing golf balls as far as his ageing body would allow on a driving range in Suffolk, but in the late summer of 1999 the rituals of retirement were still not for me. I wasn't a senior citizen with time on his hands, enjoying the solitude of the practice ground. I wasn't ready to leave the game I adore.

In my bag, a ring-tone broke my train of thought. Elsie was calling to say that Newcastle wanted to speak to me urgently – in London, today. Things were moving at last. The North East was calling me back. I was on my way home.

At the end of nine years of toil in Europe, rounded off with a one-year stint back at PSV Eindhoven, I was back in England, weighing my options. I had many happy memories to comfort me but no clear plan for what some people think of as the bus-pass years. Retirement was one option but neither my body nor mind were telling me to head for the golf course and the garden centre full-time. The more active the working life, I suppose, the harder it is to give up. All I really knew was that I was back in England at the end of a great foreign adventure. The only downside of our expedition was that we had missed our children desperately. That problem was solved but now something else was missing – work, the thrill of the game, time on the grass.

When the 1999–2000 season opened for business I was out of

a job for the first time since my disastrous experience at Fulham, and for only the second time in forty-nine years. It hurt me not to be involved on the opening day of the season. That magical moment when the cycle starts afresh had passed me by. I missed it. By the end of August that sense of loss was starting to gnaw at me, so I set off for Portman Road to watch George Burley's Ipswich win 6–1 against Barnsley. I was an old friend of the club and knew all the directors. I just needed to watch a game.

Naturally, I was aware that Newcastle had made a rocky start to their Premiership campaign – three defeats against Aston Villa, Spurs and Southampton, followed by a 3–3 home draw with Wimbledon. They then lost 2–1 at home to Sunderland on a wild and windy night, with Alan Shearer, famously, on the bench. The newspapers referred to Ruud Gullit's teamsheet as 'a suicide note.' In those days, in a North-Eastern derby, it was regarded as managerial vandalism to leave Alan Shearer out of the side. Amid the wreckage of a home defeat to Sunderland, Ruud faced the whirlwind of his decision to challenge Alan's status as a Geordie hero.

By now the club were joint-bottom of the Premiership and facing a daunting trip to Old Trafford to meet Manchester United, who had started their season with four wins and a draw. The outrage surrounding Shearer's demotion to the bench provided a bonanza of headlines in Fleet Street, as we used to call it. I think Ruud began to scan the room for the exit and eventually resigned. So the job of managing my beloved Newcastle United Football Club was suddenly vacant. A romantic thought floated across my mind, 'Mm, I like the look of that,' not really believing that I would ever go back to the North East. I'd been away for fifty years. It seemed fanciful to believe that the circle of my life would complete itself with a homecoming at the club I had watched through dazzled eyes as a young boy from Langley Park.

As Ruud cleared his desk and Steve Clarke took temporary charge of the team, I did not pick up the phone or tout myself for the job in any way, but ultimately my name was linked to the position. The pundits were joining the dots – 'Bobby Robson's just come home after nine years spent abroad, he's not working, he's a Geordie lad. There's the solution.' The earliest speculation all stemmed from the press. Hand on heart, I didn't speak to a soul to give the Newcastle directors the impression I was waiting for my phone to ring. Whenever the media asked me to declare my hand, I simply said, 'Look, I'm home now. If they're interested in me, all I can say is I'd be interested in speaking to them.'

Several days went by and the list of names linked with the post seemed to grow. It wasn't just Bobby Robson's job any more. Candidates were popping up in all directions. By the time ten days had passed since the Sunderland defeat, I took the absence of a call from the club to be a silent rejection – too old, maybe. I was sixty-six. I thought the moment had passed. There were no noises, no smoke signals in the trade. I was inching my way towards the point of acceptance we all reach when it's plain that a job we covet has been set aside for somebody else.

Cut to that golf range near Ipswich, where I was practising my swing, quite alone, and Elsie's voice saying, 'Freddie Fletcher's been on the phone. They're coming down to London to see you, today.'

'Today? What, right now?' I exclaimed. Freddie was the chief executive at St James' Park and was to become a good friend. 'Well, I'd better get myself home, then.'

I threw my bags in the boot and drove home to change. Elsie handed me the address of a house in London where we were to meet, cloak and dagger style. By then, excitement was starting to take a hold. Despite the lengthening list of candidates appearing in the press, I knew there were actually very few suitable and available contenders. Freddie's willingness to come to London with such haste told me I was in with a shout.

When I strode through the door of the house, which had been chosen to ensure maximum confidentiality, I saw Douglas Hall, the deputy chairman and biggest shareholder, Freddie Fletcher, Freddy Shepherd, the chairman, and the club solicitor. It was reminiscent of January 1997 when they had come all the way to Barcelona to see me. On the way to London I had called my investments and financial adviser, John Hazel, who sped down on a train from Colchester to lend professional guidance and moral support. We met at Liverpool Street station and talked business on the way to the house.

The initial meeting didn't go well. In fact, it was a fiasco. Here's why. Newcastle offered me a really poor salary. In fact, the offer they made me was so low that I felt obliged to say to them, 'I'm afraid I'm not going to be interested in this job.' I knew Newcastle had become a major reconstruction project and I knew what the position was worth. I also had some idea of what the club were paying some of their star players. They were way off target with the manager's salary. I said all this with some trepidation because I desperately wanted the job. All I wanted was for them to make me an offer that reflected my own experience as well as the scale of the task in hand.

They knew it was a paltry opening pitch. Their assumption must have been that I was financially secure after all those years of continental football and so wouldn't haggle over the terms. They thought they could get me cheap. They offered me £400,000 a year, at a time when Alan Shearer, I believed, was on around £3 million.

So there I was, caught on the horns of a dilemma. The club were sinking, the club were sick, the club required rejuvenation, and they were offering a paltry reward to their potential saviour. It might not seem a trifling amount to you, dear reader, but in the context of Premiership management positions, it was miles below the going rate. It was also way below what I had been earning at PSV and Barcelona. In those circumstances, a football manager, or a player, is motivated not by greed but a sense of fair play, of his market value relative to his experience and expertise.

Later, I found out what the players were on. Marcelino, who was signed by Ruud but barely played, was on £1 million a year. I was being offered less than half of what Marcelino was getting for sitting on a bench. I was offering them my experience, my knowledge and every pulse of my energy to save the club.

'Give it to somebody else,' I told them, as I left the room. 'If you're paying that sort of money, you won't get knowledge and experience, and you'll go down to Division One.'

After my grand tour of the Continent, I came home feeling I was a better coach and a better person than I'd ever been. I had more to offer than at any time in my forty-three years in football management. I was more mature and knew more of the top players than ever before. You never know everything, of course, but boy, was I well equipped. It was stalemate, however. They went away, I went away, and after some to-ing and fro-ing I finally agreed to go to St James' for a basic salary of £500,000. I also negotiated a half million pound bonus to be paid if we stayed up. So I actually became manager of Newcastle United with a chance of earning £1 million, but I'd had to fight them hard to get to seven figures.

We started out together on a twelve-month deal, which might seem rather half-hearted or token on their part but, in truth, I wasn't concerned about the length of contract. I felt I could pull Newcastle back from the edge of darkness and win over the directors. I knew I could prove my worth. This has been one of the themes of my career, the belief that I would always repay a new employer with success. Proving myself became a reflex. I would drop the results right in front of the directors and say, 'There you go, told you I could do it.'

Strangely, I had never worked in the Premiership, which replaced the old First Division in 1992, yet the urge to compete in the new English League had been eating away at me all the time I was on the Continent. I watched the new élite League develop from my vantage point in Europe, and I liked what I saw. It looked exciting, full of passion and vigour.

At that point in my life, I didn't want a long-term appointment.

'Look, I'll work my socks off for Newcastle for two or three years, we'll get re-established in the North East, and we'll see how it goes,' I told Elsie. 'I'll be happy to pull out after two or three seasons if it doesn't work out. Let's see if I can save Newcastle from relegation.' So I signed in that frame of mind. The length of contract was irrelevant.

I had always been a Newcastle supporter. It was my club. My dad, my brother Ron and I were first in the queue at the ground for home games. When, as Newcastle manager, I looked across the banks of faces at St James' Park, I saw my dad. Every fan out there was my dad. All the time I'd been abroad – throughout all my time in football, in fact – there was one result I looked for. 'How have Newcastle got on?' I would ask at teatime on every Saturday of my life.

In our meeting, the board did admit that they had no war chest to hand over for team rebuilding. There had been money once, they said, but it was all gone now, spent by Kenny Dalglish and Ruud Gullit, the two previous managers. I recall very clearly Freddy Shepherd saying, 'You've got a difficult job keeping us up, and I don't think you can do it. I think we're going down.' He kept saying, 'I don't think you can do it.' I don't think he was trying to goad or challenge me. He honestly believed the team was in freefall and could not be saved from calamity. When I met the technical staff, they all voiced the same opinion. They thought the club was heading not just out of the Premiership but through the bottom of the First Division as well. They thought Newcastle would plummet.

In 1998 and '99 they had reached two consecutive FA Cup finals but played extremely poorly in both. I was aware of the magnitude, the power of the club. It's the grandest of the three major North-Eastern clubs, with the biggest catchment area, and the most populous, vibrant city. The team were playing to full houses. The higher you go, the more it costs, so the extra 15,000 seats on top of the original base of 37,000 cost the club something in the order of £44 million.

There was no shortage of ambition at St James' Park, which rises like a great ocean liner from the centre of the old city. Money was tight and results were bad but the potential was undiminished. St James' is a wonderfully tribal place. The Toon Army are magnificent. Those who couldn't get tickets for home games would support the team on the road instead. They were very vocal and marvellous to play for. It was one of the top six clubs in the country, yet here we were, wallowing at the bottom of the table and heading out of the Premiership on current form.

For such a big and passionately supported club, Newcastle have endured some terribly lean times. In 1978, when I won the FA Cup with Ipswich, they were relegated with 22 points. I remember that so clearly. There I was with gates of 22,000 and no money, relying on a youth system, winning the FA Cup, while Newcastle United were crashing out of the top division. It made no sense.

A huge media circus arrived for my unveiling, which, I believe, I handled well. After England and Barcelona, I felt I could cope with these mass cross-examinations. I even challenged a reporter to a race. The tone of this chap's questions had been: 'You're sixty-six. Don't you think you're beyond it, physically?' I fixed him with a stare.

'No, I don't think so. In fact, if you fancy a hundred yard dash, I'll take you on,' I said. The offer wasn't accepted.

In the Premiership table we had a single, solitary point. It was not the best launching pad I'd ever put my bag on. I didn't know the players especially well – Marcelino, Goma, Dumas, Pistone, Maric, Charvet, Ketsbaia, young Robinson, Des Hamilton, Serrant, Robinson, Dyer, Ferguson. I didn't know what they were like either as players or as men. I felt least familiar with the ones Ruud had brought in. I needed to get on to the training ground and take a proper look.

September 1999 was the first time I met Alan Shearer, this icon of the city, and talked to him face to face. I was abroad all the while he was having his major successes with England, principally at Euro '96. At Barcelona, I had tried to buy him when he was at the peak of his success with Blackburn Rovers, in the summer of 1996. I knew his reputation and I had seen him perform plenty of times, both live and on TV, but I didn't know him as a person. I studied him closely in our first game, at Chelsea, which we lost through a disputed penalty (we should have had one ourselves, by the way), and came to a swift conclusion.

Alan had lost his movement. He had become a static player, standing with his back to goal. Imagine a penalty area. Alan was running across the face of the box – fifteen yards in one direction and fifteen yards in the other. He was making lateral runs, waiting for the ball to come to his feet. He'd lost the spins and turns and the old dynamism. I could see it straight away. A great striker faces the goalkeeper he's attacking, not his own. He faces the opposing keeper. In some games, Alan would be facing our own Shay Given 75 per cent of the time.

Ruud had been extremely wary of Alan because Alan was a major political figure, powerful within the club – more influential than Ruud himself, some felt – but in addition, Ruud sincerely believed that Alan was finished as a Premiership striker. He thought he had lost his mobility and he had. What I set out to do was restore it. At twenty-nine, Alan was young enough to recover his old lethal prowess, his old range of skills and get his dynamism back. He'd lost his game and it was simply a question of finding it again.

Alan's hold up play was brilliant. His first and second touches were excellent. He never surrendered possession of the ball and could lay it off perfectly. When the play went wide, he could steam into the box and get on the end of crosses. He was fantastically brave in the air, a great header of the ball and a good climber. Alan wouldn't know how to be afraid. It's not in his physical vocabulary. What he'd lost was his movement without the ball. He wasn't making runs down the gulleys between defenders.

I didn't treat him differently from any player I inherited. I realised very quickly that he was an exceptional guy with good character, nice to be with and good on the training ground every day. Punctuality, professionalism, attitude in the changing room, team meetings, on the bus, in restaurants – Alan scored ticks in all these boxes. You name it, he was top. I've never met a better guy. He was a fighter and brave, and would empty his physical locker for you, however hard the game. He and Gary Speed were fantastic role models. What I had to do, though, was to get Alan facing the right way again and attacking the spaces in behind defenders.

'Alan, you're not running. You're static,' I told him.

Did he resent having his faults pointed out to him? No, he didn't. He thought my relationship with him changed in my last year at Newcastle. It didn't but he thought it had. It's not accurate to say that I lost faith in his ability to keep contributing to his old standards at the highest level. From the outset, I liked him enormously. I could talk to him. He was the captain and talisman. Like me, he was pleased to have come home to the North

East. He turned down Manchester United to come to Newcastle, so I believe. In English football at that time, no greater declaration of allegiance to a home-town club could be made than saying no to Alex Ferguson.

After the initial assessments had been made, the next step was to bring in my own staff. I hired Mick Wadsworth as my assistant and Charlie Woods as chief scout. Charlie found the diamonds and I did the polishing. He was a seriously good scout. He spotted Craig Bellamy and Darren Ambrose and JJ – Jermaine Jenas. One problem in football now is that agents, not scouts, are doing all the persuading with chairmen and chief executives. When I criticise agents for the money they're taking out of the game, I know I'm clean. Backhanders have been offered to me and my reply is always the same – 'I don't want it. If I take that money, I'm cheating my club.' Charlie Woods was once offered money by an agent and came straight to me. I told him, 'Let's report this to the chairman.' Charlie had been told by a middleman, 'There's half a million pounds for you and Bobby in this deal – divide it however you like.'

In 1999, Newcastle didn't have a chief scout and they didn't have a proper network of talent spotters. Can you believe that? I made all my staff scouts as well because under the existing system the technical staff weren't going out to look at potential acquisitions. I sent mine out on Tuesday and Wednesday nights to watch games and file reports.

In my time as England manager, the FA had seven regional coaches who oversaw all the coaching courses. Mick was the FA's regional coach for the north-west. With England, I was also director of coaching. Along with Charles Hughes, I was responsible for the coaching centres and the centres of excellence, so I had a joint role. I started Lilleshall with Charles Hughes, and the summer coaching courses there. Dave Sexton was the first resident director. The idea was that the best young players would attend a national academy. Terry Venables, Glenn Hoddle, Kevin Keegan and Sven-Goran Eriksson were not expected to get involved in that line of work. I worked to a blueprint, to produce excellence. That's how I spotted Mick.

At Newcastle, we didn't have our own training ground. Instead, we had access to a facility at the Riverside near Chester-le-Street. It was council ground and people used to walk their dogs there. Before that we had rented a training ground that was student orientated, and had to share dressing rooms and training areas. At the Riverside, when I arrived, I had no office and we had fifty players using one pitch. The ground was heavy in the winter, which was fine if you wanted to run to build up stamina but as a football surface it was awful. The reserves were forced to train on ground that was disgraceful, and I mean disgraceful. Training facilities had been one of the club's blind spots. Nobody complained. I believe Kenny objected a bit towards the end of his time but nothing was done.

I left the chairman in no doubt. 'Look, the club has got no chance when we're training in these conditions. We're never going to develop young players. We're never going to improve their skills. In the winter we can't do any worthwhile practice. You've just got to find new training facilities.' I hammered the point home time and again.

Two years later, in my third season, we escaped these abject conditions. The club found an area of government land at Little Benton, signed a 120 year lease and got cracking. We levelled and re-seeded it and laid new pitches. The two squash courts were converted into a multi-purpose gym for power and speed training and we also had an indoor pitch, which is vital in the North East. In winter, at the Riverside, we would often struggle to keep the ball on the pitch because it was being kicked into the wind the whole time. Sometimes you'd have solid frost for two days and would be unable to do a thing.

I remember one day in January or February, when we went to play Charlton, trying to prepare the players on a pitch that was as hard as nails. I couldn't let Alan Shearer or Gary Speed – or anyone else for that matter – train on that kind of surface. All I had was the synthetic running track that ran round the edge of the pitch. So I set up little five-a-side goals on the track and played games of six versus six. We were a big Premiership side, going to Charlton Athletic, practising on a running track.

To get a licence to set up a Premiership academy, which was granted by the FA Premier League, we needed to fulfil certain criteria relating to coaching, training and facilities, and we were a long way off meeting those. So Newcastle United, which existed in the middle of a hotbed of young talent, had no academy to attract the region's finest players. It was awful. We had access to thousands of schoolboys but nowhere to bring them – hopeless.

Before we could address these vital structural reforms, though, my Newcastle career kicked off with that visit to Chelsea. Although we lost 1–0, I told my players after the game, 'If you give me that every week, we'll get out of trouble. We'll get up this League.' They had played with plenty of spirit against good opponents. I watched Shearer, Speed, Dabizas, Dyer, Solano, Lee and Barton and felt I had some decent ammunition with which to go into battle.

At Stamford Bridge that day I received a tremendous ovation from both sets of fans. It was the first time I had worked at an English football ground for about ten years. Out on the pitch, by the dug-out, I had been chatting away when I suddenly registered an announcement over the PA. 'Back on English soil . . .' the voice was saying, and then I became aware of an eruption of applause.

'This is for you,' someone said.

'Oh, bloody hell, right, right . . .' I said, and responded with waves to this amazing ovation.

With one game under my belt, I headed back to Europe for a UEFA Cup tie at CSKA Sofia, which we won 2–0. It was useful to go abroad with the players at that point because on European trips you spend more time with them, so this gave me a chance to get to know a few of them a little better. Our victory, in a difficult environment, raised morale ahead of our extraordinary encounter with Sheffield Wednesday, at home, on 19 September.

Let me start by saying that Newcastle scored their biggest win since Len Shackleton hit six on his debut in a 13–0 win over Newport back in 1946. I saw that game – it seems incredible, but I did. I was there with my father. I would have been thirteen years of age. Now here I was presiding over an 8–0 win, in which Alan Shearer, the Jackie Milburn or Hughie Gallacher of his generation, scored five.

It was an amazing day. Just about everything went right. The young centre-half, Aaron Hughes, played his first match for me that afternoon and took just eleven minutes to open the scoring. In Ruud's old squad we had plenty of defenders – Marcelino, Dumas, Charvet, Goma – but a few injuries in that department. That week, I had been offered Colin Hendry, who was an immensely experienced defender, and been tempted to bring him in. I recall going to see Hughes, who was only a kid at the time. John Carver and Steve Clarke had told me he was a shy boy of nineteen or twenty who wouldn't impose his authority on the pitch as perhaps he should, but who was a very astute reader of the game.

'Listen,' I told young Aaron, 'we've got a choice. I've got a centre-half problem on Saturday. I can gamble, throw you in, see how we go, or I've got a chance of bringing in Colin Hendry. How do you feel about it?'

'Well, I'd like to play,' he said.

'I'm sure you would, son. How's your confidence? How do

you feel? It's a home match and the team's not doing very well. Can you handle that pressure?'

Sheffield Wednesday were down with us at the foot of the table. Their strikers, Gilles De Bilde, who had been with me at PSV, and Gerald Sibon, weren't bad. In the end I told young Hughes, 'I'm going to play you on Saturday. At Ipswich, I developed the club by giving young players a chance. I've seen you a couple of times on the training ground and I like what I see. You've just got to be tougher, a bit more alert. Go out there with stacks of confidence and play with your courage.'

Aaron played extremely well and headed a goal from a cross by Kieron Dyer – the first goal of his career. I was sending a message to the club – I would invest in youth, I would build for the future. Shearer had not scored in open play for ten games, but that day he landed five. I felt for poor Danny Wilson, the Sheffield Wednesday manager, as he watched his goalkeeper, Kevin Pressman, disappear under an avalanche of our goals.

In truth, the scoreline was somewhat misleading. With Temuri Ketsbaia and Duncan Ferguson in and out of the side through injury, I felt we needed more firepower up front. Aside from those two and Alan Shearer, we had Paul Robinson, whom Ruud had brought into the side against Sunderland at Alan's expense. With the greatest respect, Paul fell short of authentic Premiership standard. He was a long way below Shearer.

'Look, I need a striker, I must have one,' I told the chairman. The two Freddies could see I was doing a good job and appreciated the fact that I hadn't complained about the shortage of transfer money.

'Pick a striker and come back to us,' they said.

Mick Wadsworth and I put our heads together and came up with Kevin Gallacher, a player I had always liked. He was frail but fast, and Shearer needed a 'quickie' alongside him. Freddie looked into it and learned that we could prise Gallacher from Blackburn Rovers for about £500,000. Kevin was an honest, busy player, had a good character and trained properly. He would complement Shearer by racing beyond defenders. While one centre-half was trying to nail Gallacher, Alan would be left with a one-on-one with the other and so improve his goalscoring prospects. For that reason, not least, Kevin was ideal for our needs, and they had already played together when Alan was at Blackburn.

In those early weeks, I tried hard to acquaint myself with the local media. The regional press are exceptionally powerful on Tyneside. They weren't quite the squawking menagerie of Barcelona, but the Newcastle papers, TV and radio stations were nevertheless a hotbed of news, comment and gossip. I felt I was developing a good rapport with local reporters but I could not always rely on their support.

A regular visitor to the chairman's office was Alan Oliver, the chief football writer at the local *Chronicle*, and he was often in the privileged position of being able to run transfer stories about players I had mentioned to the chairman when the information was known to no one else outside the club. Unfortunately, towards the end of my five years at the helm, the *Chronicle* did not help me much.

However, I was consumed by the job of moving us up the table. In my thirty-two Premiership games that season, we won fourteen, drew nine and lost nine, rising from joint-bottom to eleventh place when hostilities ceased with a 4–2 home win over Arsenal in May. There were some notable highlights, apart from the annihilation of Sheffield Wednesday, especially a 3–0 home victory over Manchester United on 12 February when Shearer and Duncan Ferguson were really hitting it off.

Duncan, for all his qualities, was habitually injured. When I arrived he was one of thirteen injured players. With the team in trouble, I felt that one or two of them were taking liberties. So one of the first things I did was to tell the senior physiotherapist, Derek Wright, 'I want to see every single injured player, with you, in my office,' such as it was. I fired the questions. What was the injury? When did it occur? How long have you been out? What's your treatment? Are you coming back in to the training ground in the afternoon? How many sessions are you having a day? I made sure every question had been asked of each player, and then demanded of Derek, 'Look, you have to make it less easy for them to get home in the afternoons. If they've got kids to pick up at four o'clock, they can't do it if they need treatment.' As a manager, sometimes you need to be cruel to be kind. You have to get players off their backs and on to the field of play. If they're playing and contributing, they can go home in the afternoons. They have that incentive. Faced with an unacceptably long injury list, it was no good being Mr Nice Guy. It was time to be ruthless.

When Duncan and Shearer got going, the two of them were awesome. Duncan scored a terrific goal in that 3–0 win over Manchester United. I liked him. He called a spade a spade. He was a smashing lad. He didn't play a lot of football that season, but when he and Shearer linked up in sixteen consecutive games they struck thirteen goals between them. Duncan had a tremendous range of attributes. He had a good first touch, a strong left foot and was untouchable when the ball was at head height. He would batter you in the air.

Generally, the squad need shaking up. I ran my eye all the way down the squad list and knew I wouldn't care if some of the names were erased from the roster. So in mid-February I placed thirteen players on the transfer list. We needed to bring in decent money for the ones we sold but some of the less committed members of our outfit were hard to shift. The message, though, was clear. Troublemakers and whingers would not be tolerated.

We shut them up. We told them, 'We don't want any layabouts around the place. This is Newcastle United.'

I worked away with my one-season deal and gradually imposed my authority on the team. Really, there was no Newcastle 'board' to talk to or consult with. The chairman would often say to me, 'I'll put it to the board,' and I would reply, 'Chairman, there is no board. There's you and there's Douglas Hall.' Freddie Fletcher left at the end of that year, a victim of the Save Our Seat Campaign which occurred when Newcastle asked bond-holders to either give up their seats and move elsewhere in the stadium, or pay £1,350 a year to remain in their existing seats. There was a huge outcry, and the club won a high court case but scored a PR own goal. Freddie and I are good friends. To this day he keeps an eye on me.

The club could see I was expending plenty of energy. In the evenings I would go scouting for new players and I was on the training pitch every day. I was never 'upstairs' dealing with letters, faxes and paperwork. The training pitch was my spiritual home, coaching was my vocation. My uniform was a tracksuit. Performances were improving and so were results. We were gradually climbing the League. Eventually, in February, the club offered me a twelve-month rolling contract, which I signed on 18 February, otherwise known as my sixty-seventh birthday.

A useful boost to our self-esteem that season was our good FA Cup run, which ended with a semi-final defeat by Chelsea at Wembley. Gustavo Poyet shot us down with a goal in each half. The upside was that we had acquitted ourselves well. Unlike in 1998 and '99 when we had lost miserably, this time we were the better side.

Although Freddy Shepherd and Douglas Hall had appointed me, I saw very little of Douglas in that first season, or, indeed, throughout my five years in charge of Newcastle. He was something of a recluse as far as the staff were concerned. He would come to the club sometimes and I wouldn't even know he was there. He didn't once ask to see me in five years. At the same time, I knew how immensely powerful he was within the club. He called many of the shots. It would not surprise me if, in the summer of 2004 when Newcastle threw me aside, he encouraged Freddy Shepherd to give me the sack.

15

YOUR COUNTRY
NEEDS YOU – AGAIN!

GOING home to the North East to manage Newcastle was sufficiently special for a man of sixty-six, but the following autumn, in October 2000, I almost made another dramatic return – to the England tracksuit I had taken off in Italy after the 1990 World Cup. My country, apparently, needed me, and I was eager to answer the call.

The story begins at Wembley with rain and a resignation. Dear old Wembley, braced for the wrecking ball that was meant to flatten it within days of England confronting Germany in a World Cup qualifier. In the doomed stands, I watched Kevin Keegan's team lose a dismal match to a freakish free-kick by Dietmar Hamann, the Germany and Liverpool midfielder. I love international football and I hate missing England matches. Like the rest of the crowd that day, I trudged home from Wembley digesting the news of Kevin's sudden resignation. Taunted by England supporters, as I and other England managers had been, Kevin had announced to the players in the dressing room that he was quitting with immediate effect.

I thought no more about it, not in a personal sense, at any rate. Howard Wilkinson assumed temporary command for the trip to Helsinki the following Wednesday for a qualifying match with Finland, which we drew 0–0. England had one point from a possible six at the start of their mission to qualify for Japan and South Korea in 2002. The question of who would guide them through the next stage of a troubled campaign did not intrude on my work at Newcastle until the chairman called me in after we had played Everton at home on 21 October.

'I'll be straight with you. The Football Association have been on to me requesting your services but you're not going,' he announced. 'We've just brought you back here, we're pleased with you, you're doing a great job and we're looking for continuity and stability. We've told them "Forget about him". You can't do it part-time. This is a big club and you haven't got the energy to do both jobs. There's a lot of work to be done here. You're under contract and we're not letting you go.'

'Fine,' I said. 'If that's how you feel about it, I accept what you say. Mind you, I'd like to do it, and I can do it for a while.'

'You're not doing it.' His final word was emphatic – end of conversation.

The FA deserve praise for the way they went about making their approach. On the Wednesday prior to my conversation with Freddy Shepherd, I had been at Manchester United to see them play PSV in the Champions League, and had bumped into Adam Crozier, the FA chief executive, and David Davies, his executive director. As we chatted away, neither mentioned that an approach had been made to Newcastle, which, of course, was the right way for them to conduct their business. Adam and David were dead straight. I spoke to one person and one person only about the England job and that was my chairman.

Later, when I ran into Crozier again, at a function, he said, 'You remember when we met at Manchester United? We had approached your club before that night. I didn't dare mention it to you, even though the request had already gone in. If the chairman had given us permission to talk to you, we would have made a formal approach, but I didn't want to do any improper tapping-up.' That's how straight Adam Crozier was when England were in need.

From my heart, I can say that I was profoundly disappointed

not to be able to go to my country's assistance. I still possessed reserves of energy and by now the club was in the ascendant. There was a long way still to travel but I was quite sure we would be safe from the jaws of relegation at the end of that season. I had every reason to believe that we would import new talent again in the summer of 2001 and build and build towards success. Let me reaffirm, so there is no doubt, that football clubs are not resuscitated overnight – unless, that is, you have access to Chelsea's inexhaustible wealth, in which case you can stroll around the market saying, 'I'll have him, and yes, I think I'll have him as well while I'm at it . . .'

While the club was stable and making progress, I felt I could have handled the England job, the intricacies of which I knew so well from my eight years in the post. By the time I left the FA in 1990 I knew the role inside out, and I was familiar with every single player in the country from senior to Under-17 level. For me, it held none of the terrors that seemed to send so many candidates rushing to their keyboards that autumn to issue statements distancing themselves from the job. In troubled times, and with our participation in Japan in some doubt, the FA evidently wanted a pair of safe hands.

In my disappointment, I at least had plenty to console me. I was engrossed in Newcastle United and getting on better and better with my players. I was out on that training ground every day. Elsie and I were repatriated in the North East. Our roots had been re-established quite nicely and life was good, so I didn't sulk. I felt I owed a debt to Newcastle for bringing me into the Premiership, and I had the team placed in a challenging position just outside the top four.

By way of a digression, I felt we had the makings of a decent national side, despite all the pessimism and the turmoil. In fact, there has never been even a two-year period in England when we have failed to produce good players of one sort or another. In

Kevin's last game, we were simply out-thought by Germany, who played three in central midfield to our two. Hamann's hastily taken free-kick had us in a pickle – not concentrating – and before we knew it David Seaman was scooping the ball out of the net. These weren't terminal flaws. They could be rectified. There were good players in our side that day: Seaman, Adams, Beckham, Owen and Scholes among them.

After the 'no' from Freddy Shepherd, the FA trawled the inter-national market for Kevin's long-term replacement. To find him, they went to Sweden, via Rome, to hire the country's first foreign coach, a contentious move that had much of England debating the rights and wrongs of going overseas for help. As an ex-England manager, I was asked for my opinion and I placed myself in the large camp of football people who felt there had been no need to look beyond these shores. Nationalism had nothing to do with it. I just felt it was a wrong move. No offence is intended to Sven-Goran Eriksson. We are a big football nation with more professional clubs than any league in the world. With our strong foundations, we simply didn't need to leap on a flight to Rome to find Kevin's replacement.

Sven, whom I knew and liked, had not been a national coach in any country, so there was no validity in the suggestion that he was being hired for his experience. I felt that plenty of English coaches could have done a perfectly good job. Sven didn't know the English players he was about to take charge of, although he was intimately acquainted with our style of play. Overall, though, his results have been creditable.

When the new man was unveiled and the country demanded meat to put on his biographical bones, a light was shone on our encounter at Ipswich, when Sven was an aspiring student of the game back home in Sweden. In those days, he wrote to me for advice and I invited him over to see how we did things at Portman Road. He studied our practice routines and wrote them all down on charts on a flip-board. I didn't mind him cribbing my methods. He was a nice guy. I even invited him on to the bench for one of our games. He spoke decent English and could chat away quite merrily.

Ipswich won the UEFA Cup in 1981 and the following year the club Sven was managing – IFK Gothenburg – took over from us as champions. They took the trophy from us in person, by special delivery. David Rose, the Ipswich secretary, and I took it to the final so that it could be presented to the winners. We carried it in a box on to the plane, stored it in the overhead luggage compartment and then carted it to the match, where we passed it on to the UEFA delegates. So I've handed a few things over to Sven in my time.

It did amuse me that, nine days after Freddy Shepherd refused me permission to take the job, Sven marched into the FA on £3 million a year, while I was on £500,000 at Newcastle. Needless to say, the chairman never said, 'Oh, by the way, Bobby, we'll adjust your salary to compensate you for having to say no to the FA.' There isn't a major footballer in England today who wouldn't have used that situation to enhance his earnings. Say Barcelona had come in for Alan Shearer and we had told them to go away. I'm quite sure Alan's agent would have demanded a meeting with Freddy Shepherd to ask for a pay rise to compensate him for the money he had surrendered by staying put. That principle would not have applied to me, as manager. I wasn't that type of guy, either. If I had taken the England job and steadied the ship in qualifying, I have no doubt they would have offered me the position full-time.

At St James' Park, meanwhile, I was continuing my purge of unwanted players, and doing good business, too. Sometimes, players who are surplus to requirements have to be pretty much given away. To earn some money for them is quite a feat. During my career I've always been conscious of the need to bring money in while writing cheques in the opposite direction. At Newcastle, I was never told exactly how much we were receiving for discarded players because the chairman was so hands-on. He kept those details to himself. I had to keep asking him to glean any information at all.

'How much did you get? Did you get three million? Did you?'

'Yeah, I got three,' he would reply. Conversely, each time a player was moved in or out of the club there would usually be a full discussion between manager and chairman. If the chairman wanted to shift a player for financial reasons alone, he would always seek my approval.

In the summer of 2000, I understood we took £4 million from Everton for Duncan Ferguson, plus another £3 million for the Italian left-back Alessandro Pistone. Duncan had cost us £8 million to buy but I wasn't unhappy about the size of that shortfall because we could never be sure Duncan was going to play a sufficient number of games. With him leaving, Shearer celebrating his thirtieth birthday, Ketsbaia not being the player we wanted, Robinson not being quite up to scratch and Kevin Gallacher being a short-term acquisition, we needed a top-notch striker to enhance our armoury.

That brings us to Carl Cort, a 6ft 4in twenty-two-year-old who had come through the ranks at Wimbledon and played for England at Under-21 level. I saw Carl Cort play several times and warmed to him, as did Charlie Woods, my chief scout. Carl was good in the air, with a good spin and a strong shot, better on the deck than he was upstairs. Alongside Shearer, I thought he would traumatise Premiership centre-halves. I watched him towards the end of the 1999–2000 season in Wimbledon's 3–0 defeat at Bradford City – a freak result, in the sense that every single Wimbledon player was superior to his Bradford counterpart.

Tottenham were pursuing Carl quite hotly and I was told they had made a bid of £11 million for him and Ben Thatcher, the Wimbledon left-back. We didn't want Thatcher and persuaded Wimbledon to sell us Cort on his own for £7 million. He was young, athletic, and I thought he was going to become a great Newcastle player. He and Shearer started brilliantly. He had pace and a good turn. He looked the ticket. On his home debut – a 3–2 win over Derby County – he drew a good response from the crowd and scored after five minutes, and Shearer rated him.

We weren't to know it but we were merely witnessing a brief flourish at the start of a dispiriting year. The problems began in late September when we travelled to Leyton Orient for a Worthington Cup match, in which Carl pulled a hamstring. From that day on, his time at Newcastle was a catalogue of disasters, the poor lad. He went from one injury to another and we could never get him right. These weren't phantom ailments. They were genuine physical setbacks. The medical department and I kept saying over and over again that Carl was cursed.

The hamstring injury required an operation and it went wrong. Carl developed an infection and ended up with a green and yellow open wound that would not heal. That cost him four months on the sidelines. His Achilles heel went next. My God, it was frustrating. Carl Cort fell apart in front of our eyes. His spirits began to flag and at times that boy was desperately low.

Finally, we had him sound and playing in a practice match when Marcelino, of all people, loomed from behind him and rocked him with a tackle. Carl was long-legged, slightly Bambi-esque, and in the impact of that challenge his knee went. Yes, he tore the ligaments in his knee. The dark irony of this latest mishap was that Marcelino was having terrible injury problems of his own. So one recuperating player crocked another. Carl was a lovely boy but it all just went horribly wrong for him. After the Marcelino incident, the chairman went crackers. His arms went up and the frustration poured from his mouth in characteristically lurid terms.

When we finally conceded defeat over Carl Cort's medical chart, we took £2 million for him from Wolverhampton Wanderers. Dave Jones, the Wolves manager, was often on the phone, enquiring about Carl, and in the end we decided we couldn't keep nursing him through his injuries. We had to yield some return on our investment. Everyone at the club loved Carl, the other players and the medical staff especially. I felt so sorry for him and looked after him as best I could. It's spirit-crushing for a professional footballer to come in to training every day but not be able to play. When I asked Dave Jones about him, some months later, he said, 'We like him, he's doing very well and we have no regrets,' so there was some semblance of a happy ending to his time on Tyneside.

Carl's age and potential fitted my preference for age and promise. In all my years in management I hardly ever bought old players. I've always believed in looking forward. My squads have always been equipped with young legs and an edge of freshness, hunger and vitality, but you need the balance. You need mature players, some Steady Eddies. At Newcastle, they were Shearer, Speed, Solano and, before them, Robert Lee and Warren Barton. My intention was to buy British wherever possible because I had lost a bit of faith in the idea that the answer to all our problems could be found overseas.

I have no reservations about Henry, van Nistelrooy, Vieira, Zola – the list goes on and on. Those players have enhanced our game and our culture. They've been brilliant. Before the great bonanza of the Premiership, we never had players such as that in our country. When I bought Muhren and Thijssen to Ipswich, and when Ossie Ardilles went to Spurs, they were exotic additions to our footballing stock. In those days, you couldn't find players with their attributes in Britain. What we've been guilty of in recent years is buying ordinary players from abroad, who haven't been better than the equivalent English players in the same position. So all we've done is knock the English player out of a contract, out of an opportunity. Money comes into it because often it was cheaper to buy overseas than in the domestic market. We do over-price our own players sometimes. Broadly, English football ought to be importing special foreigners, not ordinary ones.

That 2000–01 season – my second in charge – was disfigured by injuries. We ended up finishing eleventh once more, despite being fourth in mid-October and sixth on 20 January. A run of five defeats in seven matches between 31 January and 14 April undermined our assault on the top six places. We had four big injury losses – Shearer missed most of the second half of the season, Dabizas went out with a cruciate ligament injury, Cort played just three of the first twenty-eight games and Dyer missed the last eleven Premiership matches.

With the reconstruction project well under way, it was apparent that we had some big personalities around the place. Kieron Dyer, who had been bought from Ipswich for £6 million, was undoubtedly one. Before Ruud pounced, my contacts at Portman Road had told me about this quick little kid they had coming through. They said he could run all day. When I inherited him, I formed a high opinion. He was a bundle of energy and had terrific physical condition for someone so light. He could skip over the ground. He wasn't a great passer – or not a long passer, anyway. He would run twenty-five yards and pass it five. Robert Lee, in contrast, would run five yards and pass it twenty-five. That was the difference. Kieron wasn't sure of his ability to make pinpoint passes, so instead he would run the distance and then give the ball, but he seldom gave it away.

He could wriggle between the two central defenders and work himself into some excellent positions but he wasn't a natural finisher. That was something we always worked on. In training, he would dispatch the ball brilliantly and look very accomplished in and around the penalty area. In matches, he just wouldn't pull the trigger. He would end up side-footing it or dispatching weak shots.

He wasn't a great tackler, marker or header of the ball. His talent lay in running the ball from midfield to all points of the pitch. His left foot wasn't as strong as his right, but he was an astute short passer and he could run tirelessly. I wouldn't like to play against him, as a defender, because he would make my life hell.

Defence was one of my main concerns that season. There was plenty of traffic in that department. Over the course of the whole season we sold Howey and Charvet, and Alain Goma to Fulham for a reported £4 million, and acquired Andy O'Brien from Bradford City for £2 million.

In the meantime, Sven had taken over from Peter Taylor, England's second caretaker manager, and conjured wins over Finland, Albania and Greece to put us within striking distance of Germany, who were six points clear at the top of World Cup qualifying Group 9. How I would have loved to travel to Munich in September, as part-time England boss, plotting revenge for Italia '90.

16

JEKYLL AND HYDE

CRAIG BELLAMY, who many think of as the *enfant terrible* of the Premier League, is a strange boy, a great player wrapped round an unusual and volatile character. He can be delightful one minute, then walk on to the pitch and begin snarling at the referee, but I consider the decision to buy him from Coventry in July of 2001 to be one of my most successful forays into the Premier League's transfer market.

As a creative and dynamic force, Bellamy had always excited me. I tried to buy him the year before we were finally successful in bringing him to St James' Park. I had been to see him play for Norwich, and I think the chairman had been told, by people to whom he listens, what a good player he was, so he was not slow to support my attempt to poach him away from Norfolk. One of the people Freddy Shepherd looked to for advice was Paul Stretford, the agent, whose judgement he always seemed to respect.

My first move for Bellamy came around the time we received an offer from Everton for Duncan Ferguson, in the summer of 2000. On that same day, Bellamy was going across to Coventry to sign. I left several messages for him that day to say, 'Don't sign for Coventry just yet. Give me twenty-four hours.' My thinking was that if Duncan Ferguson was out of the club by then, we would have the money to spend on Craig, but Craig's answer was that it needed to be sorted out that day. I begged for twenty-four hours but he wouldn't give it and the deal was signed.

However, there was a twist. That morning, Duncan had come into my office in a highly agitated state, brandishing the local paper.

'What's all this? Ferguson for Everton? I don't want to leave Newcastle. I like it here. I'm buying a house. I love playing with Shearer. I don't want to go. I'm happy here. We've got a good team. How dare this journalist say I want to go to Everton?' On and on he went.

'Are you saying you don't want to go to Everton, Duncan?' I asked calmly.

'That's exactly what I'm saying.'

'Right, well, I'll ring the chairman and tell him you want to put your shirt on Newcastle and don't want to go to Everton.'

'Exactly. Exactly right,' Duncan affirmed.

I gave the chairman the full run-down on the scene in my office and said the story in the local paper hadn't come from Duncan because he knew nothing about it.

'Duncan wants me to ring up Alan Oliver from the *Newcastle Chronicle* and accuse him of giving false information to the public,' I concluded.

That night – the day I tried to sign Craig Bellamy – I was at home when the phone rang, about 10 p.m. It was the chairman.

'You won't believe this,' he said.

'What won't I believe?'

'Right at this moment, Duncan Ferguson is on his way to Everton Football Club to sign for them.' I couldn't take it in.

'Chairman,' I started, 'you heard me tell you what Duncan said to me – about the Everton story being rubbish. Are you saying that in eight hours the whole scenario has changed?' Apparently, it had.

The next morning I phoned Craig Bellamy as fast as my fingers would allow but it was too late. So I lost Ferguson and I lost Bellamy, all in one day. It was typical of Duncan to change his mind so dramatically.

Meanwhile, Bellamy moved to Coventry but at the end of the season they were relegated and then couldn't afford the £6 million transfer fee or the wages he was being paid in the Premiership. Twelve months on from the day they snatched him from me, they put him up for sale.

'What do you think?' asked the chairman.

'Buy him,' I said.

'But he's had a bad year,' said Freddy.

'I know,' I said. 'It's because he's been playing outside-left. He can't play there. He needs to play through the middle, off a main striker. He's got pace. He wants the ball behind defenders. No one would catch him. He needs to improve on his finishing but I think we can achieve that. We'll have him practising on Tuesday, Wednesday and Thursday, and he'll score because he'll get in positions that not many Premiership strikers can.

'On top of that,' I continued, 'he's got the will,' and he has. He's got this fire, this spirit. He knows where goals are scored – in behind defenders – so he was constantly trying to manoeuvre the ball into those positions. I considered him to be superior to Michael Owen. He could run, check, turn, receive the ball to his feet and beat an opponent when he was running at them one on one. He had a feint and double feint, and could slide a team-mate in. He loves to score but if he can't he'll pass. I like that about him. He's a very, very good player despite his persistent knee problems, his volatility and his foul language. A cruciate knee ligament injury and tendonitis were the biggest entries on his medical chart.

If Craig Bellamy wasn't such a gifted footballer, you would turn your back on him, because he's a nightmare of a boy. You'll have a fight with him every day in training. Graeme Souness,

The Nou Camp was a cauldron when Real Madrid came to town. It was Catalonia against Spain. This was a game I had to win.

Ronaldo was a joy to work with on the training pitch – I could even keep up with him for a yard or two!

Chatting to the King of Spain soon after my appointment as Barcelona manager.

I lost my job to Louis Van Gaal after one season, despite winning the European Cup Winners' Cup, the Spanish Cup and finishing second in the League.

Ronaldo, a lethal striker and a loveable guy, scored the goal that gave me my second European trophy as a manager.

PSV sidetracked me for a second stint in charge, just when I thought I was coming home from Europe for good.

The dream job – fifty-three years after I first watched Newcastle, I'm the team's new manager, in the dug-out as we take on Chelsea at Stamford Bridge.

Newcastle v. Arsenal, May 2000. Arsene Wenger and I exchange thoughts on life in the Premiership.

Craig Bellamy brought pace and ingenuity to our attack, as well as trouble off the pitch. Here he makes his debut in August 2001, against Sunderland.

Sir Alex Ferguson and I share a laugh. We're old-school football men in a game that can become too serious.

Renewing an old acquaintance with Manchester United's Ruud Van Nistelrooy, whom I managed at PSV.

Jermaine Jenas, a real star of the future, shares my birthday. I'd swap my number for his. Freddy Shepherd is standing behind.

Jonathan Woodgate (*left*) never gave me a moment's trouble. I think he'd learned his lesson. Here we're consulting physiologist Paul Winsper.

We gave Patrick Kluivert a chance to resurrect his career.

Alan Shearer, a Geordie legend, in action against PSV. Sometimes I had to force Alan to take a rest.

The club, supporters and council clubbed together to commission this statue of me at Portman Road, Ipswich.

Elsie and I savour my knighthood in the Queen's birthday honours list with sons Paul and Andrew in November 2002.

The Freedom of the City of Newcastle upon Tyne, awarded to me in March 2005. I called it 'the proudest moment of my life'.

Young members of the Robson clan. Alexander and Isabelle with parents Mark and Jane.

Andrew's daughters – my grandchildren – Olivia and Lucy.

Three generations of the Robson family celebrating Mark and Jane's wedding in 1987.

my successor, would back me up on that. Their relationship deteriorated so badly that Craig ended up being sent out on loan to Celtic, in January of 2005. In matches, often, it was all effing-this and effing-that from beginning to end. We talked to Craig about that a lot. We would say, 'You can't swear like this in training because if you do it here you'll carry it into matches on a Saturday afternoon, and if you do that you'll end up with a red or yellow card. You can't swear at referees. It's in the laws. You'll be sent off.'

He's a spiky little kid, very ambitious. He wants the best and he wants to win. Believe you me, there's no doubting his will to win. He's quite prepared to have a go at a team-mate at half-time. He has no fear of saying what he thinks. In fact, sometimes he says too much and comes out with opinions that are simply not correct, but it all stems from his ambitious nature. As long as he has the desire, and as long as he has that natural pace in his legs, he will always be a potent and valuable player.

With the first-team squad stable after two eleventh-place finishes, for 2001–02 I was able to start my big investment programme in youth and in pace and artistry. Signing Bellamy was a major catalyst in our rise to fourth place in the Premiership that season. He scored nine league goals for us, despite missing the last two months of the season, and provided the perfect foil for Shearer, who finished the campaign with twenty-three.

On the left-hand side of the team we'd had Stephen Glass, who possessed a good left foot but wasn't quite quick or strong enough to fill the position long-term. I looked high and low for a left-sided player who could dribble and get wide and who had pace. Like the England management, I suppose, I was scouring the leagues for an outside-left. The Premiership's best, Ryan Giggs, was un-buyable. Trevor Sinclair, who ended up at Manchester City, was not naturally a left-footed winger.

Eventually, I plumped for Laurent Robert, of Paris St-Germain, who was also excellent at free-kicks, corners and generally directing the ball into the box. Charlie saw him play and I saw him play. We realised that, defensively, he was suspect. He knew about going forward but he wasn't so smart about travelling backwards. The modern game is played both ways, but we felt we could develop him, coach him, talk him into being the player we wanted him to be. Such was our faith in our own ability to change him that we paid PSG something like £9 million to bring him over from France.

Now, let me tell you, I had Laurent Robert in my office more times than any player I have known in my whole career. I cornered him in the treatment room, the dressing room, my office and even the boardroom twice. Sometimes we even had his interpreter there for the sake of clarity. We used a flip-chart. I tried everything to make him understand his defensive responsibilities.

'Do you understand what I expect from you?' I would ask, fixing him with a stare.

'Yes, yes, yes,' would come the answer.

Then I would turn to the interpreter.

'Does he understand what I'm saying about where we move the ball, where to come, how to drop back, how to drop inside, how to slide . . . ?'

'Yeah, yeah.' The answers were always in the affirmative. My God, we spent some time on those conversations. If nothing else, they improved Laurent's grasp of English.

Whether he'll ever get the message, I really do not know but I can say for certain that in the 2003–04 season he scored eleven goals and made twenty-nine last passes prior to other players scoring, which equates to forty goals. When he's doing that, you can put up with some of the play falling back on top of you because Laurent's not doing his defensive job. That's just what he is – talented and exasperating, and a great deliverer of the ball. He would put it on the spot for Shearer, who returned to the first team after five months out, in a 1–1 draw with Sunderland in August, our first home game of the season. When we beat PSV 2–1, Laurent delivered two fantastic crosses, one for Shearer, one for Speed, both curling on to the head of the incoming player.

The player some people might mention in the same sentence is his fellow Frenchman, David Ginola. With Ginola, Kevin Keegan had faced many of the frustrations I now faced with Laurent. He thought the game was played in one half. Laurent just didn't like defending. His view of the game was that someone would defend on his behalf and then give him the ball to run at opponents. You simply can't operate that way in modern football.

When we had Jenas and Bellamy and Dyer and Robert, we were just terrific. Solano was another class act, with a good delivery rate. We had Nobby's terrific right foot for crosses and Laurent's artistry on the left. Then there was Gary Speed in the centre of midfield, as solid as ever, with his dextrous left foot. Gary and Alan Shearer are two of the most professional players I've met in my life. Give them a commendation for everything – preparation, attitude, professionalism, behaviour, setting examples, role models. You couldn't meet two better people.

Gary was a fitness fanatic. Before he went out to train he would go through his own personal stretching routine. Then he would stride out with everybody else and do the squad routine. He was hardly ever injured and was as brave as a lion. He never ducked out of a tackle and would never shirk a header, in either penalty area.

Problems with player behaviour tended to blow up when they were outside my jurisdiction. An example was Craig Bellamy going to Cardiff to report for duty with Wales and becoming involved in an incident with a nightclub bouncer. Newcastle got the blame for that one, even though Craig was on duty with

Wales. To suggest I failed to react to these transgressions is an insult. I bet I called more team meetings than any other Premier League manager. I was constantly banging on about behaviour and attitudes. 'No, you can't have this, and no, you can't do that,' I would tell them. No telephones in certain situations, no caps in restaurants, no ear-rings in training, punctuality – I was a stickler in all these areas. Imposing everyday discipline had been my life for thirty years. For the end of season walk-around, for example, I insisted that all players wore club suits, collars and ties.

One exception, I have to concede, occurred when we flew to Malaga in November 2001. A club dinner was scheduled in honour of Sir John Hall, who had a home there. Bellamy, Griffin, Cort and Dyer went out for the afternoon after training and failed to show up for the evening meal with Sir John. It was only when the function started that we realised we were four players light. Discreetly, we rang them and told them to get back to base sharpish, but the message I got back from the staff was, 'They're not returning.'

After the meal, I pulled the chairman aside and told him the story. We were in agreement, instantly, and I must say I thought the chairman was quite bold to support me so readily, given the fact that he and Douglas Hall had attracted their own adverse publicity over social activities in Spain. It must have occurred to him that if the chairman was seen to throw the book at his players, the media would revisit his own brush with the Sunday red-top tabloids, if only by way of a comparison. He could see the whole incident being thrown back in his face but that didn't stop him supporting me. He stood up for club discipline, for the manager, against the players.

We waited for the four to return, and pounced. 'There are your tickets,' we said. 'You're flying back to England. You're being sent home.' We knew it would hit the headlines, but we also knew we were right to go in hard, even though their absence at the dinner would not have been obvious to Sir John.

When the offenders eventually returned to the camp, I called them in, one by one. 'What do you think you were doing, embarrassing the club and the chairman like that? You've brought shame on us. Where is your sense of responsibility and courtesy?' Carl Cort and Andy Griffin were very apologetic. They paid their fines and assured us of their remorse.

The highlight of the first half of the 2001–02 season was a 4–3 win over Manchester United at our ground, after which Alex Ferguson made an encouraging observation. Alex declared that the Premiership's three-horse race had now expanded to four, with Newcastle joining the élite. On the touchline, I had a long and friendly conversation with Ruud van Nistelrooy, whom I had managed at PSV, but the game is probably best remembered for a less amicable meeting of minds. This was the match in which Roy Keane got himself sent off after throwing the ball at Shearer and then reacting violently when Alan apparently said something provocative in the aftermath. In his autobiography, Keane claimed Alan had insulted him but took full responsibility for his own behaviour. When confronted by Keane, Shearer stood his ground. That's hardly surprising. You can't push Alan Shearer around.

In December, we found ourselves top of the Premiership after an acrimonious 3–1 win at Arsenal, in which Ray Parlour and Craig Bellamy were both sent off. It was our first victory in the capital in twenty-nine attempts. I've got to know Arsene Wenger well since that night, but there was some rancour between us after the smoke of the game had cleared. After the final whistle, Thierry Henry descended on Graham Poll and hardly left him alone. He was complaining about anything and everything. I have the utmost respect for Thierry Henry, who's some player and, I'm told, a smashing boy, but on that occasion the defeat got under his skin and I didn't like the way he conducted himself as the teams walked off the pitch.

Arsene was pretty moody afterwards, and I just felt that they didn't take the defeat gracefully. Sometimes you have to, no matter how much it hurts. I expressed the opinion, publicly, that Arsene needed to learn how to lose. I learned that lesson myself from my chairman at Ipswich, John Cobbold, who used to say, 'Bobby, you have to love the game more than the prize. The game is more important than the prize because without the game, there is no prize anyway.' John had an attitude that was very rare, even then. he liked to win but he also thought you should be able to lose with dignity. He was right. Not only did he say it, he really believed it and he passed that philosophy down through the club. You can moan about the referee and you can whinge about the performances of the players, you can talk about mistakes or lucky goals, but if you've lost, you can't change the result. That night Arsenal expected to extend their lead and they couldn't cope with having missed that opportunity. What I said, in essence was, 'This is a great club they've got here, and what great clubs have to do is learn how to lose sometimes. They're bigger as a club if they know how to lose.'

December was a smashing month for us. In that same period we were 3–1 down at Leeds yet fought back to win 4–3. We led the Premiership at Christmas, which made us very proud.

We acquired Jermaine Jenas from Nottingham Forest in early February 2002 – paid £5 million for him, which was a record for an English teenager. Two years later, Manchester United smashed that little landmark to bits by paying £27 million for Wayne Rooney. Charlie had watched Jenas and had told me, 'You've got to go and see him. We should try to be first. Nottingham Forest know his value. He's going to cost you money but we should go for him.'

I went three times to see JJ play for Forest and liked him very much. He was nineteen and, coincidentally, shared my birthday – 18 February. By this time Robert Lee had departed and Speed was thirty-three. I needed to bolster the midfield with fresh young talent. Perhaps JJ wasn't quite ready for the first team, but after one appearance on the bench we decided to be bold and put him in the starting eleven. The team were good enough to help him through. So his first start was in the local derby at Sunderland, where we won 1–0 – not a bad way for a teenager to make his Newcastle debut. He never let us down. My word, JJ's going to be some player. He'll be an England regular, and he'll be in the side for ten years. In Jermaine Jenas, I brought to Newcastle a fantastic player with a good attitude, a nice type who'll make it to the very top.

He's a real box-to-box player, very fit and long-legged, and he gets stronger by the day. He's a comparable shape to Dyer, but longer. He's not as quick as Kieron, perhaps, but a stronger runner overall with a long stride. He needs to be a bit more selective in his passing and to spread the ball more. His passing was a bit short, a bit constrained, and I used to say to him, 'Don't be timid. You *can* hit it. Practise those fifty-yard passes. Watch Solano. He'll turn and crack it without even looking at the ball. Remember Bryan Robson. From left-half, Bryan would find the man on the opposite flank.' JJ's a marvellous player. We bought a diamond, a lovely boy who listened and learned.

If JJ had a quieter year the season after he won the PFA's Young Player of the Year award, you have to remember that he was still only twenty, playing in the Premiership, with all the physical demands that entails. Maybe he hadn't fully matured at that point, in terms of his power and strength. He has now, believe me.

Sven rang me several times to ask my opinion about JJ. My response was, 'Put him in the squad. He's not ready to start yet because he's not above Paul Scholes or Steven Gerrard, but keep him close to you. Let him learn from those two as well as Beckham and Butt. I want you to take him.' I suppose you could say I was telling him what to do but when I was an international manager, I needed club managers to speak to me the way I spoke to Sven. I needed their honest opinions. So to Sven, I said, 'Take him. He's good enough for you and he won't let you down. We'll reap the rewards and so will you.'

JJ is one the biggest reasons I was so sorry to lose the Newcastle job. I don't wish to sound egotistical, but I know what I achieved at that club. I bought good young players. When I left we had fifteen players round about twenty-two years of age. Bernard, Bellamy, Dyer, Jenas, Ambrose, Milner, O'Brien, Hughes, Ameobi – these names roll off my tongue even now. Graeme Souness walked into an Aladdin's Cave, and he knew that. He knew he didn't have a comparable treasure chest at Blackburn Rovers.

In 2001–02 we edged up towards the élite and blew some opponents away with our exuberant, pacy style. We beat Manchester United 4–3, Bolton 4–0, Aston Villa 3–0, Arsenal 3–1, Middlesbrough 3–0, Everton 6–2 and Charlton 3–0. Shearer, Bellamy, Robert and Solano were knocking them in. We amassed 71 points to finish fourth in the Premiership, just six points behind Manchester United, and had secured a Champions League qualifying spot less than three years after I had inherited a bottom-placed team. We were on our way to Europe with more money to invest – upwards, onwards.

17

THE GREAT POWERS

THE CHAMPIONS League is really an extension of international football. A manager leading his men to Juventus, Barcelona or Bayern Munich will not waste midnight oil searching for weaknesses in his opponent. He might as well chase a ghost. The path to success at this most exalted level is to build up the squad to the point where you will win six or seven of the ten outfield duels that make up a football match.

In Europe, the football feels better, smells better, stretches the mental faculties more. In the Premiership, most opponents start out with faults and fallibilities that will reveal themselves over the ninety minutes. A manager is paid to spot and exploit those frailties. You won't find them in Manchester United or Arsenal very easily, but they exist in the less formidable Premier League teams. In Europe – in the Champions League, especially – you are testing yourselves against the best teams in each league. There is no soft underbelly to strike.

This is where the connection with international football is to be found. If your country play Brazil or Italy, or even a good smaller nation, such as Romania, you start with the certain knowledge that each player lined up against you is technically accomplished and has power, pace and experience. Champions League games also require each player to hit all the high notes in his repertoire. There is no muddling through against Barcelona or Real Madrid. Mistakes are usually fatal. To survive in this unforgiving environment, you need wisdom, talent, discipline and a touch of iron in the soul.

The 2002–03 season was the year of our first Champions League adventure. Newcastle were among the European VIPs, sharing a first-phase group with Dynamo Kiev, Feyenoord and Juventus, and a second group stage with Inter Milan, Barcelona and Bayer Leverkusen.

You see my point about the rigours of the European Cup. For example, when we met Inter Milan, home and away, the centre-halves were Cordoba and Cannavaro. The right-back was Javier Zanetti. Those guys don't slip up; they don't give away stupid free-kicks; they don't make mistakes in their own penalty area; they're good tacklers; they know when to engage; they give each other good cover; they're experts at stepping up, and stepping back, and taking advantage of the offside law. They jockey, they don't sell themselves. If you try to play a little one-two to nip in behind them, they don't follow the ball, they move into position to steal the return pass. So the first problem is scoring against those top Champions League teams. You simply do not get cheap goals. Every one tends to be a pearl that leaves you thinking, on the bench, 'Well, they couldn't do much about that.'

The top Champions League clubs scour the world for people who can defend this well. They have defenders *par excellence*. The one feature common to all the great powers of Europe is that they are constantly investing in the team. My point is that it's hard for clubs outside the real élite to overcome the institutionalised excellence of the Continent's top ten or twelve contenders.

Before we could set off on the first Champions League expedition of my time at St James' Park, we needed to strengthen, to invest, to swell the ranks of young talent on our training ground. My biggest purchase in the summer of 2002 was the young European Player of the Year, Hugo Viana, for whom we paid Sporting Lisbon £8.5 million. Young Hugo turned out to be the best technical player we had at the club. What do I mean by that? First touch, delivery of the ball, an eye for a pass, an eye for the better pass (with two passes on, which one does he give, the negative one or the positive one, the safe one or the gamble?), the ability to hit it through the eye of a needle – Hugo had all that. His range was fantastic, on top of which he was blessed with a good character and could speak English.

If Hugo Viana was left out of my first eleven, it was simply because Gary Speed, Kieron Dyer and Jermaine Jenas were always a fraction ahead of him. We used him sometimes at outside-left, when we were fed up with Laurent Robert, but it wasn't Hugo's best position. We bought him as the long-term successor to Gary Speed. He just never quite got the opportunity to contribute regularly. Naturally, he became frustrated, angst-ridden. There was no bitterness in his complaints but often he would knock on my office door to enquire when his chance would come. 'Well, you're going to have to be a bit more patient,' I would tell him. 'I can't pick you ahead of Gary Speed, and I know you're out of position at outside-left, because you haven't got the pace of Laurent.'

As his disaffection grew, Hugo decided he wanted to escape Newcastle to guarantee himself first-team football, but I had to tell him, 'I can't let you do that. If I get injuries here I'm going to need you. So the answer is no.' He stayed but was never very happy. Finally, we let him go back to Sporting Lisbon after extending his contract, so that, when he returned to Tyneside, he would still have two years left with us. I believe in Hugo Viana. I really do. One day, when we beat Chelsea 2–1, he faced Claude Makelele, that tidy, tigerish holding player, and Makelele was totally overwhelmed.

At £5 million, Titus Bramble was another expensive acquisition. Now, Titus wasn't popular in some quarters on Tyneside and I have to concede that he did make one or two defensive mistakes. Of course, when goalkeepers and centre-halves make errors the ball ends up in the back of the net, but I retained a high regard for Titus. He was the best passer we had at the back of the team. He's a big lad with two good feet. In the tackle, he cleans people out. If he cuts out his mistakes, he will become one hell of a player.

Once or twice in my final season at Newcastle, Titus was absolutely outstanding. At times I would say to him, 'Forget about what's in the newspapers. Don't read them. I like you. I think you're a great player.' I called Charlie Woods in and instructed him, 'Charlie, tell Titus what you think about him,' and he did. We said, 'Forget what's in the *Chronicle*. Get out there and show what a good player you are.'

Alan Oliver was very unkind to Titus. He would write an article about Titus in March and bring up a mistake he had made last September. No journalist ever applied that unforgiving historical approach to Gary Speed or Alan Shearer or Shay Given. They only did it to Titus Bramble. I said to Alan Oliver one day, 'You've got something against Titus Bramble and I'm not having it. Now stop it, Alan.'

It's always been part of my working practice to bring players into my office and tell them what I think. The main purpose is to offer encouragement, to boost self-esteem. I want my players to share my positive outlook on life. I would say, with heavy emphasis, 'I like you. You're in my team.' That's how I would express my faith, my loyalty, especially when a player was in a trough. A lot of footballers are less secure than they appear. The swagger of the millionaire sportsman can be misleading. A lot of them are young boys, trying to get on in a very judgemental and political environment, and they benefit from regular reassurance.

That brings us to Jonathan Woodgate, whom we bought from Leeds for £9 million on 31 January 2003, the day the transfer window closed. Here was a lad who had been through turmoil. He had been involved in something wicked – an attack on an Asian student, for which he was cleared of causing bodily harm but convicted of affray – and it had hit him very hard. He turned gaunt and disappeared inside himself. He was baggy eyed and ashen. He couldn't face the public. Yet Jonathan seemed a nice sort of boy who regretted very much what he had done and was ashamed of it. I'm told that he and his family went through a terrible time.

From our end, we were looking for a dominant centre-half blessed with real class. We didn't want a stopgap, a free transfer or a defender at the end of his career. That winter, we became aware that Woodgate might be available. I recalled him playing for Leeds against Barcelona in the Champions League. He had been head and shoulders above every other Leeds player that night. We knew it was going to cost a lot of money but we felt he would repay the investment. As everyone knows, Leeds United were in a dreadful financial condition, and our chairman took advantage of their predicament, inevitably, because he's a mean, tough, no-holds-barred negotiator. When it came to transfer bargaining, Freddy Shepherd shoved compassion to one side. If he could screw the other guy, he would. He certainly did so in this case and we got the player for a copper-bottomed bargain price.

Woodgate's fitness record was out of synch with his talent. He watched a lot of games from the stands but he was young, maturing and, we hoped, moving away from a troubled phase in his life. We thought we could extract more from him than he had been able to give to Leeds. Every manager has an ego and every club thinks they can turn a player's career around. 'If he comes here, we'll sort him out. We'll treat him differently. We'll give him the guidance and support he needs. We'll work the miracle.' Everybody thinks like that. It's part of the psyche of football management.

Jonathan needed to get away from Leeds, there was no doubt about that. I suspect that the city had too many echoes and memories for him to be happy there. I knew I was signing a high-class player and I just hoped his character would stand up to the test. I met his father, who seemed very nice.

Jonathan trained and kept his head down, and we saw his quality straight away. His reputation off the pitch wasn't reflected in his conduct in a Newcastle shirt. I couldn't ever imagine him being sent off, especially for violent play. Everything he did was very clean cut. He was a tidy, careful tackler and very even-tempered. Jonathan didn't give us an ounce of trouble. We wondered how on earth he had got into that very unpleasant mêlée on the streets of Leeds.

With new players arriving, and with us qualifying for the Champions League proper by beating Zeljeznicar at the end of August, a sharp upward momentum pervaded the club, but before we could get stuck into the season, I was involved in what the newspapers invariably call a tug-of-war over Craig Bellamy and Wales. As a former international manager, I understand perfectly that no national coach can be successful unless he gets access to the best players. The three big managers I had to deal with were all Scottish – Alex Ferguson at Manchester United, George Graham of Arsenal and Kenny Dalglish at Liverpool. It's fair to theorise that none of that distinguished trio gave two monkeys about England, but nevertheless I did manage to engineer good relations with all three.

The problem with Bellamy was quite simple. He had been absent for us through injury but by the time the Wales game in Finland came around he was technically fit enough to resume playing. I told him, 'You haven't been fit to play for us but now you're fit to go and play for Wales. What happens if you play in Helsinki and come back injured?' That's what happened. Mark Hughes and I had a very good rapport. I liked him. He would ring me and I would ring him. He always listened. This time, though, I told him, 'Mark, if Craig comes back injured again, the chairman will go potty. The balloon will go up.'

We paid a lot of money for Bellamy and we had invested plenty more nursing him through his injuries. An operation in America, with flights, hotels and surgeon's fees, could set a club back twelve and a half grand. In the end, we had to tell Mark that we just couldn't tolerate Craig coming back injured all the time. It happened about three times. We just weren't getting the use of him. Craig was finding it difficult to play two games in a week, so he was coming back from a Wales game sore, with tendonitis, unable to move in training for a couple of days. It was frustrating for all of us, Craig included.

This was my most important season so far. I wanted us to make waves in Europe but it started badly. In September and October we went down to three straight defeats in Champions League group E – first in Kiev, then at home to Feyenoord and away at Juventus. We weren't bombed by Dynamo Kiev but they were just too good for us and beat us with two stunning strikes. The Feyenoord game, which we lost 1–0, should have yielded some fruit. We played well enough to earn at least a point. Then we went to Turin and found that an ordeal. We held Juventus for over an hour but went down to a brace from Alessandro Del Piero.

So there we were with no points from three games, which left us needing two home wins and a victory in Holland to stay in the competition. Well, we did a Houdini. Against Juventus at home, we achieved the considerable feat of subduing Pavel Nedved, the brilliant Czech midfielder, who had been a thorn in our side in the away leg. He was some player that night in Turin. He ran wide and through the middle and just about everywhere else on that patch of Italian turf. He was a player of such industry we couldn't hang on to him. Andy O'Brien tried to corral him while Nobby Solano tried to squeeze him from the outside-right position, but he was just too elusive. One minute we'd have him boxed in and then suddenly he would burst free. He was a ferret. Yet, at home, we managed to land some tackles on him and shut the phantom down. We saw the game out, protecting our lead from an own goal by Gianluigi Buffon, the Juventus goalkeeper. Houdini was throwing off his chains. At home to Kiev, we won 2–1, with goals from Gary Speed and Alan Shearer.

The great escape was on. At Feyenoord, in an epic match on 13 November, we led 2–0, fell back to 2–2 and clinched a place in the next round in the ninetieth minute when Dyer broke through and stroked a shot to the left of the goalkeeper, only for it to rebound to Bellamy who, with his great pace, was following up. That gave us a 3–2 lead with seconds to go, and from the touchline I pointed to my temple to encourage the players to be calm, to concentrate. So often teams get lost in the euphoria of an important goal, only to concede one immediately at the other end. This was too good to waste. Three victories, after three defeats. The chains were almost off.

Juventus won the group emphatically but we were in second place, among the top sixteen teams in Europe, with Arsenal and Manchester United. In the second group stage, against Barcelona, Inter Milan and Bayer Leverkusen, we beat Germany's representative 3–1 home and away, drew 2–2 in Italy but lost the home tie, and lost home and away to Barcelona.

The home fixture against Inter Milan will be remembered for Craig Bellamy's dismissal, in the fifth minute, for violent conduct. We had talked to Craig quite specifically about the dangers of playing in Europe, where you can't get away with retaliation or unruliness. We told him, 'These guys will attempt to upset your apple cart, and if you respond that's exactly what they want you to do, and you'll be sent off.' We were wasting our breath.

Alan Shearer had been a victim of the same underhand tactics but the referee had missed Alan's aggressive response. A defender had been hanging off our captain and Alan reacted by flinging an elbow in the direction of his tormentor. The TV cameras picked it up and after the match UEFA intervened quickly and Alan was suspended. So we lost both Bellamy and Shearer at the end of a 4–1 home defeat – not the best start to our latest campaign.

'What were you doing?' I demanded of Craig. 'They've antagonised you and you've fallen for it. When are you going to learn?'

In case anyone should think Craig was alone in being challenged, questions were also asked of Alan. It was unusual for him to behave in that way but the emotion of the match and the frustration of losing Bellamy after four minutes got the better of him, despite his widespread experience of hand-to-hand combat with Italian defenders, who can be a bit naughty in the penalty area. They'll grasp, manhandle and jostle you. They'll pull your shirt out of shape. Sometimes it's hard to put up with that kind of disruptive, irritating attention. Alan has the right temperament for dealing with the dark arts, but on that particular night something cracked.

In December, the away tie in Barcelona was billed as my homecoming and I was thrilled to be going back to the Nou Camp. On the night of the game it just poured and poured and the pitch was declared unfit. We weren't due to play again until the Sunday, so after a few discussions we agreed to play the game the following evening. This was the night when Kieron Dyer, defending a goalpost for a corner, let the ball go straight past him. We were 2–1 down when Dyer's concentration deserted him, and still fighting, but it finished 3–1 to my old club. This time, there was to be no escape and we finished third in the group behind Barcelona and Inter Milan.

Maybe we hadn't quite matured enough, as a team, to be

beating Barcelona on their own ground. Around the club, I often ran into people who thought, 'We're Newcastle United, we should be beating everyone.' Out in the middle of the pitch, the scenario is quite different. If inexperience runs up against the kind of class and experience Barcelona bring to the party, the job can hardly be described as a straightforward case of Geordie spirit and tenacity overcoming world-class talent. At this early stage of our development, the élite were simply too good for us. The eight quarter-finalists that year were Ajax, AC Milan, Real Madrid, Manchester United, Inter Milan, Valencia, Juventus and Barcelona, which, I think, reinforces my point.

My sixty-ninth birthday was upon me and I woke up not expecting the club to have planned anything special to mark the occasion. We trained as normal that day but Judith Horey, my secretary, was very clever in luring me to St James' Park. She told me the chairman wanted to see me and insisted on coming with me into the lift, claiming, 'I've got to go to the top floor anyway.' When I entered the boardroom the whole gang was there – the first-team squad and all the staff together with Elsie and members of my family. The chairman gave me a very nice inscribed silver bowl.

The figures on the page said, indisputably, that I was sixty-nine but I really didn't feel that old. Sometimes I hear myself saying, 'I haven't had a day off sick in my entire life,' and then I remember that I've fought cancer twice, which seems crazy. Elsie corrects me. 'You've been at death's door twice. What are you talking about? Of course you've been off sick.'

I was enjoying my life and my job and was still awash with enthusiasm. I was enjoying the way Newcastle were playing football and knew we were getting better, stronger, smarter. I was proud of that. The stadium was complete. The commerical side of the club was going well. I had superb technical staff. We were a couple of players short of really challenging Manchester United and Arsenal, but everything about my life was good. I suppose I felt unsackable.

I had no visions of stopping. I would wake up excited about the day. I rose every morning at 7.10 a.m. and relished getting dressed and climbing into the car because I was on my way to do a job I loved. The hour spent getting to work I used as thinking time. I would contemplate the day's training and everything I wanted to achieve with my players. The Premiership was a mighty, daily challenge. I wouldn't have changed that job for the world, even at seventy years old. Elsie and I were back among friends and relations and we loved it. I felt at peace. I felt fulfilled.

The season ended, though, with an April wobble – a 6–2 home defeat against Manchester United in the middle of three consecutive defeats, with Everton and Fulham on either side. In the Everton game, Thomas Gravesen made a horrible tackle on Olivier Bernard. Olivier collapsed, unseen by the referee, who waved play on. David Moyes, the Everton manager, stood up and shouted, 'Kick it out, kick it out,' to his players, but they carried on and scored, four passes after Bernard had been felled. We lost 2–1 that day but Gravesen should have been sent off and play halted prior to the winning goal. Moyes, who had done his best, later apologised.

Still, we finished third with 69 points, 14 fewer than the champions, United, after being top for a week in January, and qualified once again for the Champions League. In my time at the club we had finished eleventh, eleventh, fourth and now third.

Among the many discoveries I made that season was one I struggle to confess to, even now. It concerned the apparent theft of fifteen of my England caps from our home in Suffolk. This is the true story, told for the first time.

In the autumn of 2001, I was the victim of a robbery and lost some valuable possessions. The burglar had about one minute from the time the alarm went off to complete his disreputable business. He'd come through the garden and lifted the whole window out. The police would be on top of him any minute, but speed was plainly one of the villain's assets.

Eighteen months later I issued a public appeal for the return of my England caps, which carried huge sentimental value for me. I can explain why it took that long for me to ask for them back. When I checked the house after the break-in, it didn't occur to me to make sure my caps were still where I had left them. In those days, you often got one cap for a run of three games. On the peak it would say England v. Ireland v. Scotland v. Wales. So, while I played twenty times for England, I received seventeen caps, and I had given two away – one to my dad and another to my nephew.

One day, back in Durham, it occurred to me that I hadn't made sure the caps were still in the house in Suffolk. Anxiety struck me out of the blue. I resolved to check next time I was in the south and when the day came and I peered into the hiding place, my heart nearly burst out of my chest – no caps, panic. 'Hang on,' I thought, 'if they're not there, they must be somewhere else,' and I searched all over the house but with no luck.

I rang the FA and asked David Davies, the executive director, 'Did England caps have the player's name in them back in the 1950s?' My hope was that the burglar would be unable to sell them if they had my name on, and so might find some way of handing them back. David said no, players didn't have their names inscribed in their caps in those days, at which point I felt I needed to make a public appeal, explaining that I had only just discovered the awful truth.

I got them back but not by paying a ransom, as some people assumed. Not long after I made the appeal, I decided to sell the house. It had been locked up and unoccupied much of the time and had become a worry to me. We hired a local firm to clean everything out. In the loft we had cases, crockery, old sports kits, memorabilia, football boots, photographs, bits of silver. Apparently, burglars don't like going in lofts because if anything goes wrong they can't get away quickly, so it's a good place to store valuable items. Having appointed the removal firm, I went down one day to sort through the things in the attic. I brought all the bags downstairs and among them was a zip-up adidas bag. When I reached inside I felt a familiar sensation on my fingertips. At some point during my travels, I had worried about my caps sufficiently to put them in that adidas bag and carry them up to the loft. It was sheer chance that I rediscovered them because most of the bags went into storage, where they remained unopened until early 2005.

I didn't tell people how I had retrieved my caps. When they asked, I would say only, 'Don't worry, I have them back, but if you don't mind I won't tell you how.' If you move house twenty-eight times in your married life, as we have, the memory is bound to play a few tricks.

18
THE CROWN JEWELS

An URBAN myth that dogged me towards the end of my time with Newcastle was that I tried to sell Alan Shearer to Liverpool – not in a million years. I remember, in vivid detail, the telephone conversation that set this nasty little rumour on its way. The call was incoming – not outgoing – and sent me scurrying off to see my chairman within minutes of the line going dead. Into Freddy Shepherd's office I marched to make the following momentous announcement: 'I've just had Gerard Houllier on the phone from Liverpool, manager to manager, and he has offered me three million pounds for Alan Shearer.'

When I started in this business, almost all transfers started with direct contact between the two managers. Now it's chairman to chairman, chief executive to chief executive. Managers these days run the team but they sure don't run the club the way I did at Ipswich Town. Freddy Shepherd had a look on his face that suggested to me he already knew Liverpool were chasing Alan. Then he confirmed my suspicion.

'Oh, yeah, I've known of their interest for a couple of weeks,' he said.

What I ought to have said next was, 'Why didn't you tell me?' but I held my tongue. Freddy was gearing himself up for a major declaration.

'We can't sell Alan Shearer,' he went on. 'He's the crown jewels. The public would go mad.' He was right, of course.

'Fine, I understand that line of argument and I support it,' I replied. 'The next question is this. What are you going to do about Alan's contract here? If you did sell him for three million – and I'm not saying you should – I would get a striker in for one point two million whom I like very much. He's called Emile Mpenza – twenty-three years old, powerful and quick, with strong legs. He might be the future.'

'I can't sell Alan Shearer,' the chairman repeated.

'Right. Fair enough,' I said, 'in which case you'd better get his contract sorted out. Don't imagine that Alan Shearer is ignorant of the fact that Liverpool are trying to buy him. If I know, you can be sure Alan's agent does.'

My reasoning was that Alan and his representative, Tony Stephens, would soon come into the chairman's office to say, 'If you've stopped me going to Liverpool, I think I'm entitled to another year on my Newcastle contract,' and Alan had every right to think that way. By saying no to a move, Newcastle had no option but to extend Alan's stay by a further year.

That was my reading of our situation, and I went on to argue that the same principle should apply to Gary Speed, whose energy, competitiveness and honesty marked him out as a very special footballer indeed. Alan and Gary had already been to see the chairman, with their agents, to negotiate another year on their contracts. Alan would be thirty-four at the start of the 2004–05 season and Gary would be thirty-five. I was consulted both times.

'Sign them both for another year, chairman,' I had asserted. 'I'm happy with that. They're a pleasure to have at the club. Despite their age, they'll give us everything they have. They're both great lads and they're as fit as they possibly could be. If you're asking me about their ability to play regularly in the season after this one, I suppose there is a little doubt, but they've served the club well and they are brilliant boys. It's a gamble but maybe it's one we should take.'

A compromise, I thought, might be to wait until Christmas, when we would know more about how their legs might stand up to another twelve months after the current season. It was a real conundrum, a balancing act between loyalty, finance, the needs of the team and our desire to make sure Alan and Gary were treated properly – a tricky situation for the chairman and me. I assured Freddy Shepherd that Alan would be fine for 2003–04, but was unable to issue any guarantees for the season after that. In the event, Liverpool's offer was the catalyst for Alan getting the extra year he wanted from Newcastle United.

For a long time, not a word passed between Alan and me about the Liverpool approach. Although we both knew a serious inquiry had been made, it was not something either of us felt an urge to discuss, until Alan broached the subject one day.

'You didn't tell me about Liverpool, did you?' he said.

'No, Alan, because it was company business,' I responded. 'If you become a manager, you'll have to learn that you don't tell players about every offer that comes your way. It's club business. It's got nothing to do with the player. The chairman and the manager will either say, "Yes, we'll sell," in which case we would tell you, or, "No, we won't," in which case the club is under no obligation to discuss it with their player. The player is under contract, remember.' For example, Blackburn didn't tell Shearer I'd try to buy him for Barcelona.

The sole acquisition that summer was Lee Bowyer, who came to us from West Ham on a free transfer. Our only real expenditure after we had finished third in the Premiership was Lee's salary. We had watched him closely during his spell at Upton Park, where, we felt, he was a little disappointing. He had an ankle injury and had been operated on that summer. Our advice was that it was nothing serious, a short-term problem, so we elected to take a chance, on the grounds that he was a talented player, temporarily underachieving.

We saw him as a wide player, who could also excel in central midfield. On a free transfer he was simply too good to miss. Not long before he joined us, he had been the subject of a £9 million transfer offer from Liverpool but had declined their invitation to go to Anfield and had been sent out on loan to West Ham instead, a struggling side who were relegated. We knew that his subdued performances in claret and blue were not an accurate measure of his talent. We felt that if we brought him into a settled environment and surrounded him with good players, he would recover his old prowess. Needless to say, the chairman was happy because he had acquired a £5 million footballer for nothing.

There had been a flurry of controversy about Lee signing for West Ham, who are in a racially sensitive area, and it was felt by some outside the club that Glenn Roeder should have resisted the temptation on political grounds alone. Many regarded Lee as a pariah. The same objection was placed in front of us. We knew it was coming. We knew we'd take a whack but we were prepared to take the blow. We calculated that this would be a two-day controversy, after which we would all be allowed to get on with our lives. We felt we could steer ourselves and Bowyer through a few days of adversity.

Like Woodgate, he never gave us a moment's trouble. His commitment to the club was first rate and we knew of no off-the-field indiscretions to cause us alarm. At Newcastle, he led a good, sheltered life. He bought a house by a golf course, out of harm's way. As with Woodgate, I think the incident in Leeds had shocked and embarrassed him, although he concealed those feelings much more efficiently than Jonathan. It may not have been apparent from that defiant facial expression of his, but I think Bowyer had been through torture, of the internal sort, and realised he had been a fool. Without coming out and articulating his contrition to the world, I think he was ashamed. Remorse had been eating away at his spirit.

I think Bowyer had taken a decision, deep down, not to be involved in that kind of trouble ever again. He was always polite and if he ever wanted to stay in London after a game, he would always ask three days in advance. He never popped up with a late request. I rather liked the fact that he wanted to see his mum and dad when he was in London, so I tended to say, 'Fine, not a problem, son, see your parents.'

I didn't speak to him specifically about racism. All I said was, 'You've made a big mistake and you've paid for it.'

'Yeah, I have,' he replied. I followed up with a word of encouragement.

'OK, you've done it, and what you have to do now is make sure it never happens again. The club will give you support and guidance. This is a new life. Enjoy it, and tread warily.'

'Don't worry about me,' he answered. 'I've learned my lesson.'

He joined us as we were making a mediocre start to our campaign. We lost 1–0 at Birmingham to a penalty, succumbed 2–1 at home to Manchester United and were knocked out of the Champions League qualifying phase on penalties by Partizan Belgrade, which was agonising, and horribly expensive for the club. The United game is remembered for Alex Ferguson berating the fourth official and being expelled by the referee from the United dug-out. Alex had absolutely blown his top when Andy O'Brien escaped a red card for a tackle from behind on Ryan Giggs. Still steaming, Alex watched the rest of the game on a TV set in my office.

Our 1–0 win in Belgrade was creditable enough, but the return leg descended into chaos. We needed only a draw to go through but in the last minute, at 0–0, we conceded a corner. The ball was sliding out of play when Woodgate decided to chase it to keep it on the pitch – bad move. Jonathan managed to stop the ball crossing the line but the momentum of his run carried him off the pitch, and while our centre-half was leaving the field, the Partizan defender who had been chasing him collected the ball and moved it swiftly up the pitch. After a quick sequence of passes, and with Woodgate out of position, they grabbed the goal they so desperately needed – 1–1 on aggregate meant extra time and after that penalties. Incredibly, Woodgate, Shearer and Dyer all missed their kicks. We were out of the European Cup before we had reached the competition proper. Oh, boy.

A huge depression descended on the club. In the dressing room, the players could barely lift their heads off the floor. They regretted their missed chances and thought ruefully about the big Champions League games they were going to miss. It was just an awful night. The following morning the chairman asked to see me. The directors were subdued but not conspicuously angry. It was pointed out to me that the whole club had been looking forward to a fruitful Champions League campaign and that our hopes, our dreams, had now collapsed.

'I know, I know. How do you think I feel?' I responded. 'How do you think the players feel? But we're still in Europe,' I argued. 'We finished third last season and we've still got a good team. Three years ago you were on the precipice, worrying that the club would crash out of the Premiership. We all feel sick. You're sick, I'm sick. We missed three penalties. I missed out on a World Cup final through missed penalties. It's damaging, and sad, but we've got to get on with it.'

Although we'd tumbled off the highwire of the Champions League, there was still the safety net of the UEFA Cup, and we did well in that competition until injuries emasculated us in the semi-final.

We recovered from our poor start in the League but found it a long climb from sixteenth place, in the first week of October, to our eventual resting place of fifth. All season long I grappled with disciplinary problems that were not of my making. It's an affront to me personally to allege that there was no order during my time at Newcastle, but I have to concede that there was an element – and Kieron Dyer was part of it – that was rather too fond of a good time. What that good time was I don't quite know because I wasn't with them twenty-four hours a day and I didn't go out socially with the players. No doubt they got away with things I didn't hear about, but whenever I did find out I would take the offender to task.

Dyer was connected with – but certainly not involved in – the Grosvenor House affair, in which a young woman made allegations of rape against a group of Premiership footballers. The charges were later dropped.

It all came about after a Friday night game in London against Arsenal. We decided we wouldn't train back in Newcastle on the Saturday morning. Instead, we'd make everyone come back on Sunday night for training on Monday morning. We flew down and were due to fly back. Several players asked if they could remain in London after the match. Lee Bowyer wanted to see his family in London, and Dyer and Bramble told me they wanted to visit their parents in Ipswich. That wasn't a problem.

'Be back on Sunday night, in good time,' I told them. 'Don't come back on Monday morning. Arrive the night before so you're fully prepared, and not tired, for training the next day.'

JJ asked permission to go home with his parents to Nottingham, where they and his girlfriend lived – again, not a problem. In all, about seven players didn't board the plane back to Newcastle. What I didn't know was that some of them were telling me lies. Kieron and Titus didn't go home to see their parents in Ipswich. They stayed in London for the Saturday night. There was no problem with Jenas or Bowyer, or with Hugo Viana, who remained in the capital for the weekend with his wife to shop and see the sights.

Kieron had used his credit card to book hotel rooms for a

group of people, including Titus, who ended up on the wrong end of an extremely serious allegation. Kieron wasn't out and about with the group who got themselves into trouble. He was elsewhere. He wasn't involved in any shape or form. Nevertheless, football was suddenly confronted by the most awful headlines: 'Seven Premiership stars in rape claim'. It exploded on the game.

In the frenzy that followed, the names of Titus and Kieron both cropped up. Since we were the club that people liked to make assumptions about – Bobby Robson's 'brat pack' and all that – we took the full backlash, although the names of the accused were spreading more by gossip and innuendo than by hard fact. We bore the brunt.

The police came up to Newcastle and wanted to interview just about everyone who had been down to Highbury, even players who were hundreds of miles away, tucked up in bed. Even I was interviewed. I've got a newspaper headline that I still look at with incredulity: 'Robson quizzed in rape case'. Can you believe that? Anyone not knowing the background might have jumped to the most damning conclusions.

Shearer was highly indignant when the request was made to interview him. 'I'm not going to be interviewed,' he said. 'Why do they want to interview me? I got on the plane. I went home. The night that thing happened I was three hundred miles away.' He was upset and deeply offended.

The chairman, however, asked us all to meet the police and provide our statements. He wanted us to offer full cooperation. So, yes, I was quizzed but 'Robson quizzed in rape case' I found hard to take, even with my experience of learning to ignore scurrilous newspaper headlines.

The Grosvenor House affair was out of control from the day the story broke. There was so much exaggeration and so many discrepancies in the reports of what happened, but it was very upsetting for those of us who got dragged into it from hundreds of miles away.

Eventually, life returned to normal. In January we adjusted the playing staff, releasing Nikos Dabizas to Leicester on a free transfer, Carl Cort to Wolves for £2 million and Nobby Solano to Aston Villa for £1.5 million. The Solano transfer was the only contentious one, and was badly misunderstood by some observers. We had a surfeit of players who could play in that wide right position – Nobby, Ambrose, Bowyer and Dyer, who had played in that role for England. In my opinion at that time, Solano remained potent on free-kicks, corners and crosses, but had stopped penetrating the space behind defenders. Knowing he could no longer manoeuvre the ball round a full-back or beat him for pace, he had become a static figure, too dependent on his ability to cross from a stationary position.

He was neat, tidy, got the ball, gave it, got it back, played it square and didn't lose it, but he could no longer get down that touchline and force his defender on to the retreat. He was keeping young Darren Ambrose out of the side and I wanted to correct that anomaly. Ambrose was twenty. Solano was thirty. We'd had the best of him. He was on a big salary and for that reason the chairman was delighted to move him on. It was good housekeeping. Add the transfer fee to Nobby's salary and his move to Aston Villa was worth £2 to £3 million to the club. I don't care how big the organisation, if you have a large squad of highly paid players, a duty exists to spend the money wisely and to make economies where surgical cuts are not harmful to the team. This one wasn't because we no longer needed Nobby Solano. Where the chairman let me down was in failing to support me when the criticism started rolling in. He was happy to take the money from Aston Villa but rather less eager to defend the sale in public, when some people on Tyneside began insisting that I had made a mistake. I would have liked him to say, 'This was a club decision, a business decision, and it was the right one for New-castle United.' In retrospect, maybe I should have pressed him harder to address the budgerigar noise you get when you sell a popular player. The local paper would have been the right forum. It would have helped me enormously if the public had seen me to have his support in that decision.

Another problem with Nobby throughout his time at the club was his international tie-up with Peru. In the early days he was making frequent trips back to Lima and returning unable to play in our next match. We gave him a new contract on the assumption that he would cut down on international football, and cer-tainly not play in any of the friendlies that were littering the international calendar. He gave us that pledge when he signed the new deal but the temptation became too great for him and he was soon on planes to Peru again. He would play for us on the Saturday, fly on the Sunday, play for his country on Tuesday or Wednesday and then arrive in Newcastle on the Friday night in no condition to perform for us on the Saturday afternoon. I used to say to him, 'Nobby, son, when you come back from Peru on the Friday, I can't play you the following day because you just can't do it for us. When that happens you end up letting us down.' In a typical season he might miss five or six weekend games for us for that reason.

I don't mean to be critical of him as a person. He was a smashing boy and I liked him very much. He used to bring his cornet in and play it in the dressing room, much to the delight of the other lads. When I took over, he was one of my seven blue-chip players. I wish him nothing but the best. With his declining pace, though, we had to let him go but then Ambrose picked up an injury. Some used that as another excuse to criticise me for selling Nobby, but I stand by the decision. Besides, the truth is that Nobby was happy to go to Villa Park because he could see the competition building up on his side of the pitch.

He saw Ambrose's talent. He saw Bowyer's industry and tackling. He saw Dyer's pace. He saw all that and realised he would be better off elsewhere.

Later that season, on 24 April, our paths crossed again outside the Riverside Stadium, where Middlesbrough had entertained Aston Villa. Solano was sent off just after half-time, and as Charlie Woods and I slipped away ten minutes before the end to beat the traffic, we came across Nobby in the car park, fully dressed, with a Peruvian friend, loading his bags in to the boot. Inside, his team were drawing 1–1 and were fighting for the win, which they eventually got, thanks to an eighty-ninth minute goal by Peter Crouch.

'Hello, Nobby, what are you doing?' I asked. It turned out that the next day he was making one of his rushed trips back to Peru. 'Shouldn't you be watching the match?' I continued. He evidently didn't think so and I left him to load his bags. That's the modern player for you.

During that season, we continued to attract the worst kind of attention. Think airport departure lounges and you imagine people slumped on chairs, reading, listening to music and waiting for planes to take off. You don't associate airport waiting rooms with Premier League footballers throwing chairs at their coaches but that's what happened before our trip to Mallorca for a UEFA Cup match in late March 2004, when Craig Bellamy and John Carver, our head coach, got into an altercation while I was giving a press conference in an adjacent room. It was early morning and the players had been ushered into a private room, where tea, orange juice and biscuits were waiting. In this tranquil environment, an explosion occurred.

The gist of it, I believe, was that Craig was rude and vulgar to John, and the row escalated to the point where Craig picked up a chair. I knew nothing about it until I joined them after the press conference, by which time the fracas was over. David Geddis was standing by the door as I tried to enter, and he leaned against it to stop me coming in, whispering through the crack, 'You're best out of it. Don't come in.' Bellamy was very upset.

'I'm not having this. I'm not going on this trip, I'm not going to play,' he was saying, swearing his head off.

'Look, I don't know what's taken place here, but I will investigate,' I told him. 'If you pull out of this trip, it will be an even bigger scandal. Let's get this thing under control and keep it internal. Sit yourself down, get your mind right, get on the plane and let's play this football match.'

Later, John told me, 'We had a disagreement. I hit him. He deserved it.'

As it turned out, we won the tie 7–1 on aggregate, and Craig made a great play of the fact that John had been the first to congratulate him when he scored. In the same interview, Craig played down a reported confrontation in a Cardiff hotel the previous week, calling it 'absolutely nothing'.

When Graeme Souness took over from me, it wasn't long before Bellamy was testing the boundaries with his new manager. That's putting it mildly. 'You effing prick' is what Craig was reported to have said to Souness after Graeme had taken him off in one of his early games. Craig never said anything like that to me in our four years together. He used to swear a lot but I wouldn't have tolerated him being abusive to me. In the subsequent confrontation, Graeme is said to have grabbed Craig by the throat. Although our relationship was tempestuous, Craig and I never went to such extremes.

19

THE TWELVE DAYS

I T WAS 10 a.m. on the day of our UEFA Cup match against Valerenga when I broke the news to Alan Shearer. Shola Ameobi was to replace him in the team that night. Alan was being told to take a rest in a game we felt we could win without him. He's a tough guy with good character, which is why he hates missing even a single match. That morning at the team hotel he took my decision on the chin. Later, though, he landed a diplomatic blow of his own.

My decision to withdraw Alan from the starting eleven that day was entirely sound and reasonable. Our scouts Charlie Woods and David Mills had been to watch Valerenga play and had filed a report describing our third-round opponents as a relatively mediocre bunch. They expected us to come through the away leg unscathed, provided we performed to an acceptable standard. Armed with that information, and studying the fixture list for February, I made up my mind to leave Alan on the bench.

We had played Middlesbrough on the Saturday and had won 2–1, with goals from Shearer and Bellamy. After the Valerenga match we were scheduled to face Portsmouth at Fratton Park on the Sunday. So off I went to find Alan. Surprised, he asked why I was leaving him out.

'Well, I could say, "I'm the manager" – that's why, Alan,' I responded, 'but in addition to that, we don't need you. According to my report, we can get by without you. You played against 'Boro on Saturday and you're playing again on Sunday. I want you in the dressing room, as captain, but you're not going to play.' Alan was thirty-three years of age. On this occasion, Shola could take over his duties.

'Fine,' Alan replied. 'I'm disappointed but I understand.'

'It's not easy for me to tell you you're not playing,' I went on, 'but you have to remember that there are times when Michael Owen, Ruud van Nistelrooy and Thierry Henry don't play.'

Alan played more games than any other Premiership striker I could think of. He was the only one who didn't take breaks and his main rivals in the Premiership were much younger than he was. I told him that. I tried to make him understand that, for a man of his age, trying to play in every single match was self-defeating. His competitive nature was admirable, on the one hand, but also an obstacle when I wanted him to step back from the firing line.

That morning I thought he had accepted my decision, however reluctantly. The complication arose after the match, which we drew 1–1, when Alan complained to the press about being left out. I felt he shouldn't have spoken to the media like that after the game, and I told him so. In my diary I wrote: 'Barcelona element in the press.'

In Catalonia, I had twenty élite players. Each time I put six-teen names on the match sheet, four were disappointed. The Barcelona press would go straight to the four who had been left out to get them to complain about the manager. That would provide them with the day's story – Robson wrong, Robson unpopular, or whatever they chose to say. The press survived on grumbles and rumours. They would get nothing from happy players. So when I talked to my Newcastle players about the importance of keeping quiet and of mutual respect, I had my Barcelona experience in mind.

The result had been slightly disappointing, of course, and that might be why Alan felt more inclined to grumble as he mingled with reporters after the match. His words kicked up quite a bit of dust. I had to ask myself if Alan would have complained if we had won the match. In the team hotel he had accepted my decision with good grace.

As I've said, it was a masterstroke to bring Alan Shearer back to Newcastle, and he was a wonderful leader of men, an example to all professional footballers, but there were times in 2003–04 when I could see him toiling, and I wanted to protect him wherever possible by forcing him to take a rest. In the course of our discussion after the Valerenga incident, I asked him to put himself in my position.

'Look, Alan, one day you're going to be a manager. What will you do to the player who complains to the press about your team selection, the way you complained about mine? Would you let it go, or would you have a word with him about it? Would you say, "I don't think you should have done that"?'

To his credit, he saw the logic in what I was saying and acknowledged that he, too, might one day find himself in my situation.

Sometimes, in my office, I would invite a player to sit on my side of the desk, walk to the opposite side of the room and then ask him how he would deal with a problem he had just given me. That way he could start thinking outside the box of his own concerns. He could see the team as an entity, not a collection of individuals all pursuing private agendas. I emphasised to Alan after the Valerenga game that everything I did was in the best interests of the club and that, as a result of my decision to leave him out, he would be fresh against Portsmouth that weekend. On top of that, I reminded him that I needed to bring Shola on as a player.

'He's going to replace you one day,' I said. 'How's he going to develop if he doesn't get a chance? Remember the time someone gave you a chance in your early days at Southampton?'

The storm around Newcastle United was not abating, however. Three days later, with the Nobby Solano issue put to bed, another 'transfer' caused terrible ructions inside the club. In February, we allowed Lumana Lua Lua to go to Portsmouth on loan but did not stipulate that he should sit out our game against Pompey at Fratton Park on the last day of the month. I repeat, we had a very hands-on chairman who didn't tell me everything. I had agreed to let Lua Lua go out on loan, but, in addition to paying his wages, Portsmouth had consented to a small loan fee, in the region of £100,000, which entitled them to play him in any game they chose. With that freedom, they were hardly likely to spare our blushes when the two teams met on that Sunday afternoon.

The deal was done at boardroom level, which was the way of things at our club. The directors took care of all the financial and contract issues. Again, it was the direct opposite of how it had worked for me at Ipswich. At St James' Park, under the modern system, those who ran the club didn't want me to know how every pound was being spent, how much the agent was getting, and so on. I had mixed feelings. On the one hand it saved me an awful lot of headaches. Equally, Freddy Shepherd never once interfered in team selection. I had complete control over the players, how and where we would travel and all pitch-related issues.

Down on the south coast, we were winning 1–0, thanks to a Bellamy goal, and with Lua Lua in the Portsmouth side, you can probably guess what happened next. In the dying seconds, Lua Lua snatched at a half-chance and the ball was suddenly rippling the back of our net – 1–1, pandemonium. I walked into the dressing room to find my players going berserk. Gary Speed, especially, was raging.

'I've run my sodding bollocks off and then this happens! He shouldn't have played in the game. He's scored and we've lost two points. I'm sick of this!' Gary was inconsolable.

'Hang on, hang on,' I said.

'Lua Lua shouldn't have played,' Gary exclaimed and Alan Shearer weighed in to support Gary.

'I understand how you feel,' I sympathised, 'but it's not the fact that Lua Lua has scored that ought to be bothering us. It's the fact that Portsmouth have scored in the dying seconds – our concentration went AWOL. It hurts more because it was Lua Lua, I agree with that, but it could just as easily have been the centre-half. We turned our backs on the corner. If we'd picked him up and done the job properly, he wouldn't have bloody scored. That's the issue. He could have been Bill Smith. We've let Bill Smith score a last-minute equaliser on the edge of the box. That's what we should be upset about, not what his name is.'

So it was an awful three days. First I had to contend with Alan Shearer's remarks about being rested for the Valerenga match, then I had a row with the players about Lua Lua's goal for Portsmouth. As if to add to the pile, the next morning, an article appeared in the *Journal*, quoting Steve Harper, our reserve goalkeeper, as saying: 'I've got to play now or never.' I recorded it in my diary, adding, 'while on a great contract'. The fact was that Shay Given was a better goalkeeper, but Steve Harper had lost sight of that. He had used the *Journal* to inform us he was fed up with playing in the reserves. What he was forgetting was that the club paid him extra to compensate him for the frustration of having to play second violin to Shay Given. That article further inflamed an already delicate situation at the club.

That afternoon I visited the chairman, who was livid at the reaction of the players to the Lua Lua affair. On this occasion, I felt inclined to support him. 'Chairman dead right on both counts,' I wrote in my diary. At that stage, Lua Lua was our fourth-choice striker. As the chairman pointed out, why should we have been worried about facing a striker who, at his own club, was fourth choice behind Shearer, Bellamy and Ameobi? If the players were going to be upset, the chairman argued, should they not be upset that a fourth-choice forward had beaten them with a pot shot? That was a good point and he was right. Lua Lua was a tricky little customer, but it's not as if we singled him out as a threat in the pre-match team talk. At five to three nobody was saying, 'Christ, keep an eye on Lua Lua, don't let him turn,' but by five to five he had become this huge menace who should not have been on the pitch. My players were hiding behind an excuse. The following day I called them into a meeting and declared my support for the chairman's position.

'Next time, you deal with him, like you deal with van Nistelrooy and Thierry Henry and Pires,' I said. 'We failed, not Lua Lua. We failed.'

What a week. Just to cap it off, I had a row with the chairman about the state of our pitch, which was atrocious. The previous Saturday, I had called the surface at St James' a 'pig of a pitch'. The chairman didn't like that. He thought I was using the state of the turf to defend the performances and an angry debate ensued. I was within my rights to point out that between 7 January and the end of the season we were unbeaten at home, on a pudding of a field. There was no basis to his claim that I was blaming poor home results on the playing surface. Five huge issues cropped up in a week – the joys of football management.

Despite the upset over the Valerenga draw, we were motoring in that season's UEFA Cup. On 14 April we followed up our 1–1 draw at PSV Eindhoven with a 2–1 home victory that put us through to a semi-final against Marseille. In the home leg we drew 0–0, but faced the away game without Woodgate, Bellamy, Jenas, Dyer and Bowyer, who was on the bench but not sufficiently fit to start. The previous Saturday, we had beaten Chelsea 2–1 in a magnificent match with two wonderful goals from Shearer and Ameobi. Our mood was good but our injury problems wretched. We were OK at 1–0 down, but then Didier Drogba scored his second and the match seemed to slide away.

After the game, as the club regrouped, nobody at boardroom level said hello to me. In front of one or two of his personal friends, the chairman said he'd had the most miserable night of his life. 'How do you think I feel?' I protested. I tried to argue that it's extremely hard to win matches at that level when you're missing so many influential, game-shaping players. Sir John Hall, I'm told, travelled back to the airport with some disgruntled supporters who moaned about the result and the performance. As a former chairman of the club, Sir John couldn't take the heat being directed his way. So, I'm told, he began agreeing with the fans. For a man of his repute and standing to start turning on his team for losing a UEFA Cup semi-final with five players absent was extremely disappointing to me. He should have been above that – but he wasn't.

In my diary I find the following entry: 'Chairman in an ugly mood after the match, unhappy. Not a kind word. Not much sleep during the night. Missed the big players.'

Two days later, Arsene Wenger rang me to express his sympathy.

'Bobby, I understand what happened to you out there,' he said. 'We wouldn't have won that match either without five of our best players.' Arsene and I agreed that to win European semi-finals you have to have all the quality at your disposal down on that pitch.

'I know that,' I told Arsene. 'It's the people around me who don't understand.'

I don't know how many teams start the UEFA Cup because the qualifying system tends to change, but I have the figure sixty-four in my head. When you get to the semi-finals, sixty clubs have fallen by the wayside. You're one of the four best teams in the competition. The survivors that season were Marseille,

Newcastle, Valencia and Villareal. After the semi-final, people forgot that we had knocked out PSV and Mallorca, 7–1 on aggregate, in the preceding rounds. We just happened to meet Marseille at the worst possible time.

The turbulence unleashed in France continued all the way to the last kick of the season. On 9 May, our 1–1 draw with Wolves, who had been relegated, let loose another little storm. It was a disappointing result, I acknowledge. Who would have expected Alan Shearer to miss a penalty with four minutes to go? Before kick-off, I announced to the team, 'Win, lose or draw, injured or fit, I want us out there in suits, shirts and ties to do our walk around and say goodbye to the supporters for the summer.' We still had away games at Southampton and Liverpool, where we drew 1–1 to finish fifth and secure a UEFA Cup place, but this was our last home game and our last chance to pay tribute to the fans who had followed us at home and abroad all season. We always did a walk around after our last game at St James' Park but this particular one went wrong. In previous seasons we had saluted maybe 40,000 people. This time about 5,000 were left in the ground. It was a real shock. 'Look, lads, we're still doing it,' I told the players. The 5,000 who stayed were fantastic. The problem was that 35,000 more had disappeared. On the same day, Leeds United had been relegated and 35,000 Leeds fans had given the players a terrific send-off. For some reason, our public deserted us, and it shocked us. I wasn't angry with them. If you pay your money, you're entitled to express your opinion. I was just surprised.

After the game I did my usual TV interview and then relaxed, believing that the cameras had stopped rolling. Ian Payne was holding the microphone. When the formal part of the conversation had stopped, Ian asked, 'How do you feel?'

'How do I feel? I've just watched thirty-five thousand Leeds fans cheer them after they were relegated.' That's all I said. I didn't condemn our public, I didn't swear, I didn't say anything derogatory. I was just fighting for my team. I felt sorry for them. At that point, we could still have won a place in the Champions League. All I meant was, 'I feel really bad. Look at Leeds and then look what's happened here.'

I was caught on camera and the pictures and sound were beamed into the press suite. Hazel Greener, our press officer, rushed in, saying, 'Bobby, Bobby, you've been caught on camera comparing our fans with the Leeds fans.' The press had jotted down my remarks off the TV monitors. Together with Hazel, I instructed them that what I had said was completely off the record and not intended for use. They huddled together and agreed not to report it. All the national newspapers accepted that I had been speaking off the record and agreed that it would be improper for them to report my words. However, one paper disregarded that agreement. Alan Oliver rang me.

'We've got to print that story,' he said.

'Oh no you haven't,' I said. 'What I said was off the record. It's not in the *Mail*, the *Sun*, the *Telegraph* or any other national paper. So why do you have to print it?'

Alan's reply was that his editor felt it was an important story.

'Don't abuse my trust, Alan,' I responded. 'Why should you be different?'

The *Journal* didn't use the story but I was being told the *Chronicle* would, so I called the sports editor to protest. The chairman was also known to phone the local paper from time to time. If they carried anything he didn't like, he wasn't averse to giving the reporter an earful down the line.

Alan Oliver's article appeared in the *Chronicle* that afternoon. They were the only ones who published it. Every Newcastle manager has had problems with the local press. Keegan, Dalglish, Gullit all suffered. If the chairman had made a small gaffe like that, it wouldn't have seen the light of day. His influence would have carried the day inside the paper's office. I do not know whether he tried to stop it but once the *Chronicle* carried the story, everyone else followed it up and it became a huge local talking point.

There were echoes of the Nobby Solano affair, when I had to defend the decision to sell him to Aston Villa all by myself. The only saving grace was that many of the supporters who had stayed behind to applaud the team wrote to me to express their disappointment with those who had left the ground before the lap of honour. They felt the team had been abandoned at a point when we were still in with a shout of finishing fourth.

I rang Alan Oliver and said, 'I'll never forget this, Alan, and I'll never forgive. As far as I'm concerned, our relationship is diminished. You were the only one.'

The sands were shifting beneath my feet. Towards the end of that season, Charlie Woods came into my office.

'Bobby, you won't believe this, but David Pleat has been on and wants to know what's up with Lee Bowyer,' he said. David was the director of football at Tottenham Hotspur.

'David Pleat's been on the phone asking what?' I replied, incredulously.

Charlie ploughed on with his story. 'David was asking whether Lee is injured or something. He said, "The reason I'm asking is that he's been offered to me."'

'The kid's worth four million,' I erupted. 'Who's offered him to Spurs?'

Charlie had the answer – 'The chairman.'

Freddy Shepherd had apparently rung David Giess, Bowyer's agent, saying, 'Get him out of this club. I want him out. I'm not paying his salary,' and so on and so on. He hadn't come to me for my opinion or asked, 'Are you happy with Bowyer?' I realised Bowyer wasn't playing very well and so did the chairman, but his response was to take the law into his own hands.

So what did the agent do? Naturally, he rang round clubs asking whether they might want Lee Bowyer. Tottenham and David Pleat were on his list. David's response, of course, was, 'We can have Bowyer for nothing? That's nice,' and he phoned Charlie Woods, doing his homework. This was on the Tuesday or Wednesday, at a time when I was considering playing Bowyer on the Saturday.

'Go and get Bowyer and bring him in,' I told Charlie. A few moments later Bowyer appeared in my office.

'How do you feel?' I asked.

'Pretty low,' he replied.

'I've just been told that my chairman has offered you to Spurs,' I told him. 'What do you know about it?'

'I assumed it was your decision,' Lee said.

So I told Lee the story of how David Pleat had rung Charlie, and finished with a promise.

'I'm telling you that I know nothing about it,' I said. 'I understand you haven't played very well, son, and that it has not gone as well for you here as you would have liked, but for the chairman suddenly to decide he wants you out, without discussing it with me, is out of order, and I'm not having it. It wasn't my decision to try to sell you. In fact, the reason I brought you in here was to tell you I'm thinking about playing you on Saturday.'

If I had picked Lee for the Saturday match without knowing what the chairman had done, he might have ended up loping about the pitch, thinking, 'What difference does it make, the manager wants me out anyway.' My relationship with Bowyer would have been destroyed. I never told the chairman I knew he had tried to sell Lee behind my back. On the day I was dismissed, Freddy Shepherd still didn't know I knew.

Despite all the aftershocks from Marseille, two days later, on 8 May, twenty-four hours before we drew 1–1 with Wolves, the chairman had been in my office expressing strong support. In my diary, I noted: 'Wants me to stay for at least another year.' He had said, 'Look, I'm an honourable man. Whatever happens, you've got at least another year.' That's how I remember what he said and I wrote: 'What are the ramifications of that? He's showing strong support for me, at the moment.'

'Oh well,' I thought, 'if I do well, I've got a chance to stay on beyond the summer of 2005,' but on 20 May, after a meeting, a much darker entry appeared in my journal: 'Told I will not be here beyond next season.' What Freddy Shepherd said that day was, 'This is your last year, Bobby, you're going, and Charlie Woods will be going, too.' Something had changed in those twelve days.

During that period, we had drawn three matches, against Wolves, Southampton and Liverpool and, ironically, had risen from sixth place to finish fifth. On the final day of the season, 15 May, we had to hold off Aston Villa. They were playing Manchester United while we travelled to Anfield to face Liverpool. It was still possible for Villa to deprive us of fifth place and, with it, the UEFA Cup place. Manchester United were guaranteed third place, regardless of the result at Villa Park, so I rang Alex Ferguson and joked, 'Alex, I hope you're fielding a full-strength team tomorrow.'

'Don't you worry about us,' Alex replied. 'We're Manchester United. We play to win, whatever the circumstances. I can't field a weakened side. Tell your players that if they do their bit, I'll do mine. I'm going for a win at Villa Park, as I always do.'

'Thanks very much,' I said, and passed the details of our conversation on to the players. 'Manchester United will play to win. Now that's what we have to do,' I told them. The cost of the call was money well spent. At once my players dropped the mistaken belief that United would be half-hearted against Aston Villa. They won 2–0 and we led 1–0 at half-time, before

Michael Owen equalised on sixty-seven minutes. For Liverpool, Steven Gerrard was outstanding. Midway through the second half, he hit a cracking thirty-five-yard pass right through the middle of our two centre-halves and Owen, spinning, nipped in behind and equalised with a one-touch finish. It was a great goal. Gerard Houllier, the Liverpool manager, and I were both on our feet.

'Gerard,' I called over, 'why don't you take the boy Gerrard off? He's murdering us.'

'I can't do that,' Gerard called back.

'Yes you can,' I said. 'You've already qualified for the Champions League. If we get a point today, we finish fifth and qualify for Europe.' I was joking, of course. We held on for the point.

Taking the Marseille game into account, the trip to Liverpool was our fifth game in fifteen days and four of those were away from home. No wonder we became a bit 'leggy' in the final twenty minutes at Anfield.

Plainly, the club were hugely disappointed not to have qualified for the following season's Champions League but, by May, Liverpool had become pretty much unassailable in fourth place. A UEFA Cup adventure is very enjoyable but it's not like going to Bayern Munich, Juventus and Real Madrid. Nevertheless, I still felt that to qualify for Europe for the third year in succession was highly creditable. When I joined Newcastle in September 1999, playing in Europe was beyond the club's wildest dreams. We had been on the precipice of going into Division One. I consider it a feat to have made it into Europe in years three, four and five of my time as manager.

To ascend from the bottom of the Premiership to mid-table safety is comparatively easy. It's the next bit that's hard, just as the final third of Everest is the most taxing part of the climb. The teams in fourth, fifth and sixth are confronted each year by the formidable barriers of Arsenal, Chelsea and Manchester

United. Each time you improve the squad, make refinements, take the club forward another few steps, those three rivals are doing the same. The big three don't stand still to admire the view, not for a second. They will add a piece to the jigsaw when they need to. Jose Antonio Reyes moving to Arsenal is an example. So to go from fourth to first is immensely difficult.

A curious feature of our season was that we won just twice away from home in nineteen attempts and drew twelve times. For the ten months of the campaign, we analysed this discrepancy endlessly. Five or six times we conceded goals in the last three minutes of play, which cost us two points each time. I remember Alan Shearer coming in after one of those games, sick to his bones, saying something like, 'I don't know, it must be the discipline at this club. We're losing winning positions right at the end, and people are getting in scrapes off the pitch as well.' He was highly agitated, frustrated.

'You're right, Alan, I agree with you,' I said. Alan is a married man, highly respectable. Like me, Gary Speed and others, he was embarrassed about some of the headlines we had attracted in 2003–04. 'Go home, behave yourself man, you can't behave like that,' was our message to the troublemakers. The game has changed so much since I was at Fulham and West Bromwich Albion. Then, we didn't have the money to buy flash cars and champagne. If a top Premiership player is presented with a £500 bill for pink champagne these days, he'll hardly notice what he's signing. If it's £45 a bottle, who cares? I didn't have spies in the city, but the chairman was always well informed if a player was seen out indulging himself in the clubs or bars of the town. My message, consistently expressed, was that there is no substitute for self-discipline. However much I laid down the law, it was up to them to control their own behaviour.

I gave them an example. 'The club rule is no mobile phones in the dressing room. As manager, I'm not in the dressing room the whole time, so I can't always be there to ensure the club rule's not broken, but I know that some of you are using your phones in the dressing room. If you see a team-mate doing that, you need to say to him, "Hey, that's against the rules, put that phone away." Why don't you create your own discipline, from within?'

While I tried to counter-balance the disappointment about our fifth-place finish with a measure of realism – as well as optimism for the season ahead – the rest of football got on with praising the 'Invincibles' of Arsenal for going through a whole league season unbeaten. Respect, admiration, wonderment – those three words sum up my feelings for Arsene Wenger and his team. It was an incredible feat to play thirty-eight Premiership games undefeated.

Some days, you're simply not at your best and those are the times when defeat creeps up on you, sometimes by the most slender margin. I've lost matches where we have been comfortably the better side. Arsenal seemed to avoid that scenario. A key factor was the avoidance of mistakes in defence. Their goalkeeper, Jens Lehmann, was capable but not the best in the League, which tells you how good the four defenders in front of him must have been. A lot of Arsenal's success was due to strong, disciplined, defensive attitudes, not just along the back four, who were expert at recognising danger, but also from the two in central midfield, the two pistons. This pair would compensate for the fact that Pires and Bergkamp seldom chase back to regain possession. Up front, the Gunners possessed a lot of pace and artistry, plus penetration through the middle. They had willpower. They had everything.

Not long after Arsenal won the League, Jose Mourinho answered the call from Roman Abramovich, the Russian billionaire, and replaced Claudio Ranieri as Chelsea manager. I called him to see whether he would like to meet and one night, at my house in London, after the Chelsea deal was confirmed, I opened my front door to find Jose with two Portuguese members of his coaching staff.

'You have two guys on your staff, Mick McGiven and Steve Clarke, who are good, honest people,' I told Jose that night at my house, 'dead straight, and they don't want your job. They're there to help you. They wouldn't get your job anyway, so you don't need to fear them. Steve and Mick are very nice people.'

Secretly, I was slightly afraid for Jose because he was coming into an environment he knew little about. English football is an idiosyncratic world in which every game amounts to an avalanche of pressure. That's simply not true of the Portuguese league, where Jose's Porto might be facing Estoril or Academica. The questions raced across my mind – will the players take to him, what will the press think, will he settle down? Results are the only real criterion, of course, and results certainly went Jose's way. I had no need to feel protective. My fear was misplaced.

20

UNDERMINED

O N THE EVE of what turned out to be my final month as Newcastle manager, Freddy Shepherd was asked by a football writer whether there was any chance of me staying on beyond the summer of 2005. His answer had all the shocking clarity of a bullet being fired. 'No,' he told the *Guardian*'s Michael Walker, and in that moment I became, in the eyes of some, a sitting target.

Sir Alex Ferguson had taught us all about the dangers of announcing an impending retirement too far in advance. The message it sends to the players, the staff and the supporters is that the boss is on his way out. Alex later reversed his decision to stand down and immediately began regaining his authority, which, some felt, had slipped in the weeks and months when Manchester United's players were starting to look beyond him to the future.

My chairman's declaration was published on 31 July – a fortnight before our opening game of the season. If I were still the Newcastle manager at seventy-three years old, Freddy Shepherd had joked, the club 'would be in the *Guinness Book of Records*'. He also took a swipe at my transfer record.

'Bob's spent about seventy million pounds,' he said, 'and that's more than Wenger. We have always backed the manager. We have been big spenders but now we have got to make sure we get value for money – that's a nice way of putting it. Carl Cort didn't make it, Hugo Viana didn't make it, Christian Bassedas, the Argentine midfielder bought in the 2000–01 season, didn't make it. There comes a point where you say, "That's enough. We must have value for money." Were not going to be anyone's mugs any more.'

This brutal and, I believe, wholly inaccurate summation of my record knocked my legs away. He didn't mention the tens of millions of pounds I had brought in through sales. I wonder why he chose that moment, that point in the calendar, to confirm my departure. When I read his comments, I just wished he hadn't said those things. With one cold word – a single 'no' – he let the players know I would be gone in ten months. That was bound to diminish my authority. Naturally, I challenged the chairman.

'Look,' I said, 'I understand you telling me I'm in my last season here, but my understanding was that we would make some sort of announcement when my departure was imminent. We would do it together. We'd do it properly, make a joint statement,' but we didn't do it that way. The chairman merely belittled my position.

I had deluded myself into thinking I would be asked to help with the succession. When the time was right, I could have helped the chairman choose the next Newcastle manager. That was my vision and I had told him so. 'When the time comes for me to leave, I'll leave, don't worry about that,' I said, 'but before I do, I'll help you find the next guy to keep this great club going.'

My own attitude to retirement was that I would go only when my legs, heart and mind were not working simultaneously, when I could no longer get round the pitch or face the battle. I was still rising at ten past seven each morning and could hardly wait to get to the training ground. I was fine. I still had the need to work with players and be at the football on Saturday afternoons.

In retrospect, I can see that the political tides were turning against me from the moment the chairman told me on 20 May, in confidence I wrongly assumed, that this would be my last campaign. On 13 May, Charlie Woods, Gordon Milne, Russell Cushing and I had met with the chairman, and I had presented a list of ten major issues I felt we needed to discuss – incoming players, outgoing players, the pre-season programme, that sort of thing. I tried to persuade him to invest in a system called Prozone, which was going to cost £120,000 for two seasons. Many other top clubs had this invaluable device for dissecting individual performances and technical nuances. He was not keen. His mood was hostile. He called the season 'unsatisfactory'. I tried to stay calm and stick up for my players.

'Any other business?' the chairman asked at the end.

'Yes, extra money for my staff,' I responded.

I've never been one to look only at my own financial position. I've always tried to fight the corner for my colleagues. In the summer of 2003 I asked the club for £10,000 for each of my technical staff – making £100,000 in all – and repeated that request twelve months later. 'Without them, this club can't run,' I pointed out. I'm still waiting for the reply. Also on my list of concerns that day was the fact that the chairman had taken a table at the Football Writers' Association dinner but not invited me.

On 24 May we met once more. This time the chairman seemed reluctant to wade too far into the transfer market. On my shopping list were a full-back, a striker and a centre-half. I also liked the look of a young lad who was making a name for himself in Yorkshire.

'James Milner? He's the crown jewels at Leeds, we won't get him,' the chairman grumbled. 'And don't talk to me about Stephen Carr, the Tottenham Hotspur right-back, because he's not available. They've told me he won't be allowed to leave.'

We bought both players during the summer, Milner for £3.6 million and Stephen Carr for £2 million.

'Alan Smith,' I announced. 'I need a striker. Alan Smith would be a good option for us.' By then Mpenza had become unavailable. Unbeknown to me, during that discussion, Douglas Hall was upstairs, yet the chairman did not mention his presence to me, and Douglas made no attempt to come down from the fifth floor to the fourth to say hello. I found out later that he was at St James' Park all that day.

Alan Shearer was still on several shopping lists. Celtic and Blackburn Rovers both expressed an interest in snatching him off us that summer. What I said to Graeme Souness at Blackburn and Martin O'Neill at Celtic was, 'Look, we went through this last season with Liverpool. We feel we'd be selling the Tyne Bridge. The public would go crackers. More importantly, Alan is going to finish his top-flight career with Newcastle. If you wanted to speak to him after that, then fine, he may listen to you, but for the moment, he's going nowhere.'

Bolton Wanderers provided me with a moment of light relief when one of Sam Allardyce's assistants made what I considered to be an illegal approach for Alan. One afternoon, my mobile answer machine rang me with a message. It was our friend from Bolton, who had mixed up my number with Alan's, and was leaving a flirtatious message on my mobile in the mistaken belief that he was actually speaking into Alan's. His purpose was to fix up a meeting with our captain. I've no doubt whatsoever that he was trying to tap-up Alan behind our backs but what a cock-up on his part. He should be more careful whom he dials.

Bolton did manage to poach Gary Speed from us, however, and therein lies another tale of how disjointed the manager–chairman relationship had become. On our tour to the Far East, John Carver suddenly informed me, 'We've had an offer for Gary Speed from Bolton.' I knew nothing about it, so I went in search of the chairman for clarification. On no account did I want Gary Speed to leave. First I caught up with the player himself.

'Gary, what's all this about you wanting to go to Bolton

Wanderers? I know nothing about it. The chairman hasn't mentioned it to me. When John Carver told me an hour ago I was aghast. What do you want to go to Bolton for?'

'The club are going to let me go,' Gary said. 'If you don't know anything about it, you'd better see the chairman.'

'As far as I'm concerned, you're not going to Bolton Wanderers,' I told him. 'You're staying here.'

That Saturday night, the day of our game, I tried the chairman's room, reception, the restaurant and the bar. Eventually, I was told he was out. I was so angry I sat in the foyer, waiting, for half an hour. Finally, the chairman's figure appeared in the doorway and I confronted him there and then. Under cross-examination he denied all knowledge of Gary's impending move.

It was heading into the realms of farce. The next step, naturally, was to go back to Gary. I spoke to him on our flight from Hong Kong. 'The chairman says he knows nothing about this Bolton thing,' I said and left it there. We arrived back in Newcastle on the Monday morning and, early that afternoon, the chairman called me.

'Gary Speed's in here with me, he wants to see you. He wants to say goodbye,' he said.

'What?' I exclaimed.

The deal had been completed that morning. Fifty years in the game have taught me that you cannot construct a transfer in four hours. The idea that a player of Gary Speed's calibre can be sold in four hours is absurd and yet I was being told throughout the weekend that the club knew nothing of Bolton's interest in one of our most valued players.

'Gary, this is not my doing,' I told him. 'I want to keep you.'

Having let Hugo Viana go back to Portugal, to play more football, we had lost two left-footed midfielders. I needed to plug that hole and so, when my indignation had subsided, I gave the chairman four names – Nicky Butt, Michael Carrick, Mark

Van Bommel and Sean Davis. 'Why don't you bring Carrick in, he's talented, and he's a Geordie,' I suggested but the chairman was reluctant to pay West Ham £3 million for Carrick's services. His view was that he could acquire him for £500,000 in the January transfer window. Freddy Shepherd honestly believed that Carrick would not move to any Premier League club but Newcastle. He was in the last year of his contract at Upton Park – hence Freddy's belief that West Ham would have to unload him for a reduced sum in January. I told him, 'Look, chairman, if another club comes in and pays West Ham the money they're looking for, they will not turn that money down.' Michael Carrick signed for Tottenham Hotspur that summer.

In the meantime, we urgently needed a replacement midfielder, and Butt and Van Bommel both scored highly on my list. It was imperative that we replace Gary Speed with someone mature, experienced, educated, someone who could handle the big time. So that led us to Nicky Butt.

Kieron Dyer offered a glowing opinion. 'Boss, I like him. He's tough and a good passer. He'll go to one club only from Manchester United and that's Newcastle,' Dyer insisted. Two years earlier, Butt had been terrific for England at the World Cup. I asked Alex Ferguson about him, only to be told that Alex would expect to receive £5 million before letting him go. 'I'll pass it on to the chairman,' I told Alex. The chairman was especially keen on Butt, but not at £5 million. At twenty-six he would have been worth the price but not at twenty-nine or thirty. The beauty of Nicky Butt was that he was more defensively minded than the other midfielders I had. He could lurk in defensive positions while Dyer, Bowyer, Jenas and the others marauded.

Laurent Robert could be a tree or he could be a weed. We never knew what to expect with Laurent, so we bought Milner to make that left-sided position more competitive. He was bought for the long term. I had watched him the previous year, playing for Leeds, and he had shown enough flashes of ability to make me think he would develop into a very good player.

Despite the chairman's comments to the *Guardian*, we still liked Hugo Viana. I saw one paper describe him as a flop. He wasn't a flop. If he was, why did we re-engage him on another year's contract, to come into effect when he returned from Sporting Lisbon, where we allowed him to go on loan?

Then there was Patrick Kluivert. That season, I knew I was going to have to rest Alan Shearer at some point. Plainly, I had nothing against Alan but I had to deal in facts. There comes a time when even the greatest players can no longer perform at the very highest level. I knew we were going to face that possibility with Alan and I recall saying one day to the chairman, 'Supposing you sack me, or I retire tomorrow, the biggest problem the next manager is going to have is resting Alan Shearer, if he feels he has to. How is a young manager going to do that? I will because I've got the bottle, but could a young manager do it?' His teamsheet would amount to a suicide note.

If the need arose, I knew how I was going to handle the discussion. I was going to ask Alan a question, man to man – 'Would Alan Shearer the manager now pick Alan Shearer the player for every game? Knowing the alternatives – Kluivert, Ameobi, Bellamy, Dyer – would you pick Alan Shearer every single time?'

The day I replaced Alan in a pre-season friendly against Celtic that summer, he expressed real displeasure. He was not abusive or even impolite. He was just unhappy. As he left the field, he remarked, 'So you don't want me to play ninety minutes any more, do you not?'

'Alan, sit down,' I replied, 'there are other players in the team.' If he's going to be a manager, and a player comes off and says what he said to me that day, how will he respond?

We paid no money for Kluivert, although his wages, I gather, were exceptionally high. I did all my homework on him, phoning the people who would know whether he represented a sound investment. Jose Mourinho was among those I spoke to. When it came to selling ourselves to the player, I told him, 'Patrick, you will love it here. It's a vibrant city, a football city. It's made for you. You've got to get yourself back to where you were. You've got to forget about Barcelona. You've got to forget about nightlife. You're at a critical age. You're twenty-eight and this is your last big move. Fail here and you will fail everywhere. If you don't succeed at Newcastle, you're finished.'

He got my message, I think. He is intelligent and I took to him. His talent was never in doubt, and he was six years younger than Shearer. Curiously he had never had a serious injury. He was a good professional in the dressing room. Against Aston Villa, when we were 2–1 up at half-time, Patrick urged his team-mates, 'Come on, lads, we're in a good position here. Let's not throw it away. We need this victory.' A manager can deliver that message himself but it's reassuring to hear a player with real authority take it upon himself to make such a positive announcement. Shearer and Speed often did it.

During the season that the directors had all been so aggrieved about, we had played twelve games in Europe, all of them televised. We had finished fifth and qualified for Europe for the third consecutive year. In a bad year, so called, we were still able to bring in Milner, Carr, Nicky Butt for £2.5 million and Patrick Kluivert on a free transfer.

Aside from Euro 2004, in Portugal, where I went as a commentator for ITV, I went to the training ground every day that summer. The chairman gave me permission to take my annual holiday during the European Championship, where, I felt, I was going to be able to see all the top European players in one go. We set up shop at a hotel on the Expo site in Lisbon, where Terry Venables, Des Lynam, Ally McCoist, Peter Reid, Mick

McCarthy, Gazza, Gary Lineker, Alan Hansen, Mark Lawrenson and I generated plenty of camaraderie. I also bumped into Arsene Wenger, Gerard Houllier and Alex Ferguson, who joined me for a charity golf day.

I liked the Czech Republic a very great deal. For them, Pavel Nedved was outstanding. The day he went out of the match after twenty minutes was the day their hopes expired. How Greece won that championship, I'll never know. Somehow they managed to beat France, the Czech Republic and Portugal, twice, through sheer organisation – incredible. I thought England's performance overall was no better than average. I base that assessment on the fact that we couldn't retain possession. To get the ball forward and behind defenders requires great skill, but you can't always achieve it with one pass, which is often what we tried to do. Many of our match-winning players were quiet for long periods – Gerrard, Scholes, Owen, Beckham. As a coach, you rely on those players in big tournaments.

The exception was Wayne Rooney. His hold-up play, his vision, passing and finishing were all first-rate. Some of his play was that of a twenty-seven year old, ten years above his actual age. Charlie Woods had told me two years earlier about this exceptional kid at Everton, but warned me that it was going to be impossible to extricate him from Goodison Park. In Portugal, he demonstrated Paul Gascoigne's brand of confidence and precocity. He was afraid of nothing – a totally natural player with a man's build and awesome power and maturity for someone so young. He reminds me of one of those starlets Argentina are so good at producing, Maradona most obviously. These guys had strength, pace and self-confidence, and almost a dismissive attitude to the opponent.

I couldn't have known it then, but Rooney was to feature in one of the great Newcastle transfer dramas. It started with Jonathan Woodgate, our classy but injury-prone centre-half. As the new season approached, we decided that Woodgate's latest injury needed more attention and elected to send him to Germany to see a specialist for an exhaustive two-day examination. One Wednesday afternoon, after training, I took a call from the chairman.

'I've had an offer for Woodgate,' he said. 'It's fifteen million. What do you think?' Wow! I tried to assemble my thoughts.

'Well, it's a lot of money, I appreciate that. I also appreciate that he's not fit and not playing,' I said. 'But it's equally true that you can't replace a player of his quality. I can't see one out there.' I liked Jonathan a lot. His attitude was first class. He was one of the players I enjoyed seeing walk into the training ground. The chairman and I discussed his injury record at length. Maybe a change of club, a change of environment, a change of training routine might help him overcome his persistent physical problems.

'Tell you what,' I said to the chairman, 'I'll think about it.'

'How about this, then,' he responded. 'Would you let me buy Rooney?' Those were his exact words. 'Would you let me buy Rooney?'

'Rooney? You won't get Rooney, chairman. He'll cost you twenty-eight million and we haven't got that kind of money.'

'No, but I might get him for twenty million,' he replied. 'If we got fifteen million for Woodgate we would only need another five.'

'Chairman, I would never stop you buying Rooney. He's the best young player in Europe. I've just seen him prove it at Euro 2004. He was sensational. The best thing about buying him would be that he's young. He's long-term. It would be great for the long-term future of Newcastle United. But I should point out that I've already got Shearer, Bellamy, Kluivert and Ameobi. Rooney would make five strikers.'

'That's your problem,' the chairman said.

'Yes, I know, and I can handle it.'

Despite my assurances to the chairman, it remained true that five into two just didn't go. The club were hardly likely to pay £20 million for Rooney and then leave him on the bench. So my four existing strikers would have been competing for just one place. That might mean Alan Shearer dropping out of the team some days, because I was always a big fan of Bellamy, but before we went down that road, I wanted to be sure we could afford a centre-half to replace Woodgate.

'Can we have Rooney and get a defender as well?' I pressed the chairman.

'Yes you can,' he said. Sometimes he was straight as a die and very helpful. I have to say that. Those were the times that kept me going.

In the short-run I felt we would be all right because we had Andy O'Brien, Aaron Hughes and Titus Bramble at centre-half. As long as we brought a full-back in, Hughes could go to centre-back – hence the importance of signing Carr, whom I admired very much. He was a good footballer with good strategic sense. If my chairman was offering to get me Wayne Rooney, I was hardly likely to say no. I love strikers. I'm like Alex Ferguson in that respect. I once sat with him in my office, talking about this and that, when Alex said to me, 'I just love strikers, you know, Bobby.'

'So do I,' I said, with some justification. I've coached Ronaldo, Romario, van Nistelrooy, Lineker, Beardsley, Shearer, Mariner. I've always had great strikers around me.

'I always like to have four top strikers at my club,' Alex went on.

'So do I,' I chimed.

These were potentially momentous days but the news was seeping out through the normal routes. Selling Woodgate was bound to inflame public opinion, so the chairman went on the front foot with a now famous declaration: 'Next week, the club will make a signing that will rock the world of football.' On the Friday afternoon, I tuned in to Sky TV to see Alan Oliver talking about Newcastle's bid for Wayne Rooney. It certainly wasn't me who leaked that juicy piece of information.

'The public will be gobsmacked,' declared Alan, which left me wondering how on earth Alan Oliver knew who was coming next to Newcastle? Under media questioning I kept my mouth shut. I had no intention of discussing our possible transfer activities in public.

Meanwhile, I needed a new centre-half and I knew how difficult it was going to be to find a replacement of Woodgate's calibre. Arsenal's Sol Campbell? Ledley King from Spurs? Rio Ferdinand? Hardly. I quite liked Anthony Gardner, another Tottenham centre-half, but I made no headway in pursuit of him; nor could I have persuaded Middlesbrough to part with Gareth Southgate, who had just signed a new contract. The élite centre-halves were proving impossible to buy.

Off stage, there were other rumblings. When Newcastle were linked with Rooney, Manchester United received the shock of their lives. They had to take seriously the possibility that Rooney would move to Newcastle instead of Old Trafford, where most experts assumed he would end up. My understanding is that Manchester United had no intention of buying Rooney quite yet, although they were sure they would be able to acquire him when it suited them. Suddenly they rushed to the table and the price shot up to £25 million plus, which gave our chairman something of an image problem, as the Proactive agency, who handled Rooney, were also close associates of our club. Freddy Shepherd's son, Kenny, works for Proactive. Football has become more and more of a family affair these days. When we signed Patrick Kluivert, for example, I went to the boardroom to discover Douglas Hall's seventeen-year-old son, John, who is a nice lad, playing a minor role in the ceremony.

Our season began on Saturday, 14 August with a short trip to Middlesbrough. Sad to say, the start to my sixth Premiership campaign was preceded by an outbreak of conjunctivitis and a one-man mutiny by Kieron Dyer. The conjunctivitis was evil. At the training ground, the dressing rooms and restaurants were ruled out of bounds as we tried to stem the spread of the condition, which causes a nasty inflammation of the eyes. Lee Bowyer was one prominent victim. At the same time, Darren Ambrose was out injured. I took the decision to take the most experienced midfield I could summon to the Riverside Stadium to face Steve McClaren's team. That meant fielding Dyer on the right, JJ and Butt in the centre and Laurent Robert on the left. In training for the game, Dyer played in the wide right position and was poor. At home that evening, I received a voicemail message from him: 'Boss, can you ring me? I don't want to play wide right in the game against Middlesbrough.'

I didn't ring Kieron back. The next morning I waited for a knock on the door that never came. Finally, I went looking for him. In essence, he refused to play in the position I had chosen for him. 'I can't do well there, it's not my best position,' was the gist of what he said. I tried to reassure him. Part of the reason I allowed Nobby Solano to leave was that Dyer had performed well wide on the right. He's quick. He can go past people. His final ball wasn't as good as Solano's but he was adept at getting behind defenders. If he put his mind to it, Kieron Dyer could play anywhere except left-back and centre-half. He was adamant, though.

'Are you refusing to play?' I asked. 'Are you telling me that if Sven-Goran Eriksson picks you to play outside-right for England next Wednesday, you're going to refuse to play for your country?'

He couldn't answer that one. He hadn't thought that far.

'Right, I can do one of three things,' I said. 'I can suspend you and fine you for refusing to play. Or I can make you play. Or I can put you on the bench and use you wherever I need to, which may be at outside-right. I'm going to choose the last one. You're sub and you will come on wherever I tell you to come on. I could fine you two weeks' wages but the reason I'm not going to do that is that I don't want a disciplinary issue overshadowing the opening Saturday of the season.'

I knew what the public would have said: 'Oh, here we go, another nightmare at Newcastle, another case of indiscipline.' I didn't want that. It wouldn't have been right for our club or our supporters. So I chose to say nothing outside our private conversation, not even to the chairman, who, in fairness to him, had given me a free hand to manage the players as I saw fit. I protected Kieron Dyer and I protected the club, but what did he do? The news leaked out but not through me. There I was putting my job on the line to protect the club while Dyer was disclosing the details of our confrontation.

In the game, finally, I started with James Milner, who was eighteen years of age, in Dyer's place, and Kieron eventually came on at outside-right. We drew 2–2, after conceding a goal from the last pass of the match with ten seconds to go.

The next morning – the Sunday – Kieron sent me a text message: 'Boss, will you tell Sven my head's not right, I don't want to be picked for England.' Needless to say, I didn't accede to that request. Sven picked his England squad that evening and Dyer was included. In all my time managing him, Dyer didn't quite do anything to warrant us putting him on the transfer list but there was always a feeling that if a big club came in for him offering serious money, we would have been tempted to sell. At times he was scintillating. At times I loved him. He could run and run and burn people off. At other times, he was quiet on the field, wouldn't put his foot in, wouldn't head the ball, didn't sparkle.

After the Middlesbrough match we lost 1–0 at home to Spurs and then Norwich came to St James' Park for a Wednesday night game. We were 2–0 up but drew 2–2. First Shay Given made a rare error and then we failed to deal with a corner. After the match, Sky pounced on Craig Bellamy. If I'd known they were going to ask him about the Wayne Rooney story I would have refused the request to interview him. Craig, who had scored, was upset by the result and blurted out that he would consider his own position if Rooney came to town – more bad headlines.

In the Aston Villa game, four days later, Kluivert played instead of Alan Shearer, who was told the night before that he would be on the bench.

'Why?' Alan asked. That was always his first response to being left out. Again, I replied, 'Well, I could say it's because I'm the manager, Alan, but I won't say that.' Instead, I pointed out to him that he had started the first three games of 2004–05, against Middlesbrough, Spurs and Norwich, and that I also had Kluivert, Bellamy and Ameobi keen to contribute. I wanted to retain Bellamy's pace, while Kluivert, who scored against Aston Villa, had yet to start a Premiership match in a Newcastle kit. I wanted to see how he would get on, playing a full ninety minutes.

'You're very much involved, Alan, but I'm leaving you out today. You played last Saturday and you played on Wednesday, so you've had two games this week. This would be your third game in eight days. You've just turned thirty-four.' He took it pretty well. It was just that he wanted to play every game.

In the event, Kluivert scored a great goal but we lost 4–2 to David O'Leary's team. Those two were the last goals Newcastle scored with me as manager.

21

HELLO AND GOODBYE

RADIO silence. No response to my calls. On the Sunday after our 4–2 defeat at Aston Villa I tried, without success, to contact the chairman. It was highly unusual for him not to call me back. Still, I was neither suspicious nor even concerned by his failure to respond. I dialled his number not knowing I had less than twenty-four hours left in the job.

We were fifteen days into the new Premiership season and there were a couple of issues I needed to discuss, including the match at Villa Park and our urgent need for a new centre-half. The transfer window was about to close and I had sent Charlie Woods up to Scotland that weekend to see Jean-Alain Boumsong of Rangers and Celtic's Bobo Balde. The discussion would come soon enough, I thought, and on the August bank holiday Monday, I rose earlier than usual, setting off for the training ground to be in before nine. When my mobile phone rang, the voice of Tony Toward, one of the club's administrators, came down the line: 'Russell Cushing called and said the chairman wants to see you in his office at nine thirty this morning.'

'I've just passed the club and I'm on my way to the training ground,' I told Tony, 'but don't worry. I'll carry on to the training ground, have a cup of coffee with my staff and be at St James' by nine thirty.' Being so close to work, I thought the best plan was to get my staff together and give them their instructions for the day.

'Just keep the fires burning until I get back from meeting the chairman,' I told my coaches. 'I've just had a call. We're trying to get a centre-half in – it's probably about that. If I'm not back, make sure the players are on the training pitch by ten thirty.'

Not for one second did I entertain the possibility that the gallows were being erected for me up at the old stadium. In retrospect, there was one disquieting aspect of the chairman's summons. Why had Russell Cushing called Tony to get him to ring me? That was odd. The chief operating officer didn't have the courtesy to ring me himself to tell me the chairman wanted to see me? I assumed it was merely a failure of manners, and pulled into the club car park in a businesslike frame of mind. I strode into Freddy Shepherd's office to find Joy, his secretary, the chairman and Russell Cushing, which again was somewhat strange, given that it was a bank holiday. Even then, I was not apprehensive as I took my seat.

'Good morning, chairman,' I said, opening the batting. 'Any thoughts about the centre-half?'

Freddy Shepherd's face turned red. Then he uttered a single sentence.

'I'm relieving you of your position.'

Silence descended. No words would come.

'Why?' I said at last.

'Results.'

'Results? We've got another sixty games to go, chairman.' He handed me a letter.

'So it's a fait accompli, is it?'

More silence. My mind was reeling. Slowly, I recovered some semblance of poise. I asked him straight, 'What are we going to do about my contract?'

'Well, we'll have to honour it.' That phrase struck me hard. Not 'will' honour it, but 'will have to' honour it. I didn't like his choice of words one bit. He told me to get in touch with my solicitors. I thought it would be sorted out in a week. In the event, it dragged on through the whole season and into the summer. Although they did pay me my monthly salary, which was fine, it took all season, until June 2005, finally to settle my contract. This was despite the fact that the chairman had told John Barnwell, the head of the League Managers' Association, the previous September, 'If three Geordies can't sort this out quickly, there's something wrong with us.' If I had been sitting in Freddy Shepherd's chair that day, when he dismissed me, with all his power, all his access to the club's financial might, I would have said to the departing manager, 'We will honour your contract, and here's your cheque.'

I walked out, angry and bitter. Outside, I wanted to stride back into that room and play merry hell. Alone again, I was spitting blood. The whole five years went flashing past my eyes. The overwhelming sensation was of something precious being snatched away from me, something I had built, something good. 'Bloody hell,' I mumbled to myself. 'I've just bought Stephen Carr and young Milner. Kluivert could well turn out OK.' Patrick had played pretty well at Aston Villa. The names shot through my mind – Bellamy, JJ, young Ambrose, Shay. I'd worked hard to get us into Europe again and, after four Premiership games, I was being denied the chance to take the team back on to the Continent. It had all been grabbed away from me.

I was about to enter a period of life that I can only really describe as a kind of bereavement. Certainly grief was at the forefront of my emotions as I wrestled with the injustice of what they had done. First, though, I had some hoops to jump through, some rituals to enact. Auto-pilot took over. The next, sad step was to return to the training ground to break the news to the staff. 'What do I do, who do I ring?' I asked myself in the car but as I strode into Little Benton people were already digesting the news of my dismissal. It had been announced on television. The news had travelled faster than I could in my car. As it was international week, all international players were away with their countries and the first person I ran into was John Carver.

'John, assemble my staff, will you? Not the players, but my coaching staff.'

'I lost my job today,' I told them. 'I've just come to say hello, and goodbye. Look, John,' I finished off. 'I have to leave now. At some stage I'll get Judith [my secretary] to clear my desk. I'm afraid I haven't a clue who's coming in next. I'll come back, maybe on Friday, when all the players are back from international duty, to say goodbye to them.'

Then I called Elsie.

'You've given them your life,' Elsie said calmly. 'If that's how they treat you, you're better off out of it.'

The club released a statement, which read: 'The Directors of Newcastle United wish to place on record their thanks for the way in which Sir Bobby has worked tirelessly over the past five years to try and bring success to the club . . . The club agreed, early in 2003, to extend Sir Bobby's contract by one further season. However, after careful consideration, the club decided it was in the best interests of all concerned to re-visit that decision . . . He leaves having remodelled the Newcastle team with many young players admired and coveted across the UK and Europe. The club will no doubt continue to benefit from the knowledge and experience he has given during his time here.'

By the time I reached home, the press were camped outside my house. I sat inside, numb, not knowing which way to turn. It was a modest house, not designed for a siege. Experience told me the media would spend the rest of the day out there if they had to, so I decided to step outside and say a few words.

'Look, you've all got families, you've all got homes to go to, I don't want you to spend the next eight hours outside my house. If I do one interview, will you leave it there?' I suggested. I kept it short and simple. I was disappointed. I wished Newcastle

United success. I would always be a fan of the club. Inside, I felt convulsions of shock, indignation and loss.

The football writers, who were well-informed, touted the young Birmingham manager, Steve Bruce, as my successor, but in fact Graeme Souness was in charge for the next home game, against Blackburn Rovers, the club Graeme left to take up his new position at St James' Park. Ironically, I'd had lunch with Steve and his wife in September 2004, after my dismissal, at the Villa Sol golf resort in Portugal on the day when some newspapers were announcing that he would be seeing Freddy Shepherd that very afternoon. I told Steve that the Newcastle job was a treasure trove and talked about how vibrant the city was. Anyway, it was Graeme and not Steve who lowered himself into my chair.

As the Blackburn game approached, I faced a dilemma. As promised, I did return to the training ground on the Friday to say goodbye to my players. There were warm handshakes and a little speech from me, in which I urged them to go out and beat Blackburn the following day. In the papers on that Saturday morning, JJ made some kind remarks: 'His man-management skills were excellent. He knew how to treat everyone and had a good relationship with all the other players. There was a lot of respect between us. It will take a long time for me not to call him Gaffer.'

To go or not to go to the game? In my farewell address, on the day of my sacking, I had reflected: 'Who is to say that at the next home match I won't be among the fans? I don't know where else I might go. It's been my club since my father brought me here as a kid and I'm black and white through and through. There are no better fans in the world.' But as the hours passed I felt less and less inclined to take up a seat in the private box I had rented at the stadium. In the end, I decided that my presence might create an unhealthy distraction for the team. It was hard, but I stayed away. Graeme attended with his young son but sat in the stands while John Carver took charge of the Newcastle starting eleven and Tony Parkes stepped in as caretaker for Blackburn. The Newcastle team – the first I had not picked since September 1999 – was: Given; Carr, O'Brien, Hughes, Elliott; Bowyer, Jenas, Dyer, Robert; Shearer and Bellamy, with Harper, Kluivert, N'Zogbia, Milner and Ameobi on the bench. I felt proud to be leaving so many fine players at Graeme's disposal – proud and still deeply aggrieved.

In his programme notes for the match, the chairman began: 'I would like to pay a personal tribute to Sir Bobby Robson, who parted company with us twelve days ago.' He went on: 'Sir Bobby and I parted on very good terms. We have had some great times together, we remain great friends, and I'm sure there will be times in the future when I beat him again at golf.' Given the nature of my dismissal and the club's unwillingness for so long to settle my contract, I find the bonhomie in the chairman's words that day somewhat ironic.

In the same match programme, Alan Shearer wrote in his captain's column: 'We haven't had the best of starts to the season, with no win in four games, and after the Aston Villa defeat two weeks ago, it sadly came to an end for Bobby Robson, but I want to stress that it was nothing to do with Bobby leaving me out of the starting eleven at Villa Park.

'The manager came to see me at the team hotel on the Friday evening before the game. We had a good professional discussion about it and I can promise you there was certainly no argument and certainly no bust-up. I merely asked him why, and he gave me his reasons.'

Inevitably, people speculated about Alan's role, if any, in my dismissal. I want to emphasise that I have no suspicions on that account. I can see no hidden agenda on Alan's part. I simply do not believe that he used his considerable clout at the club to have me sacked. Did the players suspect that I might be dismissed after the Aston Villa game? I don't think they did. The impetus, I believe, came from Douglas Hall, whose family own 41 per cent of the club, and Freddy, whose shareholding was then around 25 per cent.

A couple of weeks after I was fired, Sir John Hall spoke out in a television interview. The gist of what he said was, 'Bobby should have been sacked after the Marseille game.' When I read subsequently, in some newspapers, that I had 'lost the dressing room', I felt incomprehension and fury. What did they mean, 'lost the dressing room'? Towards the end of my time at Newcastle, Alan Shearer stepped out on several occasions to deny that there was any discord or factionalism in the dressing room. Granted, Alan did object when the likes of Bellamy and Dyer brought the club into disrepute. He didn't like seeing Newcastle's good name being tarnished and he told those players so. What there was, perhaps, was a lack of self-discipline from a minority of young players when they were away from the club, but it was a mistake to assume that the dressing room was packed with malcontents and cliques.

When you know in your bones that gossip is simply not true but you have no recourse, no way of puncturing the myths, it hurts you to your soul. All football managers will know what I mean. It's open season. You are out-gunned. Rumours mutate into accepted fact. Everyone claims to have the inside track. It's hard enough to lose your job without also being robbed of your reputation.

In the days that followed, I was wounded very deeply by the columns and articles suggesting that Graeme Souness had been hired to restore discipline. The implication was that I had failed to control a group of supposedly playboy players and had allowed them to run amok. In fact, there was no problem with discipline inside the club, no problem with punctuality, or behaviour on the training pitch, at airports, hotels and restaurants.

All the rules were laid down. For heaven's sake, I've been all over the world coaching millionaire players, so I know how important it is to impose standards of behaviour. If you have no control, it's simply a mess, and you can't survive in football management without control.

I was on at our players constantly about their behaviour. For example, if they transgressed the seventy-two-hour ban on going out before a match, they were fined. All the little mishaps with Kieron Dyer came at times when, legally and contractually, he was allowed to be out and about – usually a Saturday or Sunday night, sometimes a Monday, but not three days before a match.

A few weeks after I lost my job, I heard that Patrick Kluivert had been upset about losing an earring in training. Under me, Patrick wouldn't have lost it because he wouldn't have been allowed on the pitch wearing an earring in the first place. I resented the suggestion that Graeme was a sergeant major while I was an old officer easily deceived by mischievous lads. Besides, Graeme would be the first to concede that Liverpool, in his heyday as a player, was no place for monks and teetotallers. Those guys lived the life. A change of manager did not prevent Patrick Kluivert being seen leaving a nightclub in the early hours of the morning.

In the wake of my dismissal, many people rang me to commiserate, including Sven-Goran Eriksson, Alex Ferguson, Jose Mourinho, Paul Gascoigne – and Kieron Dyer. Arsene Wenger phoned a few weeks later to see how I was and to wish me well. In addition, I received 800 letters of support, including one from the Prime Minister. When I lost my job, six other people lost theirs as well – John Carver, Charlie Woods, David Geddis, Kenny Wharton, Gordon Milne and Simon Smith, the goalkeeping coach. Backroom staff are the unseen victims of a managerial change. I wish mine well and am sorry that all their hard work could not save them from the fate that befell me.

As I took stock, my instinct was to find work with another club, quickly. Even after the scarring experience of being hustled out of Newcastle, I felt the old urge to be on a training ground in my tracksuit, coaching players. I met the chairman of Sheffield Wednesday, Dave Allen, who was a nice man, but knew within ten minutes that a job at Hillsborough was not for me. Clear interest also came from Wolves before they appointed Glenn Hoddle on a six-month contract, but however strong my yearning to be back in the game, I was locked in a legal struggle with my former employers and it turned out not to be feasible for me to accept a new job while they were still refusing to settle my contract. I was stuck in no man's land.

I did manage one brief return to the dug-out – at St James' Park, ironically – for a Legends versus Celebrities match on Sky TV. When I lost the Newcastle job, I had withdrawn from the project – a 'Big Brother' style affair, based at the club's training ground, where a camera was to be fitted in every room – but the organisers wrote to me begging me to step back in. They had spent £250,000 on advertising and my name had featured heavily. Two children's charities were involved, so reluctantly I returned to the show.

Ulrika Jonsson and Neil Durden-Smith were the presenters. Our academy was converted into a hotel. Graham Taylor, Luther Blissett, a doctor and a psychologist all tried to lick the celebrities into shape. They were amateurs who loved a kickabout. By the end of the week, after twelve coaching sessions, Graham had turned them into a team with some purpose. They were young and could run. The issue was how and where they ran.

It was not explained to me that there would be a civic ceremony for me at the end of the match; nor did I know about the documentary Sky had made, which featured Arsene Wenger saying some complimentary things about me. At the end of the game, while the lads went up to get their medals, I stood on the pitch-side with my staff, and was on the verge of returning to the dressing room when an official urged me not to leave.

'Hang on, there are another couple of ceremonies yet, Mr Robson,' he said.

As applause rippled round the stadium I heard my name over the PA. Before I knew it I was being ushered up the steps to meet the Mayor of Newcastle, who was holding a ceremonial sword, which, I soon discovered, was for me. It was a symbolic gift from the Mayor. By the time I reached the top steps, Alan Shearer and the chairman, who had been sitting in the vicinity, had disappeared. I discovered later that Alan had merely retreated six or seven rows. I said a few words to Ant and Dec, who were holding the microphones, collected my sword and went back down the steps to rejoin the throng.

At a reception for all the players, the first person I saw was Alan. As we exchanged pleasantries, some newspapers were gearing up to present the 'disappearance' of Alan and the chairman as a 'snub'. One Sunday paper reported: 'Sir Bobby Robson was furious after being sensationally snubbed by Alan Shearer and Freddy Shepherd at St James' Park.' I spoke to Alan about this much later and he said he was hurt by the allegation that he had fled the scene. 'I was six rows back. I watched the presentation,' he told me.

A pattern was setting in. I was constantly having to rebut newspaper stories, whispers and innuendo about my time as Newcastle manager. There were numerous small attacks, and one or two major ones. The worst of them, pre-Christmas, was a renewed suggestion that Graeme had been brought in to restore discipline and order. Another upsetting skirmish followed the publication of a book, a picture-based biography by my old friend Bob Harris, with no official input from me, called *Living the Game*. That autumn, Bob's publishers released an updated version, including my 'dramatic departure from Newcastle

United', which they included in a chapter headed 'Betrayed'. To my horror, I picked up the *Sunday Telegraph* on 17 October to see the front-page headline on the sports section: 'Robson: Shearer betrayed me'.

I went berserk. I have never made that allegation against Alan, nor would I. If the new chapter was critical of Shearer, it was nothing to do with me. Now the sky really was falling in. Another indignity was queuing up behind. In the *Chronicle* on 20 October, Michael Martin, from the Newcastle fanzine *True Faith*, laid into me on the basis of what he assumed to be in Bob's book. It was a disgusting piece, inaccurate and indefensible. I found myself calling the sports editor of the *Chronicle*, and insisting, in a rage, that they print an apology and retraction, which they did.

Michael Martin started his article, which was headlined: 'Sir Bobby should keep quiet', with a real howler. 'News that Sir Bobby Robson is to release an updated version of his biography with the additional chapter "Betrayal", in which he is alleged to have blamed Freddy Shepherd and Alan Shearer for his exit from Newcastle United, is disappointing in the extreme.' I hadn't blamed anyone. I hadn't written the book. 'Some of the early sightings of the new chapter state that Robson felt Shearer should have done more to quell player indiscipline at our club,' the author went on. He was surmising, and surmising wrongly. The article was worthless, shoddy, gossip-ridden, and I duly received my apology, but yet more damage had been inflicted on my standing, my relationship with the Newcastle fans.

Busying myself with speaking engagements, media work and a house move, I stayed in regular contact with Michael Kennedy, my solicitor, and John Barnwell, who was most helpful and sympathetic, as I pressed my claim for compensation from the Newcastle board.

Christmas came and went with no cheque from the club. If I thought public hostilities had ceased, I was jolted out of that delusion in January, when Craig Bellamy's relationship with Graeme Souness broke down irrevocably. Before Newcastle played Arsenal away on 23 January, Bellamy had reportedly walked off the training ground, claiming to be injured, but also upset at being asked to play on the right-hand side of the team instead of in his favoured position through the middle.

The subsequent eruption kept the presses spinning for a week. Asked for a comment, I merely pointed out that Graeme's relationship with Bellamy had got off to a bad start with the throat-grabbing incident. Freddy Shepherd let me have both barrels. 'Graeme Souness has been unfairly blamed for what has happened in the past week, but the seeds of the Craig Bellamy situation were sown before he arrived at the club,' the chairman diagnosed, shortly before Bellamy was dispatched to Celtic on loan. 'Many of the problems Graeme is having to deal with are down to the way the previous manager handled discipline. If Sir Bobby Robson had taken a harder line, I am convinced we would not be facing this situation.'

That was outrageous. I was being made the chief culprit for Souness and Bellamy falling out five months after the club had shown me the door. It was an astonishing act of buck-passing, and I hope no one was fooled.

Even more bewildering was a claim made by Douglas Hall, in the pages of the *Sunday Mirror*. 'We had to get rid of Sir Bobby Robson because he would have got us relegated,' Douglas was quoted as saying. 'We were going down, no mistake about it.' I found this hard to square with the knowledge that we had finished fourth, third and fifth in my last three seasons in charge. I interpreted Douglas's remarks as an attempt to defend the club's decision to dismiss me in favour of Graeme. When the press asked me for a comment, I said, 'I'll let intelligent people make up their own minds about whether I would have led the team into the next division down.'

A few days later, Freddy Shepherd, to his credit, instructed Russell Cushing to call me and apologise for what Douglas had said. I appreciated that call. In the end, Newcastle finished the 2004–05 Premiership campaign in fourteenth position, nine places lower than twelve months before. If fifth place was 'unacceptable', what does that make fourteenth? A drop of nine places cost the club millions of pounds in positional money.

I watched these dramas from afar, and observed the infamous punch-up on the pitch between Lee Bowyer and Kieron Dyer in the Newcastle–Aston Villa match with great sadness. That week, the city had been rejoicing over Alan Shearer's decision to stay on for an extra season. The Newcastle supporters went from elation to dismay in twenty-four hours, and the contrast between the two press conferences was extraordinary. My attitude to Alan's retirement was that I wanted him to finish his illustrious career at the right time. If I have my doubts about his ability to maintain his own high standards for another season, I wouldn't challenge his desire to wring every drop of juice from his talent. He's been a great character for English football.

While Newcastle toiled in the table's bottom half, my old student, Jose Mourinho, was lifting the Premiership trophy with Chelsea. In successive seasons at Porto and in London, Jose won the Portuguese league, the UEFA Cup, the European Cup and finally the Premier League. What a remarkable story!

Among his many impressive qualities is an ability to handle big-name players. When I first used him on the training ground, my squad knew Jose had not played the game at a high level but he overcame that handicap. He had a way of speaking to star players authoritatively. At Barcelona I would ask him to tell Ronaldo not to play so deep, not to drift back fifty yards from the opposition's goal. Jose had the confidence to do that and he learned the vocabulary of the players.

Around the time I was stepping up my ambassadorial role with

Nobok, a new company that promotes sporting legends, a very special honour came my way. It followed – and, in many ways, surpassed – my knighthood in the Queen's Birthday Honours list in the summer of 2002, which put me in the company of Bobby Charlton, Geoff Hurst and Alex Ferguson.

On Wednesday, 2 March, I was summoned to the Banqueting Hall of the Civil Centre in Newcastle to be granted the Freedom of the City of Newcastle upon Tyne by the Lord Mayor, Councillor George Douglas. I was joined by a throng of family, friends and well-wishers for one of the proudest days of my life. I thought about my speech over many days and took great care in the choice of words. I told the audience: 'When I received my knighthood I really thought that's as good as it gets, but I have to say being granted the freedom of the city by the people of Newcastle upon Tyne has to be the proudest moment of my life and I stand here full of personal emotion and humility.'

I was joining Jackie Milburn, Alan Shearer and Jonny Wilkinson on the roll of eighty-five freemen whose names are carved on the walls of the Banqueting Hall. Alan and Gazza were in the audience. To celebrate, I rented a big room at the Copthorne Hotel, where sixty of us laughed and reminisced for five or six hours.

In the days that followed, a number of councillors wrote to me to say they had never seen so much emotion in a ceremony of that kind. Perhaps it was because I had talked about my father, and how he went down the pit white and came up black in an area where those two colours symbolise a city's love of football, a love that burns within me and will never fade.

AFTERWORD

CANCER came back to attack me a third time, in the spring of 2006, and this time my love of skiing saved my life – yes, skiing. On a boys-only trip to the slopes with my son Mark and grandson Alexander I had an accident that brought my latest malignant melanoma to light. An adventurous spirit has its uses. Mine drove me back to the snow after sixteen years of missing out on one of my favourite hobbies. Two major events have filled my time since I concluded my business with Newcastle United. The first was a new job as special advisor to Steve Staunton, the Republic of Ireland manager. The other was a third round of major surgery to remove a growth on my lung. Update that score to Me 3, Cancer 0.

As England manager, I went skiing every season for eight years but then came my travels across Europe and my skis stayed in the loft. When we headed to St Anton to do some catching up, I was rusty, I admit – hence two falls. The first one injured my calf and the second sent me crashing on to my chest. I knew I'd caused some damage. I could feel the air go out of my lungs.

Struggling along, I flew to Madrid to interview Jonathan Woodgate for a *Mail on Sunday* article and met up with Ronaldo, who was in fine shape. From there I went to watch PSV Eindhoven play Lyon in the Champions League at the invitation of my old friend Stan Valckx. My old pals in Eindhoven could see I was in pain and suggested an x-ray on my ribs, which revealed a faint shadow on my lung. The advice from the PSV physician Cees van der Hoogenband was that I should have a further x-ray when I got home.

Back in Newcastle, Dr John Mackay, who is now my personal doctor, could find no cause for alarm but rang PSV to discuss their findings, just to be sure. A full scan was arranged and, sure enough, a spot was visible on my lung. They stuck a needle through my back for the biopsy and a malignant melanoma was diagnosed. Without the skiing accident, it would have remained unnoticed.

It sounds calamitous, but a full PET scan confirmed I had no other growths, just the one on my lung. They removed a lump the size of a golf ball but there was no need for radiotherapy or chemotherapy. Mr Stephen Clarke, the surgeon, operated on me the day I was due to attend a twenty-fifth anniversary celebration of Ipswich Town's victory in the UEFA Cup. Elsie took wonderful care of me, as usual, but my God I felt ill after the operation. It took me two months to recover and I lost two stone.

With all this going on, I wasn't able to contribute fully to the Republic's win over Sweden, although I attended both that game and the defeat against Chile. It's a great job for me and I'll be back, helping Steve, as fit as a butcher's dog. I'll be strong. I'll be powerful.

It's amazing I've survived again, thanks to skiing. Thanks to falling over. Thanks to someone saying, 'Let us help you.' As we set out on that first day at St Anton, Mark had said to me, 'Dad, you're the oldest man on the slopes.'

Would I ski again? Oh, aye. I love it.

CAREER RECORD

Clubs – Player
Waterhouses School
Middlesbrough amateur schoolboy forms
Chester-le-Street
Langley Park Juniors
Fulham (May 1950)
West Bromwich Albion (March 1956, £25,000)
Fulham (August 1962, £20,000)
Vancouver Royals (Player manager May 1967–January 1968)

Clubs – Manager
Oxford University (coach, 1965–1966)
Fulham (January 1968–November 1968)
Ipswich (January 1969–July 1982)
PSV Eindhoven (July 1990–May 1992)
Sporting Lisbon (July 1992–December 1993)
FC Porto (February 1994–May 1996)
Barcelona (July 1996–May 1997, general manager to June 1998)
PSV Eindhoven (July 1998–June 1999)
Newcastle United (September 1999–September 2004)

Honours
CBE for services to football in 1990
Football Writers' Association Tribute Award for outstanding
    contribution to the national game 1992
British Sports Writers' Association Pat Besford Trophy for
    Outstanding Achievement in 2001
Knighted for services to football in 2002
Football Association Hall of Fame 2002
Freeman of the City of Newcastle-upon-Tyne 2005.

Trophies

1973: Texaco Cup (Ipswich)
1978: FA Cup (Ipswich)
1981: UEFA Cup (Ipswich)
1991 & 1992: Dutch League (PSV)
1994: Portuguese Cup (Porto)
1995 & 1996: Portuguese League (Porto)
1997: Spanish Cup, European Cup Winners' Cup (Barcelona)

Playing career: Club record

	League	Cup	Goals
Fulham			
50–51	1	0	0
51–52	16	0	3
52–53	35	1	19
53–54	33	1	14
54–55	42	1	23
55–56	25	2	10
West Bromwich Albion			
55–56	10	0	1
56–57	39	9	13
57–58	42	7	27
58–59	28	3	5
59–60	41	3	6
60–61	40	1	5
61–62	39	4	4
Fulham			
62–63	34	4	2
63–64	39	3	1
64–65	42	5	2
65–66	36	3	6
66–67	41	6	0

Playing career: International record

Caps	Year	Opponents	Venue	Competition	Score
1	1957	v France	Wembley	Friendly	W 4–0 (2 goals)
2	1958	v USSR	Moscow	Friendly	D 1–1
3		v USSR	Gothenburg	WC Finals	D 1–1
4		v Brazil	Gothenburg	WC Finals	D 0–0
5		v Austria	Boras	WC Finals	D 2–2
6	1960	v Spain	Madrid	Friendly	L 0–3
7		v Hungary	Budapest	Friendly	L 0–2
8		v N Ireland	Belfast	Home Int	W 5–2
9		v Luxembourg	Luxembourg	WCQ	W 9–0
10		v Spain	Wembley	Friendly	W 4–2
11		v Wales	Wembley	Home Int	W 5–1
12	1961	v Scotland	Wembley	Home Int	W 9–3 (1 goal)
13		v Mexico	Wembley	Friendly	W 8–0 (1 goal)
14		v Portugal	Lisbon	WCQ	D 1–1
15		v Italy	Rome	Friendly	W 3–2
16		v Luxembourg	Highbury	WCQ	W 4–1
17		v Wales	Cardiff	Home Int	D 1–1
18		v Portugal	Wembley	WCQ	W 2–0
19		v N Ireland	Wembley	Home Int	D 1–1
20	1962	v Switzerland	Wembley	Friendly	W 3–1

Also: Under-23 (1 cap), Football League representative (5 caps), B International (1 cap).

Management career: International record

		P	W	D	L	F	A	Pts	Pos
Fulham 67–68	League	18	4	3	11	24	48	11	22
	Cup	3	1	1	1	4	3		
	Overall	21	5	4	12	28	51		
Fulham 68–69	League	18	2	7	9	15	25	11	22
	Cup	1	0	0	1	0	1		
	Overall	19	2	7	10	15	26		

		P	W	D	L	F	A	Pts	Pos
Ipswich 68–69	League	16	7	6	3	21	18	41	12
	Cup	0	0	0	0	0	0		
	Overall	16	7	6	3	21	18		
Ipswich 69–70	League	42	10	11	21	40	63	31	18
	Cup	4	1	1	2	5	4		
	Overall	46	11	12	23	45	67		
Ipswich 70–71	League	42	12	10	20	42	48	34	19
	Cup	8	2	4	2	7	8		
	Overall	50	14	14	22	49	56		
Ipswich 71–72	League	42	11	16	15	39	53	38	13
	Cup	3	1	0	2	3	4		
	Overall	45	12	16	17	42	57		
Ipswich 72–73	League	42	17	14	11	55	45	48	4
	Cup	12	9	1	2	22	11		
	Overall	54	26	15	13	77	56		
Ipswich 73–74	League	42	18	11	13	67	58	47	4
	Cup	15	9	2	4	22	16		
	Overall	57	27	13	17	89	74		
Ipswich 74–75	League	42	23	5	14	66	44	51	3
	Cup	16	7	7	2	24	17		
	Overall	58	30	12	16	90	61		
Ipswich 75–76	League	42	16	14	12	54	48	46	6
	Cup	8	4	1	3	12	10		
	Overall	50	20	15	15	66	58		
Ipswich 76–77	League	42	22	8	12	66	39	56	3
	Cup	5	1	2	2	7	6		
	Overall	47	23	10	14	73	45		
Ipswich 77–78	League	42	11	13	18	47	61	35	18
	Cup	16	12	2	2	42	14		
	Overall	58	23	15	20	89	75		

		P	W	D	L	F	A	Pts	Pos
Ipswich 78–79	League	42	20	9	13	63	49	49	6
	Cup	13	6	3	4	17	14		
	Overall	55	26	12	17	80	63		
Ipswich 79–80	League	42	22	9	11	68	39	53	3
	Cup	10	5	3	2	19	7		
	Overall	52	27	12	13	87	46		
Ipswich 80–81	League	42	23	10	9	77	43	56	2
	Cup	24	14	3	7	47	24		
	Overall	66	37	13	16	124	67		
Ipswich 81–82	League	42	26	5	11	75	53	83	2
	Cup	13	7	3	3	24	18		
	Overall	55	33	8	14	99	71		
PSV 90–91	League	34	23	7	4	84	28	53	1
	Cup	4	3	0	1	13	5		
	Overall	38	26	7	5	97	33		
PSV 91–92	League	34	25	8	1	82	24	58	1
	Cup	4	1	2	1	3	4		
	Overall	38	26	10	2	85	28		
Sporting 92–93	League	34	17	11	6	59	30	45	3
	Cup	7	5	0	2	12	7		
	Overall	41	22	11	8	71	37		
Sporting 93–94	League	11	8	1	2	20	7	17	2
	Cup	7	4	1	2	10	4		
	Overall	18	12	2	4	30	11		
Porto 93–94	League	17	12	4	1	29	5	28	2
	Cup	10	6	2	2	19	6		
	Overall	27	18	6	3	48	11		
Porto 94–95	League	34	29	4	1	73	15	62	1
	Cup	11	8	0	3	26	4		
	Overall	45	37	4	4	99	19		

		P	W	D	L	F	A	Pts	Pos
Porto 95–96	League	34	26	6	2	84	20	84	1
	Cup	14	5	7	2	20	9		
	Overall	48	31	13	4	104	29		
Barcelona 96–97	League	42	28	6	8	102	48	90	2
	Cup	16	10	6	0	35	16		
	Overall	58	38	12	8	137	64		
PSV 98–99	League	34	17	10	7	87	55	61	3
	Cup	4	3	0	1	13	3		
	Overall	38	20	10	8	100	58		
Newcastle 99–00	League	32	14	9	9	55	36	51	11
	Cup	13	7	3	3	26	14		
	Overall	45	21	12	12	81	50		
Newcastle 00–01	League	38	14	9	15	44	50	51	11
	Cup	6	2	2	2	9	8		
	Overall	44	16	11	17	53	58		
Newcastle 01–02	League	38	21	8	9	74	52	71	4
	Cup	15	10	3	2	32	16		
	Overall	53	31	11	11	106	68		
Newcastle 02–03	League	38	21	6	11	63	48	69	3
	Cup	16	7	2	7	26	27		
	Overall	54	28	8	18	89	75		
Newcastle 03–04	League	38	13	17	8	52	40	56	5
	Cup	17	10	3	4	30	14		
	Overall	55	23	20	12	82	54		
Newcastle 04–05	League	4	0	2	2	6	9	2	16
	Cup	0	0	0	0	0	0		
	Overall	4	0	2	2	6	9		

Management career: International record*

Appointed July 1982, effective September 1982;
resigned following 1990 World Cup.

Game	Year	Opponents	Venue	Competition	Score
1	1982	Denmark	Copenhagen	ECQ	D 2–2
2		W Germany	Wembley	Friendly	L 1–2
3		Greece	Salonika	ECQ	W 3–0
4		Luxembourg	Wembley	ECQ	W 9–0
5	1983	Wales	Wembley	Home Int	W 2–1
6		Greece	Wembley	ECQ	D 0–0
7		Hungary	Wembley	ECQ	W 2–0
8		N Ireland	Belfast	Home Int	D 0–0
9		Scotland	Wembley	Home Int	W 2–0
10		Australia	Sydney	Friendly	D 0–0
11		Australia	Brisbane	Friendly	W 1–0
12		Australia	Melbourne	Friendly	D 1–1
13		Denmark	Wembley	ECQ	L 0–1
14		Hungary	Budapest	ECQ	W 3–0
15		Luxembourg	Luxembourg	ECQ	W 4–0
16	1984	France	Paris	Friendly	L 0–2
17		N Ireland	Wembley	Home Int	W 1–0
18		Wales	Wrexham	Home Int	L 0–1
19		Scotland	Glasgow	Home Int	D 1–1
20		USSR	Wembley	Friendly	L 0–2
21		Brazil	Rio	Friendly	W 2–0
22		Uruguay	Montevideo	Friendly	L 0–2
23		Chile	Santiago	Friendly	D 0–0
24		E Germany	Wembley	Friendly	W 1–0
25		Finland	Wembley	WCQ	W 5–0
26		Turkey	Istanbul	WCQ	W 8–0
27	1985	N Ireland	Belfast	WCQ	W 1–0
28		R Ireland	Wembley	Friendly	W 2–1
29		Romania	Bucharest	WCQ	D 0–0
30		Finland	Helsinki	WCQ	D 1–1
31		Scotland	Glasgow	Rous Cup	L 0–1

Game	Year	Opponents	Venue	Competition	Score
32		Italy	Mexico City	Mexico City T	L 1–2
33		Mexico	Mexico City	Mexico City T	L 0–1
34		W Germany	Mexico City	Mexico City T	W 3–0
35		USA	Los Angeles	Friendly	W 5–0
36		Romania	Wembley	WCQ	D 1–1
37		Turkey	Wembley	WCQ	W 5–0
38		N Ireland	Wembley	WCQ	D 0–0
39	1986	Egypt	Cairo	Friendly	W 4–0
40		Israel	Tel Aviv	Friendly	W 2–1
41		USSR	Tbilisi	Friendly	W 1–0
42		Scotland	Wembley	Rous Cup	W 2–1
43		Mexico	Los Angeles	Friendly	W 3–0
44		Canada	Vancouver	Friendly	W 1–0
45		Portugal	Monterrey	WCF	L 0–1
46		Morocco	Monterrey	WCF	D 0–0
47		Poland	Mexico City	WCF	W 3–0
48		Paraguay	Mexico City	WCF	W 3–0
49		Argentina	Mexico City	WCF	L 1–2
50		Sweden	Stockholm	Friendly	L 0–1
51		N Ireland	Wembley	ECQ	W 3–0
52		Yugoslavia	Wembley	ECQ	W 2–0
53	1987	Spain	Madrid	Friendly	W 4–2
54		N Ireland	Belfast	ECQ	W 2–0
55		Turkey	Izmir	ECQ	D 0–0
56		Brazil	Wembley	Rous Cup	D 1–1
57		Scotland	Glasgow	Rous Cup	D 0–0
58		W Germany	Dusseldorf	Friendly	L 1–3
59		Turkey	Wembley	ECQ	W 8–0
60		Yugoslavia	Belgrade	ECQ	W 4–1
61	1988	Israel	Tel Aviv	Friendly	D 0–0
62		Holland	Wembley	Friendly	D 2–2
63		Hungary	Budapest	Friendly	D 0–0
64		Scotland	Wembley	Rous Cup	W 1–0
65		Colombia	Wembley	Rous Cup	D 1–1
66		Switzerland	Lausanne	Friendly	W 1–0

Game	Year	Opponents	Venue	Competition	Score
67		R Ireland	Stuttgart	ECF	L 0–1
68		Holland	Dusseldorf	ECF	L 1–3
69		USSR	Frankfurt	ECF	L 1–3
70		Denmark	Wembley	Friendly	W 1–0
71		Sweden	Wembley	WCQ	D 0–0
72		Saudi Arabia	Riyadh	Friendly	D 1–1
73	1989	Greece	Athens	Friendly	W 2–1
74		Albania	Tirana	WCQ	W 2–0
75		Albania	Wembley	WCQ	W 5–0
76		Chile	Wembley	Rous Cup	D 0–0
77		Scotland	Glasgow	Rous Cup	W 2–0
78		Poland	Wembley	WCQ	W 3–0
79		Denmark	Copenhagen	Friendly	D 1–1
80		Sweden	Stockholm	WCQ	D 0–0
81		Poland	Katowice	WCQ	D 0–0
82		Italy	Wembley	Friendly	D 0–0
83		Yugoslavia	Wembley	Friendly	W 2–1
84	1990	Brazil	Wembley	Friendly	W 1–0
85		Czechoslovakia	Wembley	Friendly	W 4–2
86		Denmark	Wembley	Friendly	W 1–0
87		Uruguay	Wembley	Friendly	L 1–2
88		Tunisia	Tunis	Friendly	D 1–1
89		R Ireland	Cagliari	WCF	D 1–1
90		Holland	Cagliari	WCF	D 0–0
91		Egypt	Cagliari	WCF	W 1–0
92		Belgium	Bologna	WCF	W 1–0
93		Cameroon	Naples	WCF	W 3–2
94		W Germany	Turin	WCF	D 1–1 (lost 4–3 pens)
95		Italy	Bari	WCF	L 1–2

ECQ = European Championship qualifier
Home Int = British Home Internationals
WCQ = World Cup qualifier
WCF = World Cup finals
Mexico City T = Mexico City Tournament

*Also England B manager (January 1978–July 1982)

INDEX